**Living and Learning
with Feminist Ethics,
Literature, and Art**

Living and Learning with Feminist Ethics, Literature, and Art

Edited by
Dominique Hétu,
Libe García Zarranz,
Amanda Fayant,
and Marie Carrière

UNIVERSITY of ALBERTA PRESS

Published by

University of Alberta Press
1–16 Rutherford Library South
11204 89 Avenue NW
Edmonton, Alberta, Canada T6G 2J4
amiskwaciwâskahikan | Treaty 6 |
Métis Territory
ualbertapress.ca | uapress@ualberta.ca

Copyright © 2024 University of Alberta Press

LIBRARY AND ARCHIVES CANADA
CATALOGUING IN PUBLICATION

Title: Living and learning with feminist ethics, literature, and art / edited by Dominique Hétu, Libe García Zarranz, Amanda Fayant, and Marie Carrière.
Names: Hétu, Dominique (Professor), editor. | García Zarranz, Libe, 1979– editor. | Fayant, Amanda, editor. | Carrière, Marie J., 1971– editor.
Description: Includes bibliographical references and index.
Identifiers: Canadiana (print) 2024035771X | Canadiana (ebook) 20240357833 | ISBN 9781772127713 (softcover) | ISBN 9781772127799 (EPUB) | ISBN 9781772127805 (PDF)
Subjects: LCSH: Feminist theory. | LCSH: Feminist aesthetics. | LCSH: Feminist literature.
Classification: LCC HQ1190 .L58 2024 | DDC 305.4201—dc23

First edition, first printing, 2024.
First printed and bound in Canada by Friesens, Altona, Manitoba.
Copyediting and proofreading by Joanne Muzak.
Indexing by Pascale Hutton.

All rights reserved. No part of this publication may be reproduced, stored in a retrieval system, or transmitted in any form or by any means (electronic, mechanical, photocopying, recording, generative artificial intelligence [AI] training, or otherwise) without prior written consent. Contact University of Alberta Press for further details.

University of Alberta Press supports copyright. Copyright fuels creativity, encourages diverse voices, promotes free speech, and creates a vibrant culture. Thank you for buying an authorized edition of this book and for complying with the copyright laws by not reproducing, scanning, or distributing any part of it in any form without permission. You are supporting writers and allowing University of Alberta Press to continue to publish books for every reader.

This book has been published with the help of a grant from the Federation for the Humanities and Social Sciences, through the Awards to Scholarly Publications Program, using funds provided by the Social Sciences and Humanities Research Council of Canada.

University of Alberta Press gratefully acknowledges the support received for its publishing program from the Government of Canada, the Canada Council for the Arts, and the Government of Alberta through the Alberta Media Fund.

Contents

vii *Acknowledgements*

ix **A Letter from the Editors**
DOMINIQUE HÉTU AND LIBE GARCÍA ZARRANZ

1 **1 | Learning to Be Good Relatives**
Building Nokom's House
KIM ANDERSON, AMINA LALOR, SHERI LONGBOAT, AND BRITTANY LUBY

15 **2 | Becoming Critical**
On the Limits and Possibilities of Learning with Indigenous Womxn's Stories
MYLÈNE YANNICK GAMACHE

31 **3 | I'm Still Not Done Talking about Zombies**
JUNIE DÉSIL

47 **4 | On Living with Ghosts**
Sue Goyette's Poethics of Care
ERIN WUNKER

63 **5 | Learning to "Live with" Death**
Developing a Suicide-Affirmative Approach as an Ethics of "Living with" Suicidal People
ALEXANDRE BARIL

83 **6 | Here Is a Broken Word**
Psychosis and Ethical Accompaniment
ERIN SOROS

95 **7 | Synergies of Solidarity**
Un/Learning with Feminist Menopause Imaginaries in Canadian Writing
VERONIKA SCHUCHTER

113 **8 | Learning with Jovette Marchessault's Decolonial Feminist Critique through Her Autobiographical Relations**
ÉLISE COUTURE-GRONDIN

131 **9 | The Poethical Tao**
Chinese Canadian Situated Solidarities on Turtle Island
LARISSA LAI

153 **10 | On Trans Aliveness as Feminist Praxis**
Ivan Coyote's and Syrus Marcus Ware's Ordinary Archives
LIBE GARCÍA ZARRANZ

167 **11 | (Dis)(Re)Learning with Liz Howard's *Infinite Citizen of the Shaking Tent***
ANNE QUÉMA

193 **12 | Breathing in the "Pulmonary Commons"**
Conspiring against "Settler Atmospherics" in Rita Wong's *undercurrent*
STEPHANIE OLIVER

215 **13 | Learning Landguage**
SISSEL M. BERGH

239 **An Envoi from the Editors**
MARIE CARRIÈRE AND AMANDA FAYANT

247 Contributors
255 Index

Acknowledgements

THIS PROJECT would not have been possible without our invaluable contributors; we are immensely grateful for their stimulating collaboration and careful engagement with vital, often difficult topics.

We also want to thank University of Alberta Press for their support. We deeply appreciate acquisitions editor Michelle Lobkowicz, for her generosity, enthusiasm, attention to detail, guidance, and constant care.

Our project also benefitted from the rigorous intellectual conversation offered by the two anonymous reviewers at University of Alberta Press, whose attentive and thorough assessment of our manuscript elevated the ideas and the structure of the book.

We are also thankful to the University of Alberta, the Norwegian University of Science and Technology, Brandon University, and Acadia University for their financial support.

We also want to acknowledge the wonderful artists who let us reproduce their artwork in our collection: Syrus Marcus Ware, Sissel M. Bergh, Rebecca Belmore, Alex Janvier, and Christi Belcourt.

Living and learning with the multiple feminisms that permeate this collection have taught us that this is no easy task, as it entails a constant exercise of ethical reflection and action. As editors, we dedicate this collection to you, the reader, for your willingness to dive into its many chapters, with the paradoxes, the pleasures, and the provocations that these words and worlds propose.

A Letter from the Editors

DOMINIQUE HÉTU AND LIBE GARCÍA ZARRANZ

> I want the nations and communities we live in
> to stop holding individuals to different standards than
> they hold themselves to—to dismantle abuse and gaslighting
> at all levels, micro and macro.
> I want you to feel safe being vulnerable.
> I want us both to be safe being vulnerable.
> —ALICIA ELLIOTT, *A Mind Spread Out on the Ground*

> Biidaabin: *the first light of dawn; the past and the future collapsing in on the present; the present giving birth to radical, beautiful futures that generatively refuse heteropatriarchy, capitalism, and white supremacy and collectively live out the alternatives.*
> —LEANNE BETASAMOSAKE SIMPSON,
>   "Idle No More and Black Lives Matter: An Exchange"

Dear reader,

As we reflect on the personal and social subtexts of our book, we have found ourselves coming back to Lauren Berlant's phrase, from an interview with Michael Hardt, where they discuss the politics of a social conceptualization of love: "what it would take for people to take the risk of new relationality" (qtd. in Davis and Sarlin, 27). We are convinced that literature and art are part of the answer, that they provide key access to worlds and experiences worth the risk of new encounters and connections, worth imagining change and alternatives to injustices. Naive? We don't think so. The thirteen original contributions in *Living and Learning with Feminist Ethics, Literature, and Art*, written by emerging and established scholars and artists, position relationality at the core of critical and poetic enquiry. The contributors consider writing, whether as praxis or object of study, to be, for minoritized voices particularly, a form of risk-taking as well as an act of reclaiming and empowerment that can be costly. This ambivalence is reflected in many chapters that tackle very difficult, sensitive topics such as colonial trauma, racism, psychosis, suicide, transphobia, poverty, child neglect, environmental racism, climate change crisis, and everyday systemic violences. We thus invite you, reader, to navigate this book as a series of careful encounters with provocative modes of thinking and creating; to use it as a relational impulse for "staying with the trouble" (Haraway) through the literary and artistic approaches that our contributors mobilize and examine. We know that the majority of the analyses presented in this book are not easy, and we cautiously embrace this uneasiness in an effort to deepen the conversation about and engage the complexity of intersecting oppressions to make space for more diverse inter/subjectivities, voices, and positionalities.

Relationality, with its many ambivalences, constitutes one of the shared threads in the collection. An attention to care ethics and politics, from feminist, crip, and trans perspectives, constitutes another central pillar, connecting the chapters in various ways and framing our editorial intervention for creating this collection. As Leah Lakshmi Piepzna-Samarasinha insists, the "making of disability justice lives in the realm of thinking and talking and knowledge making, in art and sky. But it also lives in…how to learn to care for each other when everyone is sick, tired, crazy, and brilliant" (24). These relational care webs, as Piepzna-Samarasinha calls them, are grounded in the collective and the everyday, and this collection's critical and creative impulse towards the mobilization of shared and lived experience across different care struggles brings attention to ongoing public, private, and intimate relationalities. The latter demand rethinking, if not reinventing care ethics—as per the work of Hil Malatino, for instance—in line with the particularities of marginalized intersubjectivities and communities.

Accordingly, the chapters' different approaches to care theory and experience further stress how such a mobilization connects with another transversal imperative and thematic cluster in this collection, building collective spaces of resistance. This collective impetus echoes Michi Saagiig Nishnaabeg writer and scholar Leanne Betasamosake Simpson's vital question: "What happens when, instead of constantly appealing to white allies, we build constellations of co-resistance locally and internationally with those communities actively building ethical, principled and radical futures in the present, by animating and embodying those ethical systems as the intervention?" (82). Some of the authors in this book follow Betasamosake Simpson's urgent call and propose sites of co-resistance by forging engaged and caring pedagogies as well as artistic practices that are relational, collective, and, at times, imbued with tensions and contradictions. Such an engagement further echoes the collection's bringing together of diverse scholarly and creative explorations of the "poethics" (Retallack 11) of *living with* and *learning with*, phrasal verbs that showcase the vitality and complexity of the interdisciplinary fields of study. The book hence underscores the feminist urgency in which these concepts take root as the chapters offer fresh insights about the needs and costs of actively attempting to decode, revisit, understand, denounce, and resist the fast and slow violences (Nixon) that impact minoritized subjects' lives, communities, and narratives. The contributions give prominence to critical and creative voices and methods that, in the emblazing poetic words of Cicely Belle Blain,[1] are

> unfolding trauma
> gently
> building, building, growing, building
> healing
> inventing and reinventing intellectual intimacy
> existing in forbidden ways
> accidentally decolonizing
> Fucking Shit Up. (80)

Inspired by Nêhiýaw and Saulteaux educational scholar Margaret Kovach's unravelling of the complexities of self-location and purpose for Indigenous researchers, we, as editors of this book, must acknowledge that the presence and place of risks in relationality, care, and resistance also means recognizing, in humility and accountability, our responsibility and limitations. Dominique, as a white francophone Canadian settler and tenured professor living on Treaty 2 territory, is cautious of the different ideological narratives and privileges that shape her perspective and practice. Similarly,

Libe's position as a privileged migrant educated in Spain and Canada, and currently a tenured professor in Norway, prompts her to stay attentive to the ethics of self-location. The importance of positionality, with its complexities and paradoxes, is something that feminist, queer, and trans theorists continue to teach us and inform our pedagogy and methodology. We also draw further on Berlant's claim that "new social relations happen in time with different types of practices" (qtd. in Davis and Sarlin, 27) to make this "declaration of position" (Reder 8) in this letter to you. We feel compelled to add that we are not the ones encountering the most significant risk, even if our respective experiences as francophone and hispanophone women living in minority settings are not without a struggle. This book is thus about the possibility of imagining new relationalities to counter the oppressive systems in today's chaotic world. It is also about the urgency to build "constellations of co-resistance" (Betasamosake Simpson 81), as many of the contributors in this collection insist on, and about exploring new relationalities and care webs by attending to feminist ethics and poetics, which we ground in forms of situatedness, accountability, and solidarity.

As Mylène Gamache discusses in her chapter, Kovach establishes further connections with other anti-oppressive research frameworks, including feminist methodologies where "researchers are encouraged to locate themselves, to share personal aspects of their own experience with research participants" (110). This process entails a complex ethical apparatus where accountability and reciprocity are vital. At the same time, throughout the book, we insist on positionality to highlight further some of the anti-objectivity imperatives that organize the collection. As feminist scholars have claimed for decades, no knowledge is neutral or objective. In the words of Deanna Reder, "there is no unbiased, neutral position possible" (7), and this is key to the four of us, in our roles as editors, and to the contributors, in their roles as writers and creators. As such, this book asks what it means to keep living and learning to act with accountability at the sight of difference—a project that many feminist Indigenous, women of colour, and 2SLGBTQQIA+ writers and artists are firmly committed to, as shown by the chapters in this volume. Accordingly, whether directly or indirectly, each text and contributor are situated in terms of their fields, methodologies, and identities. Such careful tasks of positionality and self-reflection echo what Gina Starblanket configures as "relational accountability" and Sam McKegney calls—and does not fully trust—"strategies of ethical engagement" (81). They act as navigational tools in this book, interrogating "what it means to exist in worlds that employ entirely different or new ways of creating, understanding, and maintaining knowledge" (Starblanket 4) and maintaining an accountable hold on our respective critical and creative work.

This collection does not suggest that *living and learning with* feminist ethics and poetics relationally is always done carefully and respectfully. Cautious of the risk of moral judgement carried within current ethical and care turns in critical theory, the humanities, and the arts, we do not claim that ethics are the answer to the many crises of today's world or that literature and art carry a particular ethical responsibility. But, as the contributors demonstrate, literary and artistic productions, through form and language, can offer a space for contending with normative and dominant feminist ethics and new critical and poetic approaches to lived, imagined, and witnessed experiences of struggle. Each chapter thus relies on critical and reflexive analysis sustained by a coherent engagement with ethical, political, and cultural matters of *living and learning with*. Vigilant with and embracing the alliances and dissonances that inscribe the collection, the editors and contributions of this book attend to a feminist praxis of care that stems from a constellation of values and practices rooted in anti-racist, intersectional, and decolonial approaches and that are attuned to horizontal, hospitable, and holistic forms of making meaning. Therefore, this collective interest takes root not in the resurgence of moralizing or empathy in literature (Goldman 813), but rather in a contemporary transdisciplinary turn to care that emerges from trans studies, sociology, the medical humanities, as well as cultural and literary studies. Each discipline brings a different focus to the indispensable work of writers and artists who develop thought-provoking access to experiences and imaginaries that challenge problematic feminist methodologies and incite new ethical interventions, especially when it comes to injustice and privilege, that take root in care, relationality, and responsibility.

With this book, we want to study relations of *living and learning with* as compelling forms of encounter, engagement, and care between self and other, between human, non-human, and more-than-human worlds, and between various feminist practices today. Contributors understand ethics in the terms offered by Karen Barad's analogy of touching as "a matter of response. Each of 'us' is constituted in response-ability. Each of 'us' is constituted as responsible for the other, as the other" (215). Gamache's chapter complements Barad with Kelly Oliver's configuration of the same term to think further about subjectivity, which she argues "is, in fact, the result of, and depends upon, the process of witnessing—addressability and response-ability" (337). Moreover, in this desire to foster and interrogate "response-ability" through our motifs of *living with* and *learning with*, this collection draws on Joan Tronto's notions of responsibility and responsiveness. She defines the first as "embedded in...cultural practices" (134) and the second as "requir[ing] attentiveness...and suggest[ing] a different way to understand the needs of the other rather than to put our selves in their position" (135–136). As the envoi further illustrates, thinking with these notions is key for keeping us from the traps of empathy, objectivity, and moralization and to better understand how to be "engaged from the standpoint of the other, but not simply by presuming that the other is exactly like the self [or that] people are interchangeable" (136). Accordingly, by firmly positioning ethics at the heart of this critical and creative inquiry, we seek to think about the different possible expressions, potentialities, and limits of these relational dynamics and uneven distributions of care (Tronto; Malatino). This also means thinking with Christina Sharpe, whose work denounces the "conditions of ordinary brutality" (*Monstrous* 20) sustained by anti-Black discourses and practices—an exposure to systemic violences that further permeates Junie Désil's contribution to this collection.

The volume thus addresses a historical juncture where settler colonial violence's unresolved and ongoing legacies intersect with environmental and health crises as well as increasing levels of racism, transmisogyny, and sexism. At the same time, and as Larissa Lai pertinently puts it, the first two decades of the twenty-first century have also been marked "by the heartening if sometimes unpredictable work of social movements like Idle No More, Black Lives Matter, and anti-rape movements" (91). As such, this book aims at articulating a necessary reflection on situated critical knowledges and practices. This reflection seems particularly urgent, given the ongoing moment of Indigenous-settler reconciliation and nation-to-nation conciliation in Canada (Garneau), and Norway to some extent (Truth and Reconciliation Commission), as well as considering the worldwide persistent violence against Black, trans, disabled, and poor subjects. Another objective is to showcase, through literary and artistic analysis, important and timely feminist work that tackles crucial ethical, political, and cultural realities. When learning and reading about and with these realities, we are "continuously ask[ing] ourselves: what are the ethics of our work? How do we enter the texts that we chose to study or to teach?" (Beard 655), and what are the consequences of our choices?

In *Living and Learning with Feminist Ethics, Literature, and Art*, we look at issues about the relational and intersubjective dynamics that shape feminist praxis through literary and artistic works concerned with the structures and figures of vulnerability and oppression and the obstacles to solidarity. We bring together scholars, writers, and artists based in settler Canada, Norway, and the United Kingdom whose research and other creative practices respond to and confront dominant discourses and systems that, in line with capitalist, patriarchal, colonial, racist, transphobic, and ableist structures, exist to neutralize, silence, and burden minoritized lives with often costly and misplaced responsibility and expectations. Contributors approach literary, artistic, and cultural productions through overlapping gestures, mainly relying on different academic and critical thought forms. In turn, the contributions by the poet Junie Désil and the artist Sissel M. Bergh mobilize hybrid written and visual forms that counter anthropocentric impulses by prioritizing non-human figures, such as the zombie and more-than-human ecologies and worlds.

Other contributors complement their theoretical analysis with pedagogical concerns or self-reflexive thoughts. Chapters such as Alexandre Baril's and Libe García Zarranz's place these subjectivities at the forefront of the discussion with methodologies from feminist, trans, anti-racist, and critical disability studies. Paying heed to lives and relations historically, politically, and aesthetically discarded from Western imaginaries and knowledges, they examine what it means to "take on the responsibility to interrupt a particular violence," in Sharpe's words ("And to Survive" 173). As such, one of the cohesive threads of this book lies in the careful exploration, in Indigenous, migrant, and settler contexts, of the role and place of literary and cultural productions to challenge reductive and often pernicious frameworks of so-called objectivity while forging presents and futures otherwise. The collection attends to the ethics at stake when seeking to understand, represent, and confront contemporary experiences of *living and learning with* and the relationships, alliances, and conflicts that they entail. As Veronika Schuchter's chapter illustrates, this also means bringing into focus how these relational structures impact and are impacted by individual, sociocultural, and institutional power dynamics. This collection is thus not just about the economic, social, political, and cultural forces that perpetuate "the disqualification of the cultures of minoritized groups" (148), to echo Naima Hamrouni's words.

| To give full space to these entangled threads, and to allow the through lines of the book to really come together and reinforce the cohesiveness of the collection, we decided to organize the chapters in a single series rather than in sections. We believe this structure allows the chapters to echo one another without barriers, and we think such a strategy reinforces, in our own praxis, this exercise of living and learning with one another's ideas, with and through text and language, on the page and beyond. Accordingly, we organized the chapters in a way that highlights their singularity but also illuminates their connections, in an effort to provoke a resonance, a constellation of ideas, with other contributions.

Our collection opens with a collaborative chapter by Indigenous scholars Kim Anderson, Sheri Longboat, and Brittany Luby, and their project manager Amina Lalor. Their chapter, like several others in the collection, touches on an important question asked by Métis scholar and writer Warren Cariou: "How are stories related to land?" This question frames Cariou's discussion of *territory*, a term that signals the inseparability of land from storytelling. As Cariou argues, "If we think of land and stories as two aspects of the same phenomenon, this has implications for our understanding of Indigenous sovereignty, agency and ethics" (1). Also preoccupied with the weavings that bring together stories, land, and knowledge, Anderson, Lalor, Longboat, and Luby's piece proposes new, responsible ways for practicing and embodying good *living and learning with* as the authors discuss the building of a "Grandmother's house" in the University of Guelph Arboretum. Reflecting on the shared and individual journeys that led to their project rooted in Indigenous women's experiences of Indigenizing and decolonizing the academy, they situate and contextualize the ideas behind this "land-based research lab" that is also a "ceremonial space of relational care." They explain how the lab is benefitting from the stories and knowledge of older Indigenous women, "Aunties or Grannies" whose teachings and experiences are vital contributions.

In *Teaching to Transgress: Education as the Practice of Freedom*, a book that has greatly influenced many of us learning with radical inclusive pedagogies, the late bell hooks famously writes, "I celebrate teaching that enables transgressions—a movement against and beyond boundaries" (12). As mentioned above, transgressive feminist pedagogies often place relationality, reciprocity, and accountability at the centre of critical enquiry. These tropes form a substantial part of the collection's through lines. For instance, Mylène Gamache's chapter describes the dynamics in three undergraduate courses on Indigenous womxn's literatures taught at the University of Manitoba amidst the constraints of the COVID-19 pandemic. Gamache reflects on "the limits of co-learning with participants in colonial and increasingly neoliberalized institutional spaces," making connections with historical and ongoing economies and politics sustained by the extraction of Indigenous stories and knowledges. Firmly situating herself as an early career urban Franco-Métis scholar and citizen of the Manitoba Métis Federation, Gamache unravels the ethical dilemmas and paradoxes integral to any pedagogical practice that seeks to recover Indigenous stories and reconnect with matrilineal kinships.

The challenges to such re/connections for Black lives, along with the struggles attached to extractive practices, inform poet Junie Désil's following chapter of creative writing. Désil digs deep in her experience of witnessing Black subjects' "ongoing death," thinking with Édouard Glissant's *opacité*, Sharpe's configurations of "wake," and Allison Richardson's work on "bearing witness." Désil, through poetic prose and the figure of the zombie, imagines "ways to live with our living-dead condition" and interrogates how Black people live with anti-Blackness, poetizing an in-betweenness that "offers so many possibilities for 'living with'—not as resignation—but as a refusal, as celebration." At times keeping the reader at a distance with erasure poetics, Désil offers vignettes that subvert language and form, that challenge and demand responsibility and accountability. Playing with this "point of opacity," this chapter, like several others in this collection, contends with voices and bodies that wish to exist on their own terms.

If Désil's chapter mobilizes the figure of the zombie, Erin Wunker's piece mobilizes the figure of the ghost in her reflection on staying with bad feelings: "How do we live with ourselves, especially as complicit bystanders in the quotidian violences of the now? How do we live with the ghosts we've let down?" Writing from a place of bad feeling and thinking with feminist and queer theories of affect, Wunker offers an intimate reading of Sue Goyette's *The Brief Reincarnation of a Girl* (2015). She unravels how Goyette's collection "attends to the ethics of witnessing and the necessity of learning to live with complicity and failure, as well as offering some alternatives for understanding networks of care and response-ability." Goyette's investigative lyric poetry thus enacts a *poethics of care*, in Wunker's formulation, that problematizes how unruly stories and bodies are often medicalized or simply erased from existence.

Echoing Désil's work on bearing witness and bringing justice, for the Black communities, to the history and tragedy of real and symbolic ongoing deaths, Alexandre Baril asks, with care and responsibility, how to "provide a better accompaniment for suicidal people." To do so, he draws on a transformative justice movement "led mostly by trans and queer people who self-identify as people of colour (often also disabled/Mad) and who hope to find better responses and solutions to forms of violence without counting on state institutions" and brings together autotheory, a transdisciplinary approach, and examples from film and literature. Baril demonstrates that discourse on suicidality in anti-oppressive research and movements tends to reproduce forms of stigmatization, marginalization, and pathologization of suicidal people. His chapter explores what we can *learn with* suicidal people when their voices and stories are at the centre of the proposed interventions to suicide. Baril's contribution further develops what the adoption of such an approach implies for an ethics of *living with* suicidal people. As such, his "suicide-affirmative approach is both death-affirming *and* life-affirming."

Erin Soros's poetic piece strongly resonates with Baril's singular scholarly work: both emphasize how personal lived experience connects intimately to other collective bodies. Soros unravels the relational knowledges and interdependent connections that can emerge from research and creative work, with a focus on the ethical, environmental, and social experiences of psychosis, in her case. Soros shares her story here: "what follows will be a tender lesson emerging from a moment when I fell into madness, and a friend listened, took a step toward the threshold of what a mind cannot seem to bear." Soros proposes the formulation *ethical accompaniment* as a mode of relationality and care that exceeds the individual to attend further to repeated histories of violence against women and other minoritized populations. From Canada to the UK, Soros's testimony traces a genealogy of "historical atrocity" that leaves traces on bodies while opening the way to an ethics of relationality and accountability based on generous listening.

Turning to a different set of gendered and medical experiences that also demand new relational models, Veronika Schuchter comments on ageist and homogeneous perceptions of the menopause in her chapter, drawing on the 2017 edited collection *Writing Menopause: An Anthology of Fiction, Poetry, and*

Creative Non-fiction, edited by Jane Cawthorne and E.D. Morin, and the 2020 graphic memoir *Kimiko Does Cancer*, written by Kimiko Tobimatsu and illustrated by Keet Geniza. With the concept of "synergies of solidarity," Schuchter theorizes, from a feminist trans-inclusive perspective, the affective dimension of menopause and astutely shows the ways these kinds of life-writing foster a sense of community and challenge essentialist and normative understandings of aging women's bodies.

Concerned with a different facet of cultural and family genealogy and feminist solidarity, Élise Couture-Grondin's chapter examines Jovette Marchessault's relational autobiographical strategies of self-discovery in *Mother of the Grass* as crucial for understanding and situating the writer's "critique of colonialism from her singular position as a feminist lesbian Québécoise with Indigenous heritage." This gesture echoes ongoing efforts to both build on and caution against alliances between Indigenous, queer, and white settler feminisms. Like Désil and Wunker, Couture-Grondin suggests that storytelling is a form of witnessing and *learning with*, echoing the words of Cree/Métis/Saulteaux artist and scholar Amanda Fayant, who writes that "sewing together the stories of Indigenous women creates the fabric of resilience" (55). Bringing attention to the vital role of the grandmother's presence and teachings in the narrator's life, which also resonates with Anderson et al. "Grandmother's house," Couture-Grondin shows how the narrator's process of self-discovery and determination stems from a profoundly relational and intersubjective configuration of identity.

Shedding new light on feminist literary studies with vital insights from the field of Asian Canadian literature, Larissa Lai's chapter turns to her own creative and critical work. Lai's exercise of shuffling between personal and collective realms allows her to attend to the complexities of positionality when seeking to forge solidarities between Indigenous, Black Canadian, and Asian Canadian communities. Drawing on Lisa Lowe's work on race and intimacy, Lai examines how the work of Dionne Brand and Paul Yee—two others who also rely on ghostly figures—illustrates these paradoxical alliances in ways that can lead to greater ethical relationality. Echoing Wunker's interrogation of bad feelings, Lai pertinently asks, "Does our suffering ever excuse our incapacities to act well?"—a question that resonates with our collection's impulses.

Libe García Zarranz's chapter further denounces the uneven regulation of life and death through the ungovernable archives of Ivan Coyote and

Syrus Marcus Ware. Coyote's and Ware's written and visual worlds propose a poetics and aesthetics of trans aliveness with deep implications for feminist praxis, as shown in García Zarranz's self-reflexive letter at the end of the chapter. Thinking with the notion of aliveness as theorized in Black and trans studies grants García Zarranz the methodological framework with which to engage with Coyote's and Ware's interventions as exercises in feminist ethics and pedagogy. This chapter, in its analysis of Coyote's and Ware's activism and artistic practices, resonates with others in the collection such as Anderson et al., Quéma, Baril, and Soros, in how they bring together literature, accountability, and advocacy for thinking differently about living and learning with various experiences of struggle.

As shown in Anderson, Longboat, Luby, and Lalor's opening chapter as well as Gamache's contribution, the pedagogical moments of learning and unlearning with Indigenous feminist practices extend to lived space and to the classroom. Anne Quéma's chapter on Liz Howard's poetry collection *Infinite Citizen of the Shaking Tent* (2015) shows how such moments also inscribe the poetic and artistic realms. Quéma studies Howard's citational praxis as deeply rooted in Indigenous patterns of meaning-making, and weaves Howard's practice with that of other Indigenous artists and writers as well as Western philosophers and poets, showing the disruptive care with which Howard's poetic language unsettles Western scientific and cultural frameworks. As such, Quéma, in an effort to reflect on her position as a settler critic, carefully avoids an "assimilative drive of interpretation" by mapping the resurgence of Indigenous literary and artistic production as they accompany Howard's unsettling poetry, being and learning with Indigenous literature and art instead of reproducing and perpetuating epistemic violence.

Stephanie Oliver's contribution on Rita Wong's ecopoetry resonates with other pieces in the volume, particularly in the attentiveness to learning with Indigenous resurgence and land-based scholarship. Oliver demonstrates how Wong mobilizes a poetics of living and learning with water and air that draws on and honours Indigenous water keepers and relational models. Oliver complicates Wong's focus on water by looking at the evasive presence of air and breath in the poems. Like Quéma's, Oliver's close reading of the poems and contextualization of Wong's poet*h*ics highlights the potential of poetry for confronting environmental and human crises and for learning with Indigenous resurgence movements grounded in a decolonial feminist ethics, allowing for the imagination of new post-anthropocentric ecological and relational models.

Finally, Sissel M. Bergh's closing chapter also brings land-based artwork and artistic practices into focus, and her contribution completes the circle beautifully, touching on similar issues as the land-based work of Anderson, Longboat, Luby, and Lalor in the opening chapter as well as weaving scholarly and creative practice together. Bergh centres South Sámi language as a vital tool with which to recover erased histories and "relearn with the land." Writing from Sápmi land, Bergh's piece urges readers to question how history "is still being used to claim rights to exploit land, to create national pride, and, in our context, to erase Saami presence and the complexity of a multicultural past." Bergh's call thus resonates with other scholars and artists in settler Canada, such as Gamache, Quéma, Oliver, as well as Désil and Lai, whose work insists on questioning received conceptualizations of nation and history.

| The contributors wrote their chapters in English, but some also rely on French and Indigenous languages such as Ojibway and South Sámi, making the collection polyphonic and textured with the presence of these other worldviews. The variety of literary and artistic forms gathered in this volume, including poetry, life-writing, and durational performance, act as vehicles addressing fundamental issues that are widely discussed by Indigenous, Black, migrant, trans, and feminist scholars, practitioners, and activists worldwide engaged in anti-racist, anti-sexist, and anti-colonial theory and praxis. This edited collection hence contributes to the various forms of social justice interventions that have emerged in academic, creative, public, and popular cultural spaces. This book further exposes the limitations of discourses and practices that sustain so-called objective epistemologies and knowledges and insists on denouncing the persistence of historical patterns of oppression, domination, and complicity. As highlighted in the envoi written by Marie Carrière and Amanda Fayant closing our collection, our transdisciplinary volume thus focuses on and fuels feminist thought across genres, cultures, languages, and media, bringing together multiple perspectives at the intersection of feminist ethics, literary texts, and cultural productions.

While taking root in two conferences,[2] this volume does not consist of conference proceedings but of original chapters where contributors expand and deepen the examination of contemporary Indigenous, Black, Asian diasporic, migrant, and settler literary texts and artistic productions. If feminist ethics and positionality are at the centre of our critical inquiry, the chapters also rely on a myriad of methodological, pedagogical, and artistic approaches that interrogate and illuminate the complex interactions of feminist ethics, politics, and poetics. The chapters mobilize anti-colonial, intersectional, and feminist practices, each addressing, through a wide range of critical, pedagogical, and artistic strategies, the epistemological and historical violences that literary texts and cultural objects contain and contest.

Finally, the prioritizing of theoretical, comparative, and interdisciplinary methodologies in broaching this work is crucial to another central aim of the project, which is to foster debate and knowledge sharing among different perspectives, histories and traditions, languages, approaches, and worldviews. That is why this collection brings together essays that coherently interrogate and investigate the impact of possible cross-border alliances within feminist practices today—or "across national and cultural divisions" (10), as Chandra Talpade Mohanty might say, in which—and this is key—material, artistic, and political differences, positionalities, and specificities remain visible and accounted for. In this sense, the collection firmly advocates for the advancement of capacious feminist interventions where the voices of trans, disabled, and other multiply minoritized theorizations are integral. These tensions and possibilities further permeate artistic and cultural realms with deep repercussions for feminist scholarship, pedagogy, and praxis. The collection you are about to enter, dear reader, is firmly situated in this borderland.

Notes

1. Blain was one of the guest writers invited to our online conference The Poetics and Ethics of "Learning With": Indigenous, Canadian, and Québécois Feminist Production Today, and spoke with us on March 31, 2021. The talk, titled "Burning Sugar: A Reading & Conversation," is accessible online: https://www.ntnu.edu/learningwith.
2. In October 2018 we held an international conference titled The Poetics and Ethics of "Living With": Indigenous, Canadian, and Québécois Feminist Production Today. Then, between November 2020 and May 2021, we continued thinking collaboratively about these topics with a second conference, The Ethics and Poetics of "Learning With": Indigenous, Canadian, and Québécois Feminist Production Today, this time online due to COVID-19 restrictions. We placed the emphasis on the notions of "living and learning with" because we envisioned them as methodological, pedagogical, as well as aesthetic positions with transformative ethical and artistic consequences.

Works Cited

Barad, Karen. "On Touching: The Inhuman That Therefore I Am." *Differences*, vol. 23, no. 3, 2012, pp. 206–223.

Beard, Laura J. "Moving with and away from Reconciliation." *Canadian Review of Comparative Literature / Revue Canadienne de Littérature Comparée*, vol. 45, no. 4, December 2018, pp. 653–657.

Betasamosake Simpson, Leanne, et al. "Idle No More and Black Lives Matter: An Exchange." *Global Movement Assemblages*, special issue of *Studies in Social Justice*, vol. 12, no. 1, 2018, pp. 75–89.

Blain, Cicely Belle. *Burning Sugar*. Arsenal Pulp Press, 2020.

Cariou, Warren. "Terristory: Land and Language in the Indigenous Short Story-Oral and Written." *Commonwealth Essays and Studies*, vol. 42, no. 2, 2020, pp. 1–10.

Davis, Heather, and Paige Sarlin. "On the Risk of a New Relationality: An Interview with Lauren Berlant and Michael Hardt." *Reviews in Cultural Theory*, vol. 2, no. 3, 2012, pp. 1–27.

Elliott, Alicia. *A Mind Spread Out on the Ground*. Anchor Canada, 2020.

Fayant, Amanda. *Thunderbird Women: Indigenous Women Reclaiming Autonomy through Stories of Resistance*. 2019. Arctic University of Norway, MA thesis, https://iportal.usask.ca/record/69267.

Garneau, David. "Imaginary Spaces of Conciliation and Reconciliation." *West Coast Line*, vol. 74, no. 1, Summer 2012, pp. 28–38.

Goldman, Marlene. "Introduction: Literature, Imagination, Ethics." *The Ethical Turn in Canadian Literature and Criticism*, special issue of *University of Toronto Quarterly*, vol. 76, no. 3, Summer 2007, pp. 809–820.

Hamrouni, Naima. "Vulnerable Political Life: Distributive Justice, Critical Theory, and Critical Care Ethics." *Paradigms of Justice: Redistribution, Recognition, and Beyond*, edited by Denise Celentano and Luigi Caranti, Routledge, 2020, pp. 143–164.

Haraway, Donna J. *Staying with the Trouble: Making Kin in the Chthulucene*. Duke UP, 2016.

hooks, bell. *Teaching to Transgress: Education as the Practice of Freedom*. Routledge, 1994.

Kovach, Margaret Elizabeth. *Indigenous Methodologies: Characteristics, Conversations, and Contexts*. U of Toronto P, 2009.

Lai, Larissa. "Insurgent Utopias: How to Recognize the Knock at the Door." *Exploring the Fantastic: Genre, Ideology, and Popular Culture*, edited by Ina Batzke, et al., Verlag, 2018, pp. 91–114.

Malatino, Hil. *Trans Care*. Minnesota UP, 2020.

McKegney, Sam. "Strategies for Ethical Engagement. An Open Letter Concerning Non-Native Scholars of Native Literatures." *Learn, Teach, Challenge: Approaching Indigenous Literatures*, edited by Linda M. Morra and Deanna Reder, Wilfrid Laurier UP, 2016, pp. 79–87.

Mohanty, Chandra Talpade. *Feminism without Borders: Decolonizing Theory, Practicing Solidarity*. Duke UP, 2003.

Nixon, Rob. *Slow Violence and the Environmentalism of the Poor.* Harvard UP, 2013.

Oliver, Kelly. "Subjectivity as Responsivity: The Ethical Implications of Dependency." *The Subject of Care: Feminist Perspectives on Dependency*, edited by Eva Fedder Kittay and Ellen K. Feder, Rowman & Littlefield, 2002, pp. 322–333.

Piepzna-Samarasinha, Leah Lakshmi. *Care Work: Dreaming Disability Justice.* Arsenal Pulp Press, 2018.

Reder, Deanna. Introduction. *Learn, Teach, Challenge: Approaching Indigenous Literatures*, edited by Deanna Reder and Linda M. Morra, Wilfrid Laurier UP, 2016, pp. 7–17.

Retallack, Joan. *The Poethical Wager.* U of California P, 2003.

Sharpe, Christina. "And to Survive." *Small Axe*, vol. 22, no. 3, November 2018, pp. 171–180.

Sharpe, Christina. *Monstrous Intimacies: Making Post-Slavery Subjects.* Duke UP, 2010.

Starblanket, Gina. "Complex Accountabilities: Deconstructing 'the Community' and Engaging Indigenous Feminist Research Methods." *American Indian Culture and Research Journal*, vol. 42, no. 4, 2018, pp. 1–20.

Tronto, Joan. *Moral Boundaries: A Political Argument for an Ethic of Care.* Routledge, 1993.

Truth and Reconciliation Commission to Investigate the Norwegianisation Policy and Injustice against the Sámi and Kvens/Norwegian Finn. *Sannhet og forsoning—grunnlag for et oppgjør med fornorskingspolitikk og urett mot samer, kvener/norskfinner og skogfinne (The Truth and Reconciliation Commission Report).* 2023, https://www.stortinget.no/globalassets/pdf/sannhets--og-forsoningskommisjonen/rapport-til-stortinget-fra-sannhets--og-forsoningskommisjonen.pdf.

1
Learning to Be Good Relatives
Building Nokom's House

KIM ANDERSON, AMINA LALOR, SHERI LONGBOAT,
AND BRITTANY LUBY

Scene 1

It is a bright winter day, and the sun is bouncing off the snow in the University of Guelph Arboretum. We are standing in a circle around a star quilt we have laid out on the ground. Our gathering includes students, staff, and the architects who are helping us build Nokom's House, our (spirit) Grandmother's new home.

Nokom is an abbreviation of *Nokomis*, which means *my Grandmother* in Anishinaabemowin, and this home will serve as a research hub under the leadership of the authors of this essay. We intend for it to be a place of purpose, belonging, creativity, and knowledge sharing among all our relations. Our project, funded by the Canada Foundation for Innovation, the Province of Ontario, and our university is to build a land-based "research lab" for three Indigenous scholars: Kim Anderson, Sheri Longboat, and Brittany Luby, and with the guidance of our Indigenous research project manager, Amina Lalor. If we translate what we are doing from the language of grants and institutions, we could simply say we are building a space to learn how to be good relatives.

Enter Kim

The idea to build a research hub as a Grandmother's house first came to me in 2018 while I was fasting (a spiritual process where one spends time alone out on the land without food or water to gain clarity and purpose). The fasting camp was at Gabriel's Crossing, so named because the nineteenth-century Métis leader Gabriel Dumont once lived there and operated a ferry to cross the South Saskatchewan River. There are low hills rising out of the banks, and as I sat among the grasses looking down at the river, I reflected on how I might fulfil future community responsibilities as an aging Métis woman. Among the Métis (and many other Indigenous cultures), older women are often referred to as Aunties or Grannies regardless of blood connection, and they play important roles as teachers and mentors. They nurture and they discipline, always with your best interests in mind. They make sure to keep you on track. This is one way to be a good relative.

A few days into that 2018 fast I found myself inexplicably lost in dreams about the mechanics of theatre and performance and, oddly, wondering about Shakespeare's work as a spirit. I don't know much about theatre, but perhaps it is significant that I was fasting under the "direction" of Métis Grandmother, author and playwright, Maria Campbell. When I came out of the fast, I told Maria about my visit with Shakespeare, and she and I had a rich conversation about how ceremony involves performance and about how relations are influenced by how we organize and interact spatially. We talked about entrances and exits, how we position ourselves, how life energy moves or gets caught in particular spaces. I'm still trying to figure all of this out, but somewhere in that "all the world's a stage" moment, it occurred to me that there might be a way to "stage" a space where good relations could be enacted in the academy.

This experience coincided with my timing as a researcher poised to build a "lab." I had been thinking about how to create a space for the students and community members I work with in various research projects—what I call my kitchen table (KT) lab. KT meetings with my students typically involve cooking, eating, laughing, crying, plotting, creating, and lots of visiting, and thus any research space would need a functional kitchen and a good-sized kitchen table. As a researcher of social relations, Indigenous women's histories, and Indigenous identities, I have been inspired and captivated by the kitchen table vision of Métis Auntie and scholar Sherry Farrell-Racette, and in particular these words, she shared at the Sâkêwâk Storyteller's Festival in Regina in 2017:

> It is important to look at the kitchen beyond the female and the domestic. Indigenous kitchens are a synthesis of influences, originating in a small circle of people sitting on the ground around a central fire, moving into small log homes where the kitchen table was literally the only flat working space…Eating was the least of the activities done around our kitchen table. It was primarily a creative space, a work surface, a space for meditation and a social space…It was a space of action. Circularity and expansion (almost limitless) are implied in kitchen logic. Even the word *tawow*—most often simply translated as "welcome"—can be understood as "there is room for you here" and also implies a space on the ground. It wasn't a marginalized female space where women served men…It was a female-centred space, where men, women and children worked, dreamt and created.

Based on my own experiences working out of Indigenous Grandmothers' houses, I have come to see kitchen tables as training grounds for the next generation, and I want to investigate my own kitchen duty as an "academic Auntie." As the KT vision grew, it became clear that my kitchen would need easy access to land to facilitate land-based learning, ceremony, and connection with non-human relations.

Thinking of the strength of women's collective knowledges, I approached Sheri Longboat, a Mohawk scholar in the School of Environmental Design and Rural Development, and Brittany Luby, an Anishinaabe scholar in the Department of History, to see if they would join in creating a Nokom's House/research hub. Amina Lalor became part of the team as a research assistant while doing her master's in architecture, and later became the Nokom's House research project manager. Together we bring disciplines of history (Luby), planning (Longboat), kinship (Anderson), and design (Lalor) to build Nokom's House. We bring our Indigenous knowledges, spirits, and lived experiences to this work, and each one of us has a distinct entry point, particular lines, requisite timing, our own place to sit. This is the collective work that builds a Nokom's House.

Scene 2
Enter Amina

I joined the Nokom's House circle in 2018 as the last deciduous leaves made their journey to the earth. I had met Kim a few months prior at a symposium and we connected over ideas of decolonizing place and land. I was in the midst of my master of architecture thesis, exploring what it meant to design and build in a good way as a mixed Vietnamese Irish Métis woman living and working on stolen lands. Now, four winters since Kim first shared her vision for Nokom's House with me over coffee, I continue to reflect on the questions I posed within my thesis abstract:

> How do we, as architects, reconcile our practice within a settler-colonial context violently inscribed onto Indigenous lands? How do we confront our complicity in Indigenous erasure and honour the treaties and kinship networks that underlie our presence on this ground? Amid an escalating climate crisis, and acknowledging architecture as a land-based practice, how do we mend our relationships with the land, water, plants, and animals? (v)

I have come to learn that the broad answer to these questions rests in being a good relative. Given Nokom's House is meant to create a space to practice research in good relation, how do we ensure that our process of creating Nokom's House embodies that same practice? How might we integrate being in good relation with our human and other-than-human communities into all aspects of design and construction? This work begins with the land.

Enter Brittany

Long before human beings inhabited Earth, some say, Gitche Manitou created Sun and Moon and the stars. Plants followed. Within Anishinaabe-Aki, plants are not inanimate, unfeeling beings. They are sentient organisms, "possessing an incorporeal substance, its own unique soul-spirit" (Johnston 32). We, the beings who followed, are dependent on these Elders for survival. Consider that "without plants to take the sunlight into their own bodies and by the use of chlorophyll trap the light of the sun into a usable form of energy, no animal life could survive" (Siisip Geniusz 14). All of the food we consume is gifted by plants—even the juiciest moose burger. *Mooz* (like you and me) receives energy to live and to grow from plants. Within the Great Web of Being, energy moves from Grandfather Sun to plants to human beings. The order of Creation is not a reflection of God's favour as it is in Christian teachings wherein Adam, who comes first, names and manages other organisms. The Anishinaabe Creation Story is, instead, a reminder of our interconnectedness. From first breath, human beings are part of a network that can sustain life—if we tend to it.

But how do we enter into the cycle of giving and receiving care? Elders from my ancestral community, Niisaachewan Anishinaabe Nation, teach that relational care begins with an acknowledgement that all forms of life are equally important. We are therefore equally entitled to the wealth and services of Earth. Human beings are no more entitled to space than Porcupine or White Pine. We, the helpers of Nokom's House, do not have an inherent right to displace plant and animal relations to build a land-based learning lab. Instead, we have a responsibility to learn who calls the arboretum home, to determine how they use space, and to negotiate living well together. We have a duty to understand and to honour our interconnections.

Scene 3

We walk, repeatedly, all over the arboretum, in groups, in pairs, alone. We listen for direction, for Grandmother's way. We do ceremonies in places that have spoken to us, laying the star quilt on the grass, among the leaves, in the snow. We smoke, sing, talk to our ancestors, talk among ourselves. Give thanks. Decide. Walk again. Visit. Listen.

Enter Kim

Land-based work inevitably involves attending to spirit relations, and Indigenous spirit-based work always involves land. I have learned that we need to choose the places where we do our work by attending to what the spirit of the land is telling us. Just like we humans all have purpose and work to do in this life, so too does the land. Different lands and waters are suited to different types of work, so you need to listen. I'm learning how to listen, and in the meantime, grateful for others in the community who are more attuned, as they helped us determine the best site for our Grandmother's home.

Land and spirit work are integral to homecoming, and much of my work is about building places and spaces of belonging to facilitate that process. It's about where we are at in our histories, individually and collectively. One of the tools of colonization was to strip us of our Indigenous identities; to assimilate us so Canada would have no more Indians, and thus, no more "Indian problem." But, as it is often said, we are still here. And we can build with each other, with land, with spirit. We do this in the places where we find ourselves.

Enter Sheri

When visiting another First Nation or meeting someone for the first time, it is common to be asked "where you from?" and "who's your family?" As academics, we refer to this as our positionality. I am mixed-race: a Mohawk and member of the Six Nations of the Grand River Territory on my paternal side, and Ukrainian on my maternal side. I am a first-generation high school and university graduate, and I never would have imagined that someday I would pursue and complete doctoral studies, become a university professor, and be sitting here writing about Nokom's House and decolonization at the University of Guelph.

I should also say, I am a geographer through formal education and training: physical geography, geomorphology, and resource management related, and from universities close to home—I never wanted to venture too far, and certainly not away from the Great Lakes where I feel so connected. I worked for ten years with many First Nations, before returning for PHD studies to understand why the water crisis in First Nations existed and persisted given the abundance of freshwater availability.

Now as I reflect on my formal educational experience in geography—the study of places and relationships between people and environments—I'm amazed that I cannot recall learning about Indigenous places, perspectives, knowledges, or even histories. All were absent from the curriculum, or if present, only as a speckling of often derogatory references in relation to "discovery" by early explorers or from an anthropological or archaeological context. Certainly not with any aim to celebrate Indigenous strength, diversity, nationhood, or resilience in the present or into the future.

Scene 4

The low sun filters through a row of spruce trees on a warm May evening. The site rotates into shadow, but the warm light paints the upper boughs of a poplar tree that is no longer alive, but not lifeless. A clearing among the canopy of fluttering poplar leaves, a small flock of cedar waxwings arrive to sunbathe among its bare branches. They pick at the peeling bark, eating moths and other insects, their yellow bellies and tail-feather tips are enhanced in the golden sunlight. Their wingtips like little red jewels.

Enter Brittany

To better understand our animal relations who share the Nokom's House site, we partnered with local settler tracker byron murray. Through frequent visiting and close-looking, byron was able to identify some of our other-than-human neighbours. We learned, for example, that Porcupine (*Erythizon dorsatum*) frequented the site. byron identified "barkless patches high up in lead branches of Poplar" as well as scat, suggesting that Porcupine feasted (and digested) on site. Porcupine also travelled through the building site. byron identified Porcupine tracks along human-made trails, suggesting that Porcupine conserved energy by walking along packed snow. We could use this information to consider the question, "What might Porcupine need from us?" We learned that Porcupine had access to other foodstuffs—indeed, Poplar was just one of many trees frequented by Porcupine. In this way, building was unlikely to cause food insecurity. A poorly placed building, however, could make it more difficult for Porcupine to seek out food.

Over time, byron's visits revealed a pattern of site use. Animal beings—from Flying Squirrel to Red Fox—tended to avoid the exposed, field-like area at the northwestern corner of the site. Our animal relations found shelter among the trees. They made use of human-made trails along the tree-line that were protected from the wind. To live well together, we could position Nokom's House to preserve animal shelter (e.g., limit tree removal) and maintain established migration routes (e.g., leave existing trails open).

Of course, we also have a responsibility to care for plant beings. They provide us with food, medicine, protection, and oxygen. What can we offer in return? Field guides, software, and conversation with arboretum staff helped me get to know local flowers, grasses, and trees. Upon learning plant names, I could begin the process of studying their life cycles. By understanding healthy growth patterns, I could better position myself to identify signs of good health and distress. This knowledge was foundational to determining what plant beings might need from me during the building process. I could demonstrate care by speaking openly about the signs known to me.

Nokom's House, for example, requires a point of entry. Future users need to transition from the parking lot into the building. In order to create this opening, we will depend on tree removal. As a general rule, stressed conifers produce more cones. This is an expression of hope that the next generation may set root and survive. I sought to identify trees that might be signalling, "I am willing to make way for the next generation" through excess seed production. Two mature conifers were identified for potential removal. They were also classified as dead or dying by arboretum staff. In this instance, signals of distress were interpreted as an offer to collaborate. In return for their lives, in return for an entry point, the conifers asked that we nurture their children through planting. The University of Guelph requires us to plant two trees for each one we remove. While the University of Guelph tells us how much to plant, conifers suggest *whom* to plant.

Relational care prompts continuous dialogue with our plant and animal relations. We commit to learning their names, to uncovering their needs, and to identifying unique markers of well-being and distress. We seek non-verbal signs of need and commit to compassionate, life-oriented responses. We may err, but ongoing observation and reflection will help us to build better together.

Enter Amina

Building on this question of what it means to design and build in good relation, we must examine all the ideas, forces, and materials that will come together to form Nokom's House. One of the first phases in a typical design process is establishing the project needs. This process began with Kim's vision, conversations with Maria Campbell, and continued with informal visits on the land. Conversations between friends began to nourish the Nokom's House spirit, allowing it to grow within the local community consciousness.

In the summer of 2019, we began work with a local architecture firm, J.L. Richards and Associates, to develop an initial schematic design for Nokom's House to support an application for funding. We formally began the design process by inviting community to join us for organized engagement on the land. Our first gathering in the arboretum brought together an assortment of local Indigenous Grandmothers and Knowledge Carriers, Indigenous faculty, staff, students, community members, and non-Indigenous partners and allies. We shared our visions for a space of safety and homecoming. We pictured the activities that would unfold at Nokom's House, many of which were typically difficult to enact within the colonial spaces of typical post-secondary campuses. We would need space for cooking and feasting together, space for collaboration and conversation, space for private conversations. We would need space on the land to plant, tend to, and harvest food and medicines. We would need a sacred fire site, space for a traditional teaching lodge, a place to cook outdoors on a wood fire. We would need a comfortable place to sit with our Grandmothers and Elders, to share stories by the warmth of the wood stove, space to store food and medicines. Collectively, we determined the spatial program that we needed to carry out research work that supports the well-being of our community.

Once the spatial program is determined, the next steps are to locate the building on the site, synthesize a schematic building design with continued community input, develop the design and create detailed construction drawings and material specifications, and finally see the building through construction.

In the fall of 2020, our research team began working with the design firm Brook McIlroy and their Indigenous Design Studio to see us through the final design and construction phase of the Nokom's House project. As I write these words, we are in the midst of completing the schematic design phase, and we have committed our best effort to develop the project thus far with care for all our relations.

As earlier scenes illustrate, part of this process has been to listen and observe our plant, fungi, and animal neighbours on the land. With the architects, we located the building in an existing clearing, with an effort to not disrupt existing trees lines, areas where we have observed the most animal habitation and activity. In our planning and placement we avoided impacting the healthy trees already rooted in the site.

Caring for our relations calls us to construct sustainably. As the design develops further, we must consider how the building will perform in maintaining a comfortable environment, as well as the offsite impact of materials brought to this land to construct Nokom's House. While the impacts of these components are less visible and immediate when compared to the disruption of the Nokom's House site itself, these aspects of the design have a significant impact on our land. To mitigate the carbon impact of Nokom's House, we plan to have the building designed to meet the Zero Carbon Building standards. This means integrating passive and active strategies to minimize energy consumption and implementing renewable energy sources such as photovoltaics and biomass (wood for heating) to achieve zero-carbon-emission building operation. The design will consider how Nokom's House interacts with the sun and wind to optimize passive heating, cooling, lighting, and ventilation, minimizing the need for external energy sources. And as we continue in this process, we will consider the embodied energy of construction materials, their carbon emission and sequestration, the distance they must travel, and their impact on the community from which they are harvested. Low impact, local materials will be used wherever possible.

Building in good relation means applying an ethic of care and consideration to all facets of site analysis, community engagement, building design, and construction. Within the web of creation, we must consider our movements carefully, to mitigate disruption and create opportunities for renewal and reconnection. Constructing Nokom's House means accepting the gifts the land has to offer. Once the building materializes on the earth, creating space for work in relation, how can we extend this ethic of care into the continued operation and maintenance of Nokom's House, and give back to our communities and the land?

Scene 5

The global pandemic has made it now customary to visit with our relatives on video calls, to seek teachings across distance and time through means that might once have once felt inappropriate. So there is Maria Campbell, up early as usual, cup of tea in hand and speaking softly through the square frame of Kim's laptop. Kim and Maria are having a conversation about "what makes a Granny space." They travel from that place on the video screen to a cabin infused by the smell of Seneca root drying. Pictures of grandchildren on the wall. A lazy old dog outside. Fire. Soup. Jars of food. Flowered china, open shelves, dishes that don't match. The hide scraper. Lots of tea. A digging stick. Laughter.

Knowing you are going to be okay.

Enter Kim

Rematriating land involves making space for Indigenous women to lead, and our intention in building Nokom's House is to deepen explorations of Indigenous feminist placemaking. Nokom's House draws from the notion that in many Indigenous cultures, Grandmothers hold distinct leadership positions in maintaining the well-being of kinship and relationality. Such spaces provide a comfortable, informal, collaborative, and reciprocal setting conducive to creativity and change.

Enter Sheri

The spatial orders established through colonization have dispossessed Indigenous Peoples of their lands and defined our present-day cities and suburbs; Euro-Western spatial orders were overlaid onto Indigenous lands through acts of planning—the surveying and parcelling of land into property, the creation of reserves, and the designation of land-use for settlement, conservation, and resource extraction. Indigenous planning is situated in relationship, land-based, intergenerational, experiential, and narrative-based (storytelling).

Enter Amina

Across many Indigenous civilizations on Turtle Island, architecture has also played a significant role in knowledge transfer within communities. Traditionally, building components often represented a series of teachings and building orientations/alignments were informed by the four directions, significant cosmologies, or features in the landscape. Building forms also reflected modes of gathering and social structures specific to their nation.

Scene 6

It's dandelion season, May 2027, and yellow blankets the clearings between trees. It is a time of transformation when the leaves and flowers seem to emerge overnight. Early pollinators work their way across the field, bloom to bloom to bloom. The comforting scent of burning wood and cooking wafts on the fresh breeze to the sound of cardinals, chickadees, and gold finches. In the garden beds, seedlings have begun to emerge from the recently watered soil. The garden hose traces a line toward the porch where the poplars cast their dancing shadows. Listen. A door opens and closes, releasing a momentary bloom of excited conversation and laughter.

Inside, it's lunchtime, and the researchers, students, and Grandmothers are sharing a meal at the kitchen table. Windows offer views through the poplars and new saplings, toward the sacred fire site and teaching lodge. On the menu: wild leek soup, battered dandelion flowers, and bannock. A fresh pot of tea holds the centre of the table, Labrador and rose hip, sweetened with maple syrup from this year's harvest. We are home.

Enter Kim

For me, this work is guided by an enduring Granny spirit. As an urban Indigenous person working with youth struggling through these bleak times of climate change, pandemic, and war, one humble thing I can do is keep building with this Grandmother. For as my adopted Mishoomis (grandfather) Rene Meshake has said, "They can bulldoze our sites, but they can't bulldoze the spirit of our ancestors."

Scene 7

We are in the arboretum again, right now. Working with the architects, students, and other community. The white background of our quilt blends into the blanket of snow covering the earth, and mauve, pink and purple points emanate out from a bright yellow star in the centre. There is a basket with sage and tobacco on the blanket, and the assistant vice-president of Indigenous Initiatives at our university, Cara Wehkamp, uses the sage to smudge everyone in the circle while we sing the opening song. We choose the Strong Women's Song, suggested by Sheri because it happens to be International Women's Day. We have some loose tobacco that we pass around while Kim offers opening words and then she passes her polka-dotted egg "granny" rattle to the person beside her. As the egg goes around, each person in the circle says what it means for them to be here, and then they offer their hopes for the day and the project. One person offers a song; others are quiet and just pass the rattle along. We then serve tea made by one of our students from the local urban Indigenous food sovereignty project. We invite everyone to take some time by themselves with the site, to offer their tobacco where they feel it needs to go. After this we go indoors and begin a design workshop led by the architects.

Enter Sheri

As I think of our work at Nokom's House, what we've embarked upon, and what we've been guided by, I am ultimately sent on a journey of gratitude, personal reflection, discovery, and uncertainty...and I walk gently, patiently, and carefully, thinking of my ancestors and relations. Being sure to allow for things to unfold as they will, or perhaps more so, as they should. For if history has taught us anything as Indigenous Peoples, it is that opportunity within the colonial constructs is not without loss, significant losses, and enduring intergenerational consequences. And in this age of a renewed commitment to reconciliation, and heightened awareness of environmental justice or what I believe Onondaga Chief Oren Lyons means when he refers to our "collective consciousness," I'm cautious and aware of the path we are forging, asking myself is this a good path, am I being a good ancestor, is it within the spirit of the Two Row Wampum, of mutual respect, or of non-interference as Tuscarora Knowledge Keeper Rick Hill would explain? The Haudenosaunee Good Mind reminds me to be aware of my thoughts and intention, and to walk peacefully with all of creation. Seven-generations thinking, common to many Indigenous Peoples, grounds me in my responsibilities to past, current, and future, and not only for human beings but, as the Thanksgiving Address teaches, "all my relations."

Enter Kim

By now, we are hoping that our audience has been able to make their own connections between the building we are doing and the theme of this collection: feminist ethics and poetics. For me, these connections come from Indigenous scholars, who have helped me understand that Indigenous feminism is really about being "in good relation" (Nickel and Fehr) or, as one Auntie put it, taking up kinship responsibilities with our human, non-human, and ancestral relations (Anderson). My own Indigenous feminist approach is wrapped up with musings about how gender and life stages determine responsibility—and perhaps this is why Shakespeare's version of life stages, captured in the "all the world's a stage" lines came to me.

I return to my work to build Nokom's House, thinking about how I might do Auntie work. I circle back to thoughts about how Aunties nurture and discipline, always with best interests of younger generations in mind. I think about how they make sure to keep you on track. How they teach you to be a good relative; how they try to be one themselves. And I think these Auntie ethics can also teach us how to be a good professor, to be an effective actor in the academy. To act on the stage where I have landed.

Closing

While construction will not begin for several months, it feels good to realize that Nokom's House already exists in our collective consciousness—it has been built in our minds and spirits through visiting, through time spent with Indigenous community members as well as our non-human relations on the site. We are building collectively across time and space, for past and future generations, for our non-human relations, and for ourselves. We are doing Granny spirit's work.

We hope she is pleased.

Works Cited

Anderson, Kim. "Multi-generational Indigenous Feminisms: From F Word to What IFs." *Routledge Handbook of Critical Indigenous Studies*, edited by Brendan Hokowhitu, et al., Routledge, 2021, pp. 37–51.

Farrell-Racette, Sherry. "Storytelling: Kitchen Table Theory." Sâkêwâk Storyteller's Festival, Regina, Saskatchewan, 3 Feb. 2017.

Johnston, Basil. "The Nature of Plants." *Ojibwe Heritage*, McClelland & Stewart, 2008.

Lalor, Amina. *in a good way: (Re)grounding Contextual Narratives on Turtle Island*. 2020. University of Waterloo, Master of Architecture.

Nickel, Sarah, and Amanda Fehr, editors. *In Good Relation: History, Gender, and Kinship in Indigenous Feminisms*. U of Manitoba P, 2020.

Siisip Geniusz, Mary. *Plants Have So Much to Give Us, All We Have to Do Is Ask*, edited by Wendy Makoons Geniuz, U of Minnesota P, 2015.

2

Becoming Critical

On the Limits and Possibilities of Learning with Indigenous Womxn's Stories

MYLÈNE YANNICK GAMACHE

IT WASN'T YET KNOWN that we would be physically gathering for the last time, on March 11, 2020; or that in response to a highly infectious and vastly spreading global virus, all remaining course content would be transmitted online.[1] We had grown accustomed to gathering on Mondays and Wednesdays at 3:30 p.m. in the same physical space, a classroom on the first floor of an otherwise quiet university college, each week that winter term. On the first day of what was now a remote learning experience, participants were asked to watch the first hour of *Words for Water: Songs and Stories of Strength by Native Women*. In this audio-visual recording of an event hosted by the Whitney Museum of American Art, we encountered the resonant voices of Indigenous poets, writers, musicians, and water protectors like Layli Long Soldier (Oglala Lakota), Deborah Miranda (Esselen/Chumash), and Joy Harjo (Mvskoke). We listened to personal stories and teachings about water extending across centuries of extractive settler encroachments. We heard poetic tributes honouring those at Standing Rock who defended and protected Indigenous lands and waters from the planned construction of the Dakota Access Pipeline. It was not lost on O-Pipon-Na-Piwin Cree Nation participant Cindy Oliveira, as evinced by the response she posted to our weekly discussion board,[2] that chronic industrial contamination of Indigenous waterways and long-term water advisories on Indigenous reserves like Shoal Lake 40 could not inspire the same kind of fervor and actionable concern that COVID-19 was immediately able to garner.³ The persistence of water reminds us that Indigenous Peoples' cross-generational, place-based, and ecological knowledges can never be so easily subsumed within mainstream re-settler discourses.⁴ Cindy compared one world—where Canada's violent lack of accountability can be lived everyday by those who are left to endure colonially induced water emergencies—to another world—where strict public health measures can be immediately imposed, testing kits provided, and settler colonial borders promptly closed, as the nation-state repeatedly flexes the reach of its own carceral logics.⁵ Through the critical exchange that Cindy's response sparked, the stark contrast in responsibility, however colonial and deeply flawed, was not lost on us.

This chapter shares insights on a pedagogical approach that is both in-formation and informed by my experiences learning with University of Manitoba (UM) classroom participants in three iterations of a second-year undergraduate course on Indigenous womxn's literatures (Winter 2020, Winter 2021, Winter 2022). Winter 2020 classes took place mostly in-person until March 11, whereas both Winter 2021 and Winter 2022 classes were held exclusively on Zoom. While the course is designed to foster creative and informed readerly exchanges, I reflect on the limits of co-learning with participants in settler colonial and increasingly neoliberalized institutional spaces. The university broadly acknowledges that its campuses and research centres are situated on the lands of the Ininiwak, Nêhîthâwak,⁶ Anishinaabeg, Dakhóta Oyáte, Dene, Anish-Ininiwak, and Red River Métis. Some Department of Indigenous Studies colleagues at the UM insist that relational protocols and teachings are embedded within land acknowledgements, which are often led by or produced in collaboration with Indigenous community members. Other colleagues worry that when acknowledgements shared at university-sponsored events are not abetted by actionable commitments, these conciliatory overtures seem to imply that universities are somehow "neutral" or "placeless" sites of learning (Higgins et al. 294). At times, they even seem to overwrite the hushed settler colonialist circumstances under which the UM could, in 1877, become the first university in so-called Western Canada to found itself on Indigenous lands. The 2015–2020 Strategic Plan for the Department of Indigenous Studies at the University of Manitoba, which was envisioned by former and current colleagues in 2019, explains that the university was partly established to educate "the Métis sons of the Red River settlement" (1). It's perhaps unsurprising that Métis men would be recruited for this edification strategy, especially if efforts to dissociate Métis from their communities and First Nations kin might serve to temper the threat they posed to the nation-state's dream and vision for "Euro-Canadian dominance" (Fiola 32). The strategic plan also acknowledges that Indigenous Peoples have a complicated relationship with the university. Deep suspicion and distrust of this colonialist institution are rooted in the university's racist and exclusionary foundations, extractive research practices, alienating policies, hierarchical bureaucracies, capitalist-driven performance metrics, and historically shallow commitments to Indigenous self-determination.[7]

As an early career urban French Métis scholar, it is with caution and ongoing struggle that I assume the responsibility of guiding students in this course. I am a French- and English-speaking urban Métis whose professional development has been both expected and financially facilitated by my parents. I have also spent most of my life studying in colonialist institutions. My mother, a first-grade teacher, always insisted on education. In periods of self-doubt, she insisted that I find my intellectual community, which she envisioned principally happening through the academy. I left relatives in the Red River Valley on several occasions to pursue an MA in Toronto on Wendat, Anishnaabe, and Haudenosaunee land, a PHD in Canterbury, England, and sessional work in the Okanagan Valley on Syilx territory. I dedicated research efforts in the pursuit of abstract theoretical engagements and abstracted myself, from ties to community and place, in the process. The ability to pursue an education elsewhere diverted time and attention away from my adored grandmother, Lucile Carrière (née Beauchemin) and mother, Paulette Carrière-Gamache, both anchors in an extended network of proudly reserved Franco-Métis kin. Despite knowing ourselves to be Métis, it was somehow only upon visiting Grant's Old Mill, in my final year as an undergrad at the UM, that I learned of our relations with Métis leader Cuthbert Grant.[8] I distinctly remember my grandmother's pride as she affirmed my mother's words with her knowing smile. My studies abroad at the University of Kent meant uprooting myself away from our stories, our kinship networks, our historical contributions to Métis governance,[9] and our relations to place. My responsibility to the stories and narratives I share with students are inflected by efforts to reconnect with and ground myself in Franco-Métis lifeways, even as my two most cherished guides and educators, my grandmother and my mother, are no longer here to inform this work.

Learning with

Denendeh-based Inuk, Haitian, and Taíno multidisciplinary artist Siku Allooloo offers a resonant teaching in her story "Caribou People," which was imparted to her by Elder Ethele Lamothe while they scraped and prepared moose hide for tanning:

> Our society is full of holes now, like the ones in this hide. So we have to sew them up. When there's a hole there instead of a mother or a father, an aunty or grandparent steps in to raise the kids. We have holes in our spirituality and culture, how we relate to each other and deal with things, so we have to find ways to relearn that. You know, we lost some of our ceremonies and ways of praying, but we can learn from other cultures who still have it. You don't have any grandmothers to teach what you need to know as a woman, so you adopt a new grandmother who can teach you. So we do it like that. We sew it up. (180)

Allooloo elsewhere explains that "the work of repair...is really about paying attention to different sensibilities" (Allooloo, "RBC X WAG"). This idea emerges in the context of Allooloo speaking about her seal-skin woven art piece and poem "Akia," featured as part of INUA, Qaumajuq's inaugural exhibit: "What would the work of repair look like if framed within a creation space?" I often wonder whether the (virtual) classroom can offer momentary spaces for creative musing and relation-building. In the 2022 iteration of this course, I curated assigned material and released discussion prompts a day before class so that participants might have time to gather their ideas and ground their in-class conversations. Glimmers of reparative work intermittently took shape in students' readerly experiences, in their written creative entries, and in their engagements with one another's felt responses. I suggest that the work of learning with can be generative for many, even reparative for some, but that it is often work that is uneven and not without its own exigencies and risks.

The title to this chapter is a partly formed imperative: "Becoming Critical" intends to make clear that these stories, *on their own*, entreat from each reader a heightened capacity for critical acuity. These stories transform and change their readers. As Mi'kmaw scholar Marie Battiste (Potlotek First Nation) affirms in *Decolonizing Education*, "I am aware of the value of story and its ability to transform my research, and resist the Eurocentric frameworks that privileged other peoples' stories and analyses of Indigenous peoples' lives. It is also transforming me and bringing back life to life" (17). Emphasizing the experience of learning with, then, aligns itself with Sámi scholar Rauna Kuokkanen's work on the importance of conducting research "by" and "with" Indigenous Peoples rather than "on and for" (10), and Sisseton-Wahpeton Oyate scholar Kim TallBear's efforts to "stand with" Indigenous subjects in ways which reflect commitment to Indigenous intellectual traditions (4). I sit with students and deliberately refrain from assuming the position of lecturer in these settings, as the stories themselves are our primary teachers. Through the questions I pose and the conversations I strive to incite, I try to model as a fellow learner in action. I offer discussion prompts ahead of time in an effort to ground and foster non-hierarchical exchange. On some days, we engage these questions collectively and, on other days, participants gather in smaller groups and chat with each other. In person, I would sit and listen or walk around to try to offer gentle prompts as needed. In a virtual setting, I float between break-out rooms, only staying in place for five- to ten-minute intervals, and keep my camera off to minimize feelings of intrusiveness.

The course is designed to introduce students to "diverse Indigenous literacy contexts" (Styres 25). Every fifty-minute class unfolds around a different set of stories, poems, films, or lyrical essays as told by a particular cis feminine, gender diverse, and/or 2SQ Indigenous content creator. A chapter from Stó:lo and St'at'imc scholar Jo-ann Archibald's (Q'um Q'um Xiiem) *Indigenous Storywork*, assigned in the second week of class, reminds course participants that stories are vessels of knowledge and power that set their own relational terms of engagement: "If one comes to understand and appreciate the power of a particular knowledge, then one must be ready to share and teach it respectfully and responsibly to others in order for this knowledge, and its power, to continue" (3). In our comparative readings of excerpts from Jas M. Morgan's *Nîtisânak* and Katsi Cook's "The Coming of Anontaks," we reflect on making space for both gendered and degendered land-body connections, such that Morgan's injunction, "Don't gender and sexualize nature," need neither reaffirm nor contradict their subsequent insistence that "The prairie wind is gay af" (46). In Anishinaabe poet Lesley Belleau's "Niibinabe," we discuss efforts to reclaim space for Missing and Murdered Indigenous Relatives through the rustling sightings of Anishinaabe water-spirits, Nebaunaubae, or "being[s] of sleep," as Neyaashiinigmiing Elder and Knowledge Keeper Basil Johnston refers to them in *The Manitous: The Spiritual World of the Ojibway*. If rivers are murky sites where bodies can go missing, Belleau incites readers to honour the endurance of "murky stories" which Indigenous womxn insist on telling (51). In the winter term of 2020, students engage with Nêhiyaw poet Sky Dancer Louise Bernice Halfe's *Burning in This Midnight Dream*, yet some critically countered whether even the use of silence in her work could mitigate the reality that some stories, including the legacy of residential schools in Canada, are too horrifying to tell.

Becoming Critical

In her contribution to Linda Tuhiwai Smith, Eve Tuck, and Wayne Yang's co-edited anthology *Indigenous and Decolonizing Studies in Education: Mapping the Long View*, Kanien'kehá:ka scholar Sandra Styres affirms "critical literacy" as a pedagogical approach that involves understanding that land is "an articulation of ancient knowledges grounded in the experiences of self-in-relationship to place" (25). In Styres's view, critical literacy invites participants to learn about who they are so that they might ground themselves in that knowledge and, in turn, better understand how settler colonialist discourses and power dynamics structure both their self-understandings and their capacities to engage with others (26). The importance of positioning themselves as readers, of acknowledging and understanding their "own cultural positionalities and relations to place" (24), is an integral part of participants' work in this course. It begins in the first week of classes, with Nêhiyaw and Saulteaux scholar Margaret Kovach's insistence that self-location is a relational responsibility which "shows respect to the ancestors and allows the community to locate us" (96). Kovach echoes the importance of understanding where you come from, as your relation to community and place informs the scope and limits of your questions as well as your own understanding of truth (97). While Kovach insists that in order to begin any meaningful interpretive work, you must be in tune with yourself (97), re-settler scholar Allison Hargreaves invites participants to consider how "different responsibilities are involved for Indigenous and non-Indigenous critics" (109). Citing Emma LaRocque, Hargreaves explains that "the critic carries political responsibilities to the 'cultural and epistemic home/lands'" of the literatures with which they engage (109).

Chippewas of Nawash Unceded First Nation writer, poet, and editor Kateri Akiwenzie-Damm joins our classroom in the winter term of 2021. Kateri generously invites a slow rereading of prominent themes and motifs recurring across *The Stone Collection*, an anthology of fourteen short stories published in 2015. She speaks of picking fossilized stones in the Saugeen Peninsula and of fossilization, as the passage of time. A reference to the pulsing life energy of stones is folded into her reflection that Anishnaabemowin concerns itself with what is alive; "what is quiddity, spirit, or manitou." She speaks of stones uncovering two sides of things as an underlying theme throughout her work, where the surface may appear one way and, at the same time, otherwise. While she expands on the nature of the relationship between two feminine characters in "Picking Stones," I take a moment to jot down a question—*Is there only one acceptable interpretation for each story?* But when it comes time to articulate it, I ask instead, *What do you take to be the responsibility of the listener and the reader?* To which she justly responds, "The responsibility of the reader is to be able to arm themselves with the knowledge that will allow them to make their way through these texts with a level of understanding, so that they may comprehend more fully what is happening."

In the foreword to the 1993 anthology *Looking at the Words of Our People*, Syilx writer and scholar Jeannette Armstrong rightfully insists that "First Nations Literature will be defined by First Nations writers, readers, academics and critics and perhaps only by writers and critics from within those varieties of First Nations contemporary practice and past practise of culture and the knowledge of it" (7). As Cherokee citizen Daniel Heath Justice insists in "Reflections on Indigenous Literary Nationalism," "very simply, to understand Indigenous literatures, it is both intellectually and ethically imperative to know something about the meaningful contexts from which those literatures emerge *and* with which those literatures are engaged" (24). Similarly, Kateri insists that it is incumbent on the reader to learn "the collective, the local, the specific—in a word, the national" (Heath Justice 24–25) context that informs each story; for to ground literatures in their own place-based Indigenous politics, relations, visions, and aesthetics bespeaks, as Heath Justice argues, a commitment to the "collective continuities" and enduring significances of Indigenous futurities (25–26).

I sit with the lingering question about whether it's appropriate to encourage students to venture their own interpretations, especially when the context is not immediately available to them. I sit with the concern that in encouraging students to listen, to become attuned to their interpretive limits, to learn to detect when further context may be needed, and to take risks with the information they have, the very aims of Indigenous literary nationalist commitments may somehow become compromised. Heath Justice clarifies that Indigenous literary nationalism "doesn't insist on insularity or exclusivity, as any thoughtful reader/critic can engage these contexts in meaningful ways" (25). While one need neither be Indigenous nor engaged with community to undertake such an approach, Heath Justice insists that it must nonetheless be grounded in the "meaningful interpretive relationship between specific writers, their specific communities on specific lands shaped by specific social, cultural and political histories" (26). Most assigned literatures in the course offer signposts to indicate to readers the political nuances and nation-specific issues with which they are concerned. And while the ethics and poetics of *co-learning with* can be felt in the critical openings students report in their responses to Indigenous womxn's stories, these conditions are consistently threatened by overwhelming institutional constraints and the pervasive effects of cognitive imperialism (Battiste 158–166). As Battiste explains in *Decolonizing Education*, "cognitive imperialism relies on colonial dominance as a foundation of thought, language, values, and frames of reference as reflected in the language of instruction, curricular, discourses, texts, and methods" (161). As the institution expects instructors and students to conform to rigid evaluative structures and competitive grading schemes, instructors are all too often at risk of replicating "whitewashing" pedagogical practices in their efforts to meet these institutional demands (Battiste 162).

I observe myself struggling with an ingrained need to replicate abstract pedagogical techniques and learning expectations. I pause often and reflect about whether my demands for creative and critical risk-taking frustrates participants' oral and written contributions; whether discussion prompts are not flexible enough to address both Indigenous and non-Indigenous participants' lived experiences; and whether my insistence on MLA in-text citation practices suits the university's sterile and disassociated learning conditions. The Stó:lo narrator and teaching assistant in Lee Maracle's "Goodbye Snauq" accentuates the cold formalism of "the halls of this educational institution [which] are empty. The bright white, fluorescent bulbs that dot the ceiling are hidden behind great long light fixtures dimming its length" (13). Maracle heightens the divide between airless institutional spaces in which breathing lands and beating worlds are contemplated, while Indigenous Nations in British Columbia face relentless pressure to defend or forfeit their land titles: "Suddenly, the fluorescent lights offend, the dry perfect room temperature insults, and the very space mocks" (Maracle 22). Through ongoing settler colonial invasions, sacred Indigenous communal sites and lands are re-settled and terraformed to suit petro-capitalist and resource-extractive economies (Todd 104). A managerial approach to land as resource (Liboiron 62) and property (Miller et al. 94–95) forecloses Indigenous understandings of land as communally occupied (Maracle 16, 25), deeply storied (Linklater 152–153), and tangibly alive. While land is, as Plains Cree scholar Cash Ahenakew elsewhere affirms, alive and "agentic," its capacities to communicate through sightings and soundscapes are "not-fully-intelligible within the ways-of-knowing-and-being that we inherit within the academy" (Higgins et al. 294). Armstrong poetically conjures the N'silxchn speaker's receptivity to the land in her piece titled "Land Speaking." There, she bends the colonizer's language to convey stories—encoded within the varied patterns of N'silxchn oral and musical properties—as told by the land, which is "constantly speak[ing]" (176): "We survived and thrived by listening to its teachings— to its language—and then inventing human words to retell its stories to our succeeding generation" (176). Indigenous womxn's stories consistently call upon participants to integrate place-based philosophies and considerations into their reading-work, as these texts often work to remind us that knowledge of "land, learning, identity, and education intersect" *through* place (Styres 24, emphasis added).

Dark Matters[10]

A course like this one invites varying degrees of proximity. We were fortunate enough to gather in person for most of the winter term in 2020, which meant that we could enact our reading circles in person. Through varied coordinated efforts, we eventually lapsed into our own co-rhythms and nourished collective readings over the course of the virtual winter term in 2021. But for reasons that are varied and include the very real violence that the assigned content at times relived, the eroding effects of social distancing, two years of online learning, globally intensifying strains of white nationalism and the increasing urgencies of climate catastrophe, dynamics during the winter

2022 term understandably felt more strained and exhaustive. Several Indigenous participants reported needing to take time away from classes to care for themselves. The same few students extended gratitude for space, time, and reflections shared with one another at the end of each break-out session. While both Indigenous and non-Indigenous students noted appreciating anti-colonial and gender-attuned learning methods, the work it required—as it bears repeating—is not without its own exigencies and risks.

Over the course of the winter 2022 term, participants were randomly invited to submit online assessments and overviews of their break-out sessions as evidence of their engagement with course content. In these submissions, they outlined what was discussed with peers that day and summarized individual responses to pre-released discussion questions. Wedged in the middle of a detailed report on peer-exchanges after a Monday break-out session, a student shared with me the experience of being laughed at by her peers while she imparted her community's painful experiences of being dispossessed from their lands and relocated to suit re-settler extraction needs. As I circulate in and out of these sessions, I think I remember witnessing the encounter in question. Even now, I hesitate to share my own interpretation as my intention is neither to invalidate nor contradict her experiences in this virtual space. Immediately conscious of the two-day delay after first seeing her peer-assessment response, I apologized for failing to promptly address the situation. I confirmed that all groups would be reshuffled upon our return from winter break the following week, at which time I would also issue a generalized reminder about the importance of maintaining respectful engagement protocols when responding to peers' sensitive offerings. But any confidence or trust she may have held in this co-learning space disintegrated from this moment on. While she continued to attend each class and responded to all email proddings I sent her way, she never again turned on her camera. Aside from a few sparse private messages sent to me, she refrained entirely from engaging in communal class discussions.

I both missed and fumbled the chance to anticipate the exigencies of this situation. I failed to meet her expectations and broader assumptions that I can insulate all participants from abrupt cues in miscommunication. I wonder if this is partly what happens when parameters around respectful discussions are too relaxed, when boundaries are not suitably affirmed, when non-Indigenous students preside over break-out session discussions, or when the haze of pandemic burnout distills chances for mutual understanding. In response to an email I sent her a month later, she circled around the source of her disengagement and underlined the irony that a course like this one, on Indigenous womxn's stories, could become inhospitable to her. She projected back to me the limits of fostering anti-colonial "educational transformation" within the alienating walls of this virtual spacing (Battiste 163). Battiste elsewhere issues the reminder that "For every educator, our responsibility is making a commitment to both unlearn and learn—to unlearn racism and superiority in all its manifestations, while examining our own social constructions in our judgments and new ways of knowing, valuing others, accepting diversity, and making equity and inclusion foundations for all learners" (166). In a chapter called "Indigenous Queer Normativity" from *As We Have Always Done*, Leanne Betasamosake Simpson (Michi Saagiig Nishnaabeg) argues that Indigenous 2SQ worlds "get destroyed" when heteronormative prescriptions invade Indigenous spaces (120). I see parallels between the infiltration of damaging assumptions about the potential of anti-colonial learning spaces, as these same assumptions can end up fostering uneven and occasionally hostile learning conditions.

In the third week of classes, participants read excerpts from Alicia Elliott's *A Mind Spread Out on the Ground*, which speaks to the narrator's lived experiences of the colonialism-depression link. Participants also engage with segments of Anishnaabe journalist Tanya Talaga's *Seven Fallen Feathers*, on the systems that fail Indigenous teenagers and their communities through institutionalized racism and neglect, and the communities who mobilize to meet their own needs through extended networks of relational care. While some students were developing language for the first time to address and denounce the permutating effects of settler colonial violence, I worried that in-class contributions might alienate those with intimate lived experiences. By the end of the fourth week of term, I am overcome by participants' varying levels of dissociation and resignation. Obiishkikaang Lac Seul First Nation scholar Saaseyaa'sin Christine Sy reminded us the week prior, in "Considering Wenonah, Considering Us," that violence can always be transmitted through the telling. Her work spurs a larger question about how violence is reproduced through participants' own engagements with these narrative forms (199–200). The assignment prompt I released at the end of week three encouraged participants to take as much time as may be needed with Peepeekisis First Nation filmmaker and scholar Tasha Hubbard's documentary *nîpawistamâsowin: We Will Stand Up*, while inviting them to reflect on their own responsibility to this multilayered story and the world-building they wish to be a part of.

Métis writer and scholar Chelsea Vowel from manitow-sâkihikan (Lac Ste. Anne) joined us for a guest visit in April 2022. She energized the room with her enthusiasm and her bright reflections. While explaining how the podcast *Métis in Space* came to be produced with fellow Métis co-host and friend Molly Swain, she was quick to foreground the resounding importance of Indigenous joy. She lamented having to teach *Indigenous Writes,* a comprehensive *Guide to First Nations, Métis and Inuit Issues* she wrote in 2016, in University of Alberta Native Studies introductory courses: "I would not say that this work came out of Indigenous joy," she concedes, "though the hope was there…We're still stuck on 101-work and it's really frustrating." In her grounded efforts to write and conjure Métis futurisms which invite readers to imagine so as to act otherwise, Vowel rejects apocalypse as a starting point: "Indigenous languages and cultures were targeted for decimation; they are not 'dying out'"—adding astutely—"*slowest apocalypse ever, btw.*" In the introduction to his edited Indigiqueer speculative fiction anthology *Love after the End*, Two-Spirit Oji-nêhiyaw writer Joshua Whitehead (Peguis First Nation) explains that while this collection of short stories was initially "designed to be geared toward the dystopic…after careful conversations, we decided to queer it toward the utopian" (10). Vowel's short stories and the speculative fictions in Whitehead's edited anthology write Indigenous bodies who "flourish into being *joyously* animated rather than merely alive" (Whitehead 11). As such, both urge facilitators to reassess the literatures they choose to assign insofar as these reflect worlds, always already, which might be lived and enacted now.

Chelsea left students with the resonant idea that *"education is not the answer, action is."* As the back matter of her most recently published collection of Métis futurisms *Buffalo Is the New Buffalo* explains, "'Education is the new buffalo' is a metaphor widely used among Indigenous peoples in Canada to signify the importance of education to their survival and ability to support themselves, as once Plains nations supported themselves as buffalo peoples." In response, Chelsea Vowel asks, "Instead of accepting that the buffalo, and our ancestral ways, will never come back, what if we simply ensure that they do?" In conclusion, I similarly invite readers to linger in the active chances and clearings which Indigenous womxn's other-worlds offer, so as to ensure that the work of materializing co-learning spaces where

Indigenous joys and actions are amplified can continue, with immense caution, collective urgency, and resonant care.

Notes

1. I inherited the course Indigenous Women's Stories in the fall of 2019 upon assuming the position as cross-appointed assistant professor in the Department of Indigenous Studies and Women's and Gender Studies at the University of Manitoba. I reference the term *womxn* throughout to quite literally make space for Indigenous-led approaches to sexual and gendered orders that do not conform to colonialist binary prescriptions and invasions.
2. I received Cindy's permission to include these reflections.
3. I should note here that in her January 2021 keynote address for the international conference on the Ethics and Poetics of "Learning With," Tuscarora writer Alicia Elliott similarly insists on "the colonialism-depression link" as a way to floodlight not only the shortcomings of Western psychiatric deficit models, but also, the settler colonial structures and policies that strategically deny Indigenous communities equivalent access to food, shelter, and water.
4. I use Métis scholar Dr. Emma LaRocque's term *re-settler* here to challenge the "civ/sav binary"—which the etymology of the term *settler* requires—as well as to rightly acknowledge the First Peoples who settled and governed themselves on these lands. The term appears throughout LaRocque's *When the Other Is Me*, where it works to disturb the white nationalist mythology that European "pioneers" were the first to occupy Indigenous lands.
5. I paraphrase here a statement that was issued in May 2020 by the organizing members of the Abolition Collective who publish *Abolition: A Journal of Insurgent Politics* in collaboration with community groups based in Toronto.
6. The UM's acknowledgement includes both autonyms (i.e., Anishnaabeg) and exonyms (i.e., Cree, Dakota, Oji-Cree) and does not acknowledge the Nakoda Nation. The decision here to replace exonyms with autonyms/preferred names is not meant, in any way, to undermine the work of community advisors in the creation of this statement.
7. See, for instance, Shelly Johnson's chapter in *Indigenous Research* on Dr. Richard Ward's 1980s research project at the University of British Columbia in which 1,878 Nuu-Chah-Nulth community members participated and donated blood samples for a proposed study on arthritis. Instead of respecting the sovereignty and integrity of research participants by storing research results within the community, Ward took the vials with him when he left UBC and never shared the "inconclusive" research results with Nuu-Chah-Nulth research participants.

8. Marguerite Grant, Cuthbert Grant's sister, is our direct maternal ancestor. I write here about the way in which I came to this knowledge as a kind of tribute to Marilyn Dumont's "Our Gabriel" (in *The Pemmican Eaters* 1–5).

9. While I have much to learn of mid-nineteenth- to early twentieth-century stories associated with Métis women kin in our networks, my mother often underlined the governance roles and responsibilities of numerous direct and extended relatives. Alexis Carrière, my maternal great-great-grandfather, was co-founder and secretary of l'Union Métisse St. Joseph de Saint-Pierre (see photograph of Alexis Carrière). Damase Carrière, who is one of nine Métis who "Fell in Defence of Their Freedoms and Rights" at Batoche in 1885 and whose grave is commemorated at a shared cemetery site there, was Alexis Carrière's first cousin. We're related to Louis Riel by marriage; Francois Poitras and Madeleine Fisher's daughters, Eleanor and Bibiane, married brothers Joseph and Alexandre Riel, while their sister, Marguerite Poitras, is my grandmother Lucile's paternal grandmother. I include these brief references as it is customary and expected in Métis circles to situate yourself and your relations.

10. This subsection shares the same title of a chapter in Alicia Elliott's *A Mind Spread Out on the Ground*, where she speaks of dark matter as an analogy for racism, an oppressive structure that targets certain racialized bodies and governs everything, even as it remains "unseen" by those who both perpetuate and materially benefit from it.

Works Cited

Akiwenzie-Damm, Kateri. *The Stone Collection*. Highwater Press, 2015.

Allooloo, Siku. "Caribou People." *Shapes of Native Nonfiction: Collected Essays by Contemporary Writers*, edited by Elissa Washuta and Theresa Warburton, U of Washington P, 2019, pp. 173–182.

Allooloo, Siku. "RBC x WAG: INUA Virtual Sessions." *YouTube*, 5:20, 29 June 2021, https://www.youtube.com/watch?v=NRrowhyZIEU&t=1s.

Archibald, Jo-ann. "The Power of Stories to Educate the Heart." *Indigenous Storywork: Educating the Heart, Mind, Body and the Spirit*, UBCP, 2008, pp. 83–100.

Armstrong, Jeannette. Foreword. *Looking at the Words of Our People: First Nations Analysis of Literature*, edited by Armstrong. Theytus Books, 1993.

Armstrong, Jeannette. "Land Speaking." *Speaking for the Generations: Native Writers on Writing*, edited by Simon J. Ortiz, U of Arizona P, 1998, pp. 174–194.

Battiste, Marie. *Decolonizing Education: Nourishing the Learning Spirit*. Purich Publishing, 2013.

Belleau, Lesley. *Indianland*. Arbeiter Ring Press, 2017.

Betasamosake Simpson, Leanne. "Indigenous Queer Normativity." *As We Have Always Done: Indigenous Freedom through Radical Resistance*, U of Minnesota P, 2017, pp. 119–144.

Cook, Katsi. "The Coming of Anontaks." *Reinventing the Enemy's Language: Contemporary Native Women's Writings of North America*, edited by Joy Harjo and Gloria Bird, W.W. Norton, 1997, pp. 44–51.

Dumont, Marilyn. *The Pemmican Eaters*. ECW Press, 2015.

Elliott, Alicia. "The Colonialism-Depression Link: A Talk with Alicia Elliott." 27 Jan. 2021. *The Poetics and Ethics of 'Learning With' Indigenous, Canadian, Québécois Feminist Production Today*, https://ntnu.cloud.panopto.eu/Panopto/Pages/Viewer.aspx?id=77dee96c-859a-4500-a3e9-acbd01534079.

Elliott, Alicia. *A Mind Spread Out on the Ground*. Penguin Random House, 2020.

Fiola, Chantal. *Rekindling the Sacred Fire: Métis Ancestry and Anishnaabe Spirituality*. U of Manitoba P, 2015.

Halfe, Louise Bernice. *Burning in This Midnight Dream*. Coteau Books, 2016.

Hargreaves, Allison. "The Lake Is the People and Life That Come to It." *Learn, Teach, Challenge: Approaching Indigenous Literatures*, edited by Deanna Reder and Linda M. Morra, Wilfrid Laurier UP, 2016, pp. 107–110.

Heath Justice, Daniel. "Reflections in Indigenous Literary Nationalism: On Home Grounds, Singing Hogs, and Cranky Critics." *Sources and Methods in Indigenous Studies*, edited by Chris Andersen and Jean M. O'Brien, Routledge, 2017, pp. 23–30.

Higgins, Marc, et al. "Staying with the Trouble in Science Education: Towards Thinking with Nature—A Manifesto." *Posthumanism and Higher Education, Reimagining Pedagogy, Practice and Research*, edited by Carol A. Taylor and Annouchka Bayley, Palgrave Macmillan, 2019, pp. 155–164.

Hubbard, Tasha, director. *nîpawistamâsowin: We Will Stand Up*. NFB, 2019.

Johnson, Shelly. "Wise Indigenous Woman Approaches to Research: Navigating and Naming Jagged Ethical Tensions and Micro-Aggressions in the Academy." *Indigenous Research: Theories, Practices, and Relationships*, edited by Deborah McGregor and Jean-Paul Restoule, Canadian Scholars, 2018. *ProQuest Ebook Central*, http://ebookcentral.proquest.com/lib/umanitoba/detail.action?docID=6324728.

Johnston, Basil. *The Manitous: The Spiritual World of the Ojibway*. HarperCollins, 1995.

Kovach, Margaret. "Situating Self, Culture, and Purpose in Indigenous Inquiry." *Learn, Teach, Challenge: Approaching Indigenous Literatures*, edited by Deanna Reder and Linda M. Morra, Wilfrid Laurier UP, 2016, pp. 95–102.

Kuokkoanen, Rauna. *Restructuring Relations: Indigenous Self-Determination, Governance and Gender*. Oxford UP, 2019.

LaRocque, Emma. *When the Other Is Me: Native Resistance Discourse, 1850–1990*. U of Manitoba P, 2010.

Liboiron, Max. "Land, Nature, Resource, Property." *Pollution Is Colonialism*, Duke UP, 2021, pp. 39–79.

Linklater, Tanya. "Desirous Kinds of Indigenous Futurity: On the Possibilities of Memorialization." *Desire Change: Contemporary Feminist Art in Canada*, edited by Heather Davis, McGill-Queen's UP, 2017, pp. 149–168.

Maracle, Lee. "Goodbye Snauq." *First Wives Club: Coast Salish Style*, Theytus Books, 2010, pp. 13–26.

Miller, Robert J., et al. "The Doctrine of Discovery in Canada." *Discovering Indigenous Lands: The Doctrine of Discovery in the English Colonies*, Oxford UP, 2010, pp. 81–125.

Morgan, Jas M. *Nîtisânak*. Metonymy Press, 2018.

Photograph of Alexis Carrière. 1914. Collection générale de la Société historique de Saint-Boniface. SHSB3986. Centre du patrimoine, Winnipeg, MB. https://archivesshsb.mb.ca/link/archives119113.

Styres, Sandra. "Literacies of the Land: Decolonizing Narratives, Storying, Literature." *Indigenous and Decolonizing Studies in Education: Mapping the Long View,* edited by Linda Tuhiwai Smith, Eve Tuck, and K. Wayne Yang, Routledge, 2019, pp. 24–37.

Sy, Christine. "Considering Wenonah, Considering Us." *Keetsahnak / Our Missing and Murdered Indigenous Sisters*, edited by Kim Anderson, et al., U of Alberta P, 2018, pp. 193–214.

Talaga, Tanya. *Seven Fallen Feathers: Racism, Death and Hard Truths in a Northern City*. Anansi, 2017.

TallBear, Kim. "Standing with and Speaking as Faith: A Feminist-Indigenous Approach to Inquiry." *Journal of Research Practice,* vol. 10, no. 2, 2014, pp. 1–7.

Todd, Zoe. "Fish, Kin and Hope: Tending to Water Violations in *amiskwaciwâskahikan* and Treaty Six Territory." *Afterall*, vol. 43, no. 1, pp. 102–107.

Vowel, Chelsea. *Indigenous Writes: A Guide to First Nations, Métis, and Inuit Issues in Canada*. Highwater Press, 2016.

Vowel, Chelsea. *Buffalo Is the New Buffalo: Stories*. Arsenal Pulp Press, 2022.

Whitehead, Joshua. Introduction. *Love after the End: An Anthology of Two-Spirit and Indigiqueer Speculative Fiction,* edited by Whitehead, Arsenal Pulp Press, 2020, pp. 9–16.

Words for Water: Stories and Songs of Strength by Native Women. Whitney Museum of American Art, 1:54:44, 15 Nov. 2017, https://whitney.org/watchandlisten/35887.

3

I'm Still Not Done Talking about Zombies

JUNIE DÉSIL

WHILE THE ZOMBIE IS OFTEN SEEN as a figure to be pitied or feared, I am particularly interested in exploring the zombie not as a tragic and pitiable personage (Lauro, *Zombie Theory*) but as an opaque figure that is persistent, merciless, unrelenting, and inextricably linked to our experiences of Blackness. As I contend in my debut poetry collection *eat salt | gaze at the ocean*, I/we, am/are in fact zombies—we are haunted, our presence is a haunting—we remain spectral. Our status as "living dead" is both a representation of our adaptability and of our existence in a condition of aftermath. As such, the perniciousness of anti-Blackness, which, as Christina Sharpe contends, is a "total climate" that we live with/in, informs our status as undead.

As a Black feminist poet and writer, I often grapple with the ethical dilemma of witnessing/mourning/celebrating Black life and death. As a poet, I am always interested in exploring my positionality as a Black feminist and as a daughter of Haitian immigrants living on unceded and stolen territories, straddling the various experiences of in-betweenness in a world that devalues Blackness. The particular experience of being born "here" in these territories but ancestrally being from "there," the experience of being hypervisible as a Black woman and also invisible, and the experience of being the progeny of powerful ancestors who led the first successful Black revolution, are inscribed and carried on our bodies. My debut poetry collection crudely attempted to celebrate both Black life and death, primarily through the metaphor of the Haitian *zombi* or (American) zombie.

That said, it is not my intention to go into the history of the zombie; there is extensive scholarly work in an ever-growing field of zombie theory, a field where the zombie is recognized as having many social anxieties and ills (slavery, mass consumerism and excess, disease vector, etc.) projected onto its personage. Instead, I want to highlight the fact that the zombie figure, which was appropriated from Haitian culture, has made the transatlantic voyage onto the cinematic and literary space where it often does heavy lifting and labour in much the same way that Black *bodies* continue to toil in many of the spaces we find ourselves in.

While writing my collection I debated changing direction and keeping the research for scholarly writing, but I decided I didn't want to be an authority despite "ancestral claim." From a creative perspective, I debated writing deliberately *in the voice/from the perspective of* the zombie, but I feared not being able to come back to myself or, rather, I feared that I would become a zombie by the end of it. I debated whether I should put out all the ways that made me/us a zombie. I thought that it would be trauma porn. There was a grief that I wasn't prepared to put on paper; I was writing the collection in the midst of ongoing extrajudicial killings of Black folks, and my collection debuted three months after the extrajudicial murder of George Floyd, and in the midst of a global pandemic. I was not prepared to discuss this grief in public, and I was not prepared to see it dissected by reviewers. This decision was difficult as there is a part of me that relishes showing, telling, and sharing the excitement about the connections and deeper understanding from my delving deeper into the history of the zombie. I want to share my ongoing fascination with this figure, its permeability, porousness, and the way it straddles enslavement/resistance/power/powerlessness agency/rebellion/transmission/infection. As Sarah J. Lauro contends, "it is ontologically defiant at the same time that it is a nonentity" (*Transatlantic Zombie* 32). I see parallels between our lives as Black folks and the subject-object position of the zombie. Now, four years since publishing that collection, I still want to talk about zombies but not as a metaphor.

Recently I talked about writing the follow-up to *eat salt | gaze at the ocean* and that it would be called *i'm still not done talking about zombies*. I'm not finished witnessing our presence. I'm not done talking about my/our ongoing death. I'm not done finding ways to live with our living-dead condition. I'm not done finding ways to witness, care, and love ourselves and each other in spite/despite a world that expects our devaluation.

Ta-Nehisi Coates unflinchingly states, in his book *Between the World and Me*, that it is "traditional to destroy the black body—it is heritage" (103). Frank B. Wilderson III, in *Afropessimism*, laments, "Why must the world find its nourishment in Black flesh?" (16). Even as we are being destroyed, our deaths are violently depicted, circulated, recirculated. Allissa Richardson has written extensively on this phenomenon. In her book *Bearing Witness While Black: Americans, Smartphones, and the New Protest #Journalism*, Richardson details the long history of treating Black death as consumable; there is an insatiable appetite for seeing our deaths depicted and circulated in the most profane manner. While the devaluation of our dead bodies is not new (lynching photographs, images of dogs being set on Black protesters, distressing images of protesters being violently hosed, etc.), the viralness of images and the rise of social media render the circulation of these images ethically problematic and traumatic. Furthermore, the callousness and regularity with which these images are circulated have normalized the lack of solemn reserve that should be granted in these circumstances. Instead, Richardson calls for a shift to holding the viewing of fatal police encounters captured on cell phones, videos of vigilante violence inflicted on Black people, and other instances of violence on Black bodies as sacred. She argues in favour of limiting their circulation and presenting these images in ways that keep the breadth and scope of the circulation contained. For example, in *Bearing Witness While Black*, she explains how the National Association for the Advancement of Colored People and likely other Black publications and organizations employed the use of a "shadow archive" (176) of distressing lynching images. The shadow archive was maintained in a separate space in the newsroom, a library, or some such archival space once peak circulation of the images had been reached. As such, by limiting the circulation of these images, a sacred, respectful, and sombre gaze was preserved. Richardson debunks the myth that it is difficult to remove from circulation images that end up on the internet, demonstrating that images of white deaths are often removed from circulation fairly quickly, pointing to the lack of images available in the wake of some mass shootings; instead, portraits that show the victims' full humanity, heartwarming portraits, remain.

In the end, the great hope that cell phone footage would provide irrefutable proof of police violence on Black bodies and perhaps galvanize the public into greater support and moral outrage has not panned out. In the ongoing wake of police acquittals and rare convictions, Black witnessing through cell phone or other visual media has only added to the viral load of distressing images and continues to desensitize the white public and traumatize Black and racialized communities. Despite this double-edged sword, Richardson argues that "black witnessing" or "bearing witness while black is a specific kind of media witnessing. It is as networked, collective, and communal as the South African philosophy of Ubuntu, which states, 'I am because we are.' Black witnessing carries moral, legal, and even spiritual weight" (5). While this form of witnessing is important—providing a way to witness and tell our stories on our own terms—Richardson is adamant that limiting the circulation of traumatic visuals and centring the fullness and wholeness of the victims of extrajudicial violence, is the most ethical way to witness our deaths.

Poethics and Living With

As a poet, I deploy strategies—the written word, cadence, rhythm of sound words, the blank spaces on page, the underscored, the blacked-out texts, and the repetition—to talk about Black life and death, how we live with the haunting spectre of our death. I explore how we are not seen, recognized, mourned properly. We live with anti-Blackness, and the use of poetics is how I make sense of my world. I am drawn to Joan Retallack's insistence of the use of *h* in poetics and want to use poethics as an entry point to discuss "living with." In *The Poethical Wager*, Retallack argues that

> A poetics can take you only so far without an h. If you're to embrace complex life on earth, if you can no longer pretend that all things are fundamentally simple or elegant, a poetics thickened by an h launches an exploration of art's significance as, not just about, a form of living in the real world. That is not a simile; it's an ethos. Hence the h. What I'm working on is quite explicitly a poethics of a complex realism. (26)

As writers, poets, artists, and producers of cultural artifacts, it is our responsibility to make sense of our chaotic and problematic world. Moreover, I see an ethical responsibility that we, as artists, have as we work and create meaning. Writing and reading to make sense, as Retallack argues, is poethics. My debut collection and all other writings, the collections I read, whether poetry, novels, and academic essays, are all an attempt to make sense of our current world. In my current and ongoing work—whether I engage in opacity or writing "for us"—the act of writing is to engage with our own and others' lived experiences. More specifically Retallack states,

> Essays, like poems and philosophical meditations, should elude our grasp just because their business is to approach the liminal spectrum of near-unintelligibility-immediate experience complicating what we thought we knew. In this case, "to write" means to engage in a probative, speculative projection of the often-surprising vectors of words as they graze the circumstances of ongoing life. (48)

For Black scholar and artist Denise Ferreira da Silva, contemporary "poethics is a practice both artistic and aesthetic" ("End") that upends current strategies of racial subjugation. Poethics and, drawing on da Silva specifically, Black feminist poethics, is a way of living and thinking beyond the narrow constraints of our predetermined lives as informed by slavery, history, and so on and moving towards a space that frees us to be and live beyond—I believe—the aftermath and the wake of our histories ("End"; "Toward").

Opacité: An Ethical Claim and Framework

I often think of Emily Dickinson's poem "Tell All the Truth but Tell It Slant." The poem is generally interpreted as gradually telling the truth so as not to "dazzle" (Dungy), and as asking to look for and/or create angles and planes to talk circumspectly about truths we may not be able to handle or be confronted with. I am inclined to believe that while telling the truth slant, or being oblique, can work as a strategy, Édouard Glissant's work on opacity decolonizes the Eurocentric pursuit of truth and visibility. He instead argues for a veiled position, a stance that acts as refusal and opens up possibilities for speaking, creating, and living on our own terms. As such, Glissant deploys and enacts his right to not be understood by Eurocentric standards. Much like zombie theory, *opacité* is flexible and malleable in the ways that it can be applied to discussions of such issues as state surveillance, the position and alterity of being excluded/on the margins, as well as queer politics.

Opacité helps to formulate claims to ethical wake work, witnessing or bearing witness (Richardson) while *living with* and in a climate rife with anti-Blackness. More specifically, Glissant's use of *opacité* is an ethical position (Murdock) that we can deploy when it comes to speaking of, attending to, and witnessing our lives and deaths, while *living with* the violence of existing in our bodies. Mark V. Campbell and Pamela Edmonds contend that opacity "emerges both as a strategy of active resistance and as an alterity working against the logic of recognition and the ocular bias of Eurocentrism." As such, I see poethics and opacity as deliberate and thought-out strategies that form an ethical framework and claim when we are engaged in wake work, but also as a way to "operationalize" living with, witnessing, loving our dead and dying, on our terms, as we live with the conditions we experience as Black folks out in this world.

Sometime ago, while explaining to British Columbian writer Wayde Compton my fledgling idea of writing a collection using the zombie as metaphor to address anti-Blackness, our ongoing deaths, and so forth, he pointed out that the zombie was the only monstrous being that could be anything. Unlike Frankenstein's monster or vampires, whose lineage is decidedly European; the zombie—of African/Haitian origin—is decidedly American, embodying projected anxieties, straddling liminality as a porous inscrutable figure that is not well understood. I would argue that in some ways the zombie embodies *opacité*; the zombie defies understanding or rather defies *satisfactory* understanding. From outsiders, and readers, there is an expectation of illumination. A need for clarity and answers from the undead. Clarity and answers that may not be readily available for the audience/reader. However, as the writer/poet/storyteller, this is where I want to draw on my right and claim to *opacité*, wherein performing wake work that inevitably gets consumed by others, I embrace deliberately wanting to be misunderstood if needed and not being understood on someone else's terms. *Opacité*, then, is a necessity, a way of ethically caring for and witnessing our lives and deaths when the rest of the world refuses to, and, as Campbell and Edmonds contend, this helps "gesture, nudge, and urge us in the direction of living a Blackness vibrantly, without transparency or apology."

In the following section written in hybrid prose/poetic style, I explore the possibilities of living with the condition of being undead and living in the aftermath or wake of our ongoing subjugation. Moreover, as living dead the in-between space offers so many possibilities for living with—not as resignation—but as a refusal, as celebration (in spite/despite) and witnessing of our lives and deaths in a world that devalues our Black bodies both in life and death. In the wake (Sharpe) of the transatlantic passage, of grief, and of our ongoing deaths, as living dead, how do we live with the spectre of death haunting us, while simultaneously being *the haunting*, as zombies? Specifically, how do we live in a "total climate," a weather pattern that is decidedly anti-Black (Sharpe)? How do we live in a world that continually seeks our death? How do we live in conditions that hasten us towards our death, and that make our dying a "necessity"? More importantly, how do we ethically mourn and attend to our deaths, problematize and discuss our ongoing murders? How do we do wake work for ourselves and our community? How do we live with/in the liminal space of living dead, as zombies?

I use various vignettes in the second part of this chapter to forge my own claim to *opacité* as a right and necessity for wake work, for living with our own haunting, and as a way to write and engage in poethics. In the vignettes, I use various in/formal strategies, like writing in small caps, run-on sentences, and lack of punctuation, and I employ instances where I deliberately let my words be misunderstood, and where I deliberately use erasure poetics—hiding text under black box.

a prayer

to my ancestors each of you. birthed an iteration of me wishing as far as you could see for my freedom i did not choose my ancestors may my progeny be intentional may they choose me and sit with me witness to my witnessing teach me how to define ethics to reject that which does not serve. do you want content warning do we put up defences to not hear the sound of our loud implication the screeching of irony my ancestors teach continually so that even when the visible chains disappear the invisible ones glow so that you learn intuition early on learn to not trust even when shown. what are the words behind the words behind the words behind the gestures behind the gestures behind the silence coded silence the one that marks your station in life that scars your tongue that shortens your life expectancy or fills it with a series of near-death stressors the ones that eventually kill you? do i warn of these contents before i share the wild joy amidst the pain and the near romanticizing of resilience? do i hide and blur and obscure for my self-preservation or yours?

alongé: even in death we do not get to rest

my father and i often joke about his death (he's fine) and how he expects i'll take on the cost of burying him and arranging his affairs. i joke and say I can only afford a cardboard box—and he and i both erupt into helpless giggles. in a more recent call he tells me a Haitian joke where Haitians ask to be buried back home, quipping that here in North America you get buried upright so you never get to rest. better to spend money flying your body back home so you can be buried *alongé*. we crack up. our conversations are rarely serious, and even serious matters become a joke. i ask my father how he feels about Black people having fatal encounters with police. i see pain in his eyes even through our video chat but he chooses to ignore our well-documented murders, and double down on his assertion that if one respects police one should not experience brutality at their hands. i wonder at his amnesia. i wonder if he remembers that he told me his neighbour once called the police on him because he was "acting strange." i wonder at his forgetfulness at being hauled away violently. and i remember that my father lives with the spectre of violence lurking at his doorstep, he lives with that haunting firmly rooted in his faith that he will be protected. even in his pain, in our disagreement—a momentary pause—then we're back to cackling and making more death jokes.

except your dad isn't dead

In my inbox my publisher sends me a review of my collection written in *Discorder Magazine*. The reviewer begins with the lines: *eat salt | gaze at the ocean is a book you have to consume twice, thrice. It's possible you may never fully understand it, but you can feel it, deeper, with each re-read.*

My husband reads the review too and shares the parts of the review that stand out for him—*tautological loops: gaps in logic,*
stumbling breaths,
and racing thoughts. Until she decides to write about zombies relating them to her life
in interactions with family,
the death of her father...

He then pauses and says: except your dad isn't dead.
My father isn't dead, true. But the reviewer who admits and accepts they may not fully understand the collection, picks up on the part where a family member recognizes that my father (his uncle) is no longer a zombie.

I have no desire to correct the reviewer.
My father isn't dead, true.
My father was a zombie and
the reviewer notes further I (me) am "still, partly, a zombie."

Black witnessing

The year 2020 and part of 2021—I live on a steady diet of snuff films. My eyes sealed shut. My eyes are tightly closed. I can only read headlines from the corner of my eyes. Same with the snuff videos. I watch them like I watch horror movies, sideways, my hand over my eyes, taking in the horror incrementally, in small doses.

Long ago when I didn't know better, I subscribed to news from CNN. Like most subscription sign-ups it piles up in my inbox until I get tired and decide to label it spam and unsubscribe. Now CNN news alerts go into my junk mail.

News Alert: Ex-officer Thomas Lane Pleads Guilty to Manslaughter in George Floyd's Death.

News Alert: Biden Gives Emotional Speech after Buffalo Shooting: "White Supremacy is a Poison."

I am currently away on Cortes Island on a writing retreat. So, any news comes in the form of headlines in my junk folder. Sometimes text messages without context, softly ping, announcing their arrival:
Dear friend, I am sending you love, blessings and support during this hard time in the wake of the recent shooting...

My therapist tells me gently that I'm traumatized. It obviously doesn't seem to click despite me saying that I've been ███████████████████
██
██

I ignore text messages, but I respond to a Caucasian acquaintance who wants to e-transfer 100 dollars "because." There's no script for what's right to do. Social media circulated messages that said "pay Black women." My private Facebook group for Black folks in this soggy city is filled with queries and commentaries and debates on this practice that suddenly cropped up. Advice ranging from don't accept to "treat yo self !" (or something like this).

I want to mourn in peace. And yet it feels important to read those headlines, inscribe the names of the dead and dying in my heart, commit to memory their faces, and more importantly get a fuller picture of who they were beyond dead Black bodies.

"And have you put our weight behind its glass door to keep the ocean out? All of it?"[1]

i watched ███████████████████████████George Floyd's life ████████████████████████████ i watched ████████████ ███ Black man. i don't know what compelled me to watch this. i've never watched these. i had █████████████████████████████ █████████ the subsequent riots. i was fourteen then. in 1997, when Abner Louima █████████████████████████████ i was nineteen, █████████████████████████████████ █████████ in 2014 i could hear Eric Garner's █████████████ ███ ███ █████████ i watched the last few minutes █████████████ █████████████████████████████

i was thirteen when my grandmother died after a couple weeks on life support. After leaving the hospital, my father got in the shower and let out the longest, anguished howl calling for his mother. i'd never heard my father cry so i concluded that he must be laughing. i asked mother why he was laughing after weeks of anxious worry. *Chérie, he's weeping.*
re-memory
when George Floyd called out for his mother, i felt something pull and unravel inside
i felt my heart collapse

and i remembered my father's anguished howl
and the door that kept the ocean at bay
couldn't keep all of it out.

"How do you mourn again when you actually never even stopped"[2]

a twitter user tweeted *Like how do you mourn again when you've actually never even stopped*
another tweeted underneath *All black peoples have done in 2020 is mourn*. i'm too traumatized to actually share my grief with others who are not Black. i don't know how to explain the grief in my body and don't want to. i ignore text messages, emails, DMs asking me how i'm doing. i snooze/unfollow social media friends whose posts trigger me. i ask my husband who is racialized but not Black to shield me from non-Black friends and family; i'm not ready. he obliges.

we're in full pandemic mode so mourning is via zoom. this zoom wake-space is facilitated by a Black therapist who takes on the burden of helping us process grief and rage without payment or expectation. it's not for the faint of heart—watching yourself, watching others break down, visibly, publicly in a little square on screen. we did not have to make sense. in fact, our grief, our rage, our fears, our anxieties, our loneliness, spilled, leaked, overflowed in messy and nonsensical ways. we mourned in ways that defied explanation, that required no explanation. sometimes it's too messy. i get it. sometimes the grief is too much, exposing the grist beneath our protective layers. sometimes, we choose not to come back to the messy space of zoom mourning. some of us babble as we *re-memoried* deeply buried trauma and loss. sometimes we laugh hysterically at the most painful of things. and three hours later we close out—mostly composed. some relief, more grief, hearts pained, ready to mourn again.

living with death in a global pandemic, and racial uprising, we hold our zoom wakes.

ethical wake work and witnessing

i've been struggling to write about the ethics of wake work, ethics of poetry while attending to our deaths. i am wrestling with the label ethical and wake and wake work and feeling like an impostor and what am i doing while there is a global catastrophic breakdown and i'm in the midst of one pretending i'm fine—this is the hardest thing i keep doing.

in the midst of figuring out what does it mean to be ethical in our witnessing? writing about the vulnerable without breaking down or without being salaciously self-centred in morbid poet pain or analysis with paralysis to talk about the difficult how to live with and in the middle of multiple and ongoing wakes in the middle of our exponential extinguishment? i struggle with the cerebral discussion of opacities and poethics. i struggle with the writing and leaning into these theoretical frameworks; i'm no longer used to academia and academic writing. this used to be my shield—writing endless papers in undergrad and graduate school theorizing our social death, tamping down my creative side in favour of tightly contained writing and critiques.

i am nowhere near answering the question of how to live with our living-dead status in an anti-Black climate. or rather i am noticing that after nearly 15 pages, i have yet to put in clear terms what that is. i know this a no—no in academia, and yet this is the point of opacity for me—the right to do this on my own terms. withholding knowledge so as to protect myself and community.

in my creative/poetic/non-academic life, living with, simply means experiencing all the pain, and suffering, and joy. leaning into the experience of being Black. i am reminded again that in spite of our status as living dead, in spite of our ongoing killing we are committed to "*living a Blackness vibrantly, without transparency or apology.*" this is a refusal, a way of being, a way of surviving—positioning ourselves in ways that defy the Eurocentric need for transparency and allows us to be *human* and thrive.

cackling on zoom calls. speaking in code or code-switching so as not to divulge what does not need to be divulged. in my writing practice, out in the world it can be erasure poetry, blocking and blacking out words, paragraphs and entire pages of text. only i am privy to the words hidden behind the thick black box.

Living With

Five hundred plus years into our interrupted histories we are still here—we are revenants. Three years into and past the "racial uprisings" of 2020 we are still living with our deaths. Living with and through our undead status. What re-animates us? What gives us life? I think of the social media posts and videos that I scroll through, the algorithms now set to endless cat videos and joyous Black folks living their best lives. Sometime last year a video ("Two Black Men") circulated on Twitter, Facebook, Instagram, and YouTube where two adult Black men are sitting outside what appears to be a take-out joint. There's a black patio umbrella that covers the black metal table. There are four chairs, small wooden slatted precarious looking chairs with metal legs. They appear to have finished enjoying takeout at the table. In the thirteen-second video they are laughing uproariously. One of them is violently slapping the table with a paper bag while his companion is shaking the table hard, then moves on to shaking his companion and hitting his arm while continuing to laugh. He eventually falls off his chair, losing a sandal in the process while the one slapping the table gets up doubles over, then walks over to his fallen companion, both hands placed on his upper arm as they continue to laugh. The details are ingrained in my mind, as I have watched this video at least twenty times—probably more—laughing as hard if not harder each successive time I watched this video. It is not clear what they are laughing about; the video does not show us the lead up. I and the many viewers who are Black recognize that kind of laughter. The kind where your eyes leak liquid joy, laughter takes hold of your ribs, intestine and lungs and squeezes. You hug your sides, doubled over. You stomp your feet repeatedly as if you want to start running. You slap the table because you *cannot*. You cannot breathe, you cannot talk, you cannot stop laughing. You cannot but help to experience that *Black joy*, Black laughter—you know that laughter.

On International Women's Day (IWD—March 8, 2023), Ijeoma Oluo shares in her Substack *Behind the Book* about her grief and loss of desire to celebrate IWD. Titled "Because We Are Still Here," Oluo's piece reflects on the attacks that Black women, folks and *trans folks endure, the continued attacks on Indigenous folks, she shares her process at arriving at a middle ground of celebrating a bit, feeling into joy somewhat. Despite the continued killings of folks made marginalized by this white supremacist system, there is something to celebrate. Oluo writes, "This isn't to say that we ignore what is happening. It's just a reminder that the loss of hope and joy and present-ness that is caused by the rapid-fire attacks against is yet another tool of oppression. We live in a world that has tried to destroy us for hundreds of years, and *we're still here."* There is an unimaginable grief—as we are dragged, drowning in the wake of our ancestral inheritance. There is no prescription for our living-dead status. There is no handbook for how to mourn continually, no bullet points or briefs on how to ethically talk about our ongoing deaths. Ross Gay asks, "Is sorrow the true wild? And if it is—and if we join them—your wild to mine—what's that...? What if we joined our sorrows, I'm saying. I'm saying: What if that is joy?" (50).

I am on Facebook, trying to find a way through this essay, I have never met writer Said Shaiye. I often see his post responses to another writer Steven Dunn. Recently Shaiye posted about his experience of this year's AWP:[3] "Walking my old streets with new friends...just being Black writers in a hostile world...watching the bubble of protection form around us — laughs and shared care, natural ease, vulnerability and tenderness. Just existing."

I find myself nodding along to his reflection, doing the deep mhmmm and so I ask if I may quote him for this piece. Recognizing myself and the experiences in their post. How to explain the joy in being seen, in joining sorrows.

Further reflecting on his experiences, he writes, "I'm very grateful for all the deep conversations and the superfluous ones, too. The levity...the deep belly laughs. Black folks just carrying on. Loving one another in a way that the world is incapable of doing. That's really beautiful."

And so, without a roadmap but love and care and laughter—deep belly—laughter we witness, we mourn, we carry on for the dead and living, we re-memory the dead, we carry on the wake work in our writing, in our poetics, in our love letters to ourselves and each other. We live with not in resignation, not always in resilience, but we live with finding life, performing life, and giving life where we are constantly denied. We celebrate that we are still here, even as we straddle life-death. We join our sorrows.

Notes

1. Sharif, *Customs*, p. 11.
2. @theeglodan, "Like how do you mourn..."
3. The 2023 annual conference for the Association of Writing and Writers' Programs took place in Seattle, Washington, from March 8 to 11.

Works Cited

Campbell, Mark V., and Pamela Edmonds. "A Note from the Editors." *MICE*, "Opacities," no. 4, summer 2018.

Coates, Ta-Nehisi. *Between the World and Me*. Text Publishing, 2015.

Da Silva, Denise Ferreira. "Toward a Black Feminist Poethics: The Quest(ion) of Blackness toward the End of the World." *The Black Scholar*, vol. 44, no. 2, 2014, pp. 81–97.

Da Silva, Denise Ferreira. "An End to 'This' World." Interview by Susanne Leeb and Kerstin Stakemeier. *Texte zur Kunst*, April 2019, https://www.textezurkunst.de/de/articles/interview-ferreira-da-silva/.

Désil, Junie. *eat salt | gaze at the ocean*. Talonbooks, 2020.

Dungy, Camille T. "Tell It Slant: How to Write a Wise Poem." *Poetry Foundation*, 10 June 2014, https://www.poetryfoundation.org/articles/70128/tell-it-slant.

Gay, Ross. *The Book of Delights: Essays*. Kindle ed., Algonquin Books of Chapel Hill, 2019.

Glissant, Édouard. *Poetics of Relation*. U of Michigan P, 1997.

Lauro, Sarah J. *The Transatlantic Zombie: Slavery, Rebellion, and Living Death*. Rutgers UP, 2015.

Lauro, Sarah J., editor. *Zombie Theory: A Reader*. U of Minnesota P, 2017.

Murdock, H. Adlai. "Edouard Glissant's Creolized World-Vision: From Resistance and Relation to Opacité." *Callaloo*, vol. 26, no. 4, 2013, pp. 875–890.

Naik, June. Review of *eat salt | gaze at the ocean*, by Junie Désil. *Discorder Magazine*, CiTR, 23 June 2022, https://www.citr.ca/discorder/march-april-2022/under-review-eat-salt-gaze-at-the-ocean-junie-desil/.

Oluo, Ijeoma. "Because We're Still Here: Some thoughts this International Women's Day." *Ijeoma Oluo: Behind the Book*, Substack, 9 Mar. 2023, https://ijeomaoluo.substack.com/p/because-were-still-here.

Retallack, Joan. *The Poethical Wager*. U of California P, 2004.

Richardson, Allissa V. *Bearing Witness While Black: Americans, Smartphones, and the New Protest #Journalism*. Oxford UP, 2020.

Shaiye, Said. "I'm on the place from AWP." *Facebook*, 11 Mar. 2023. https://www.facebook.com/kimodo.shaiye.

Sharif, Solmaz. *Customs: Poems*. Graywolf Press, 2022.

Sharpe, Christina. *In the Wake: On Blackness and Being*. Duke UP, 2016.

@theeglodan. "All black peoples have done in 2020 is mourn." *X*, 28 Aug. 2020, https://x.com/theeglodan/status/1299541135568834560

@theeglodan. "Like how do you mourn again when you've actually never even stopped." *X*, 28 Aug. 2020, https://x.com/theeglodan/status/1299571635951988739.

"Two Guys Laughing at a Table." *YouTube*, uploaded by maxgaming 171, 22 Sept. 2022, https://www.youtube.com/watch?app=desktop&v=DAk00E0A8fQ.

Wilderson, Frank. B., III. *Afropessimism*. Liveright, 2020.

4
On Living with Ghosts
Sue Goyette's Poethics of Care

ERIN WUNKER

> *Bad feelings may be grounds for social transformation.*
> —ANN CVETKOVICH, *Depression: A Public Feeling*

Feeling Bad

Near the beginning of Sue Goyette's long poem *The Brief Reincarnation of a Girl* there is a set of four lines that have haunted me since the first time I read them:

> The ghost of the girl hoisted the shovel to show
> the jury what had been prescribed to her. She tried
> telling them that all she could do with this shovel
> was to dig holes she kept falling into

I do not like to think about this ghost of a girl with her shovel and her many holes and her falling. Indeed, I do not like to think about falling children or buried children. I do not like to think about children who find themselves in front of juries. But then, what does it mean for me—a white cis settler scholar—to not like to think about these and other hard things because they make me "feel bad"? Ann Cvetkovich proposes that "bad feelings" may well be "the ground for transformation" (3). Feelings denote ambiguity, the "stuff" that "spans distinctions between emotion and affect," and make space for embodied sensation, Cvetkovich writes (4). Feeling bad tells us something. Taking the time to recognize those bad feelings gives us more information. If we take the effort to parse out feeling and context, we may find means of moving into action. Following Cvetkovich, I will begin with an anecdote about bad feelings. After reading Goyette's *The Brief Reincarnation of a Girl* for the first time I felt bad. Very bad. I'm tempted to make light of something deserving of consideration, though, so let me try and stay with the discomfort for a moment. Let me try and describe it for you. After reading the collection—wrapped in its jacket of flossy pink, with a large, sweetly goofy and unblinking bear on the front—I hid in a bedroom. Worse, I hid in the bedroom with my infant daughter. Me alone in a bedroom hiding? Not a cause for concern. Me hiding with the baby? A different story. It was cause for concern, my behaviour. It bore inquiry. *What is wrong? What are you doing? What are you feeling?* Indeed. What was I feeling? Shame, horror, revolt, and anger coursed through my body after reading this book. I felt undone. I felt a visceral need to protect, to build a barricade between the world and a small creature I'd ushered into it a few months prior. When asked what I was doing and why I was so upset I struggled to put words together. I couldn't quite explain what I had read at that particular moment, nor could I explain my need for retreat. So, naturally, given my constitution, I find this fascinating and worthy of scholarly consideration. My bad feelings—visceral, emotional, out of the blue—were information about a relationship built by Goyette's collection of poetry. The first step, it seemed, was to determine what the feelings were. Perhaps then I could unfurl what they meant and what meaningful work I might do with them. What meaningful work can come from living with and learning with bad feelings? And, might this work be feminist work?

Feeling Not Quite Right

In her meditation on depression and scholarly life, Cvetkovich posits the usefulness of the concept of acedia. Properly the affective realm of Christian monks whose work was, in great part, self-scrutiny and reflection, acedia was a marker of something being not quite right. Sometimes this self-scrutiny went a bit off track, and a monk would experience acedia, which is described by the fourth-century writer John Cassian as a "weariness of the heart" (qtd. in Cvetkovich 85). While acedia has been passed over by much of cultural as well as medical writing around mental health, Cvetkovich posits that it might offer a useful location from which to think about the pervasiveness of bad feelings in the twenty-first century generally, and among literary scholars more particularly. I find myself thinking, too, about the utility of thinking about acedia for feminists. Heart weariness, indeed. In addition to a weariness of the heart and soul, acedia is characterized by "intense feelings that can lead to a powerful urge towards movement or flight" (Cvetkovich 86). Cvetkovich's scholarly interests in acedia undergird her position that "depression should be viewed as a social and cultural phenomenon," and not solely as "a biological or medical one" (86). Acedia becomes particularly useful for her when, in beginning her research, she realizes that while melancholia has been a far more studied condition acedia undergirds Giorgio Agamben's work on naming the ennui that emerges in writers of the fin-de-siècle such as Baudelaire. She discovers that David Eng and David Kazanjian riff on work by Agamben and Walter Benjamin to posit that particular forms of acedia "can occur on the brink of transition to a new society and thus that new cultures can emerge out of a sense of grief and loss" (Cvetkovich 105), and that for Teresa Brennan acedia is a significant marker in "understanding affect as shared and social" (qtd. in Cvetkovich 105). Cvetkovich ultimately aligns acedia with "political depression," which has the potential to link "emotional and political life" (106). So perhaps my bad feelings were not markers of postpartum pathologies, but something else, or something in-between. Perhaps my "heart weariness" and "urge towards flight" were "just emotions" in Sara Ahmed's sense, where there is an emphasis on the double entendre of just as in "only" and "just" as in relating to justice both for the self and for others. This comes from the conclusion of Ahmed's *The Cultural Politics of Emotion* in which she posits that cultural emotions have the potential to infuse ethics into shared social life. Perhaps my reaction to *The Brief Reincarnation of a Girl* is an indication of the shared social affect built into the beating heart of the text.

In what follows I aim to think through and with Goyette's work in order to stay with my own bad and not-quite-right feelings reading evoked, as well as to collectively brush up against these questions: How do we live with ourselves, especially as complicit bystanders in the quotidian violences of the now?[1] How do we live with the ghosts we've let down? How do we manage that slippery and performing collective pronoun "we" when "we" seem to be complicit as well as swept up in lateral violence? And, might poetry—especially feminist poetry borne of a commitment to stay with and witness bad feelings—be an animator of what Karen Barad refers to as response-ability? For Barad, *response-ability* is a term that gestures to the possibility of attending to one another across power imbalances without denying or effacing difference. It is a challenging concept because it requires expanding our affective reach. Goyette's work, which I read as deeply feminist, animates response-ability, sometimes quite literally in the form of a care-giving bear, and other times in a neatly fashioned metaphor that moves the reader from a distanced reading to an intimate engagement of bearing witness to bad feelings.

Between Facts and Feelings
The events Goyette probes in *Brief Reincarnation*, which happen to be true events, are shocking. However, they are not rupture events in Alain Badiou's sense of the term. Badiou has written extensively on the function of rupture events that occur when those social entities and forces that have been kettled burst forth into the centre of social structure and can no longer be avoided or ignored. Examples include the 2011 Arab Spring revolts, Occupy movements, Idle No More, Black Lives Matter, and MeToo movements. The events in *Brief Reincarnation* aren't even the stuff of History, per se. Rather, the events that are the inspiration or demand for the collection live more properly in that category of affective register Sianne Ngai has named stuplimity. Stuplimity, you may recall, is that ugly feeling we are all too familiar with, where stupefaction crashes into sublimity; the *whatever* that invades our psyches almost inevitably as sensory overload and overwhelm hold onto our shirttails and fall out of our pantlegs like the strange creatures in much of Marcel Dzama's work. The events that inform Goyette's work are, for me, stuplimitous. This experience of stuplimity is what carried me into a bedroom to hide. I was devastated by this poetry. I was overwhelmed. And I was so familiar with these enormous emotions that I felt undone and overcome.

Here are the facts that lay the foundation: *Brief Reincarnation* is animated by the actual death of Rebecca Riley, aged four years. Riley died of an overdose of neuropharmaceuticals prescribed for ADHD and bipolar disorder, which was topped off with codeine cough syrup. The preschooler was diagnosed as bipolar when she was just under two years old. While her parents were convicted for her murder in the first degree, the prescribing doctor, who was no longer practicing due to a judiciary review of her peers, was not tried. Rebecca's father was given life in prison. Her mother was given somewhat less time. Her siblings, who were also taking prescription drugs for a host of neurological conditions, were taken from the home.

This is a hard story, a headline story. Clickbait that overwhelms. It is a story, I wager, that you might read, feel sickened by, and turn away from (unless, of course, you are bound to it in some less-shakable way)—that's the stuplimity working. In Goyette's poetry, however, the story becomes something else.[2] It becomes not only or even Rebecca's story—Goyette is careful never to speak *for*—but it does become more public in its domain. It is investigative, and in so seeking, it becomes, I think, poetic matter in the senses that Heather Milne unfurls in her book of the same title: it is poetry that matters, and it is matter that also refers to "the materiality of language, of bodies, of the physical world of objects, ecosystems, and geographies" (5). Like the poets Milne discusses, Goyette's *Brief Reincarnation* can also be "characterized by an embracing of materialist poetics coupled with procedural and conceptual compositional methods" (Milne 5). Some of the overlapping systems that beg consideration in *this* story include poverty, biopolitics—with specific relation to the intra-operativity of Big Pharma and Western medical mental health care, and the isolation endemic to neoliberalism that upends what Ahmed calls the happiness script of the close family. I am interested in how, and to what effect, feminist investigative lyric poetry demands an ethical response from the reader. We might usefully connect this to the affective social imperative of Brennan's notion of acedia, as well as Barad's concept of response-ability. I am interested, in other words, in how an exhausted form such as the lyric can animate an exhausted reader whose depression is owed as much to public feeling (Cvetkovich) as it is to impasse (Berlant). I'll turn directly to Goyette's collection to suggest that it attends to the ethics of witnessing and the necessity of learning to live with complicity and failure, as well as offering some alternatives for understanding feminist networks of care and response-ability (Barad qtd. in Dolphijn and van der Tuin).

Elevating the Lyric

Brief Reincarnation hovers on the edge of genre. While there are indications that *Brief Reincarnation* could be usefully situated in the Canadian tradition of the documentary long poem (so named by Dorothy Livesay), I will here focus on its characteristics as an investigative lyric (Naylor) that is working with an elevated lyric perspective (Queyras, "Women, Epic, Live Wires"). Paul Naylor's *Poetic Investigations* is the site from which I borrow the term *investigative lyric*. For Naylor, the investigative lyric is one which probes the holes of history, and in so doing troubles, or amplifies the subject of the lyric voice. Naylor's investigative lyric differs from Livesay's documentary long poem insofar as it *works* historical narrative for what is missing. The investigative lyric is a conjuror of absence and an attendant witness to the missing, whereas the documentary long poem is, in Livesay's words, "conscious attempts to create a dialectic between the objective facts and the subjective feelings of the poet" (267). In short, the investigative lyric leaves room for what I see in Goyette's work, and that is an affective economy that exceeds the subjective feelings of the poet; a little bit of the acedia mobilized for community-building purposes, if you will. Working in the long poem tradition, but not neatly, it is neither conceptual enough to be avant-garde, nor strictly lyric. The collection inhabits a space of engagement that is too close to its subject to be postmodern or objective. And yet, it deftly utilizes techniques of defamiliarization to distance the reader from the real events (as if we can know what those were). Indeed, as Sina Queyras points out in a conversation with Goyette published on *Lemon Hound,* locating *voice* is a recurrent mode of poetic inquiry and innovation in Goyette's work. Each of Goyette's books appears to be "exploring the idea of voice—where does it come from?—and its relationship to syntax...It's a kind of 'after lyric' or 'elevated lyricism'" (Queyras, "Women, Epic, Live Wires" 9). Citing the work of Lisa Robertson and playwright Marina Carr as companions in this syntactical reaching, this grasping after, this elevated lyricism, Queyras observes, "casting out into the world, into history, away from our small bodies can lead us even closer to the bone, can't it?" *Brief Reincarnation* takes us close to the bone, indeed. Let's look at particulars. Let's be attentive to perspective and voice. Let's creep in and observe the opening scene:

> The girl refused to be afraid when she climbed
> on high things. Her mother shaved the legs of the furniture
> and, along with some cough syrup, stewed it
> with a few of the girl's father's beer caps. The girl spit
> a whole parade's worth of bicycles bells back at her
> and pranced around in her diaper. The mother sat in the closet,
> lit a candle, and located the doctor with binoculars.

> The doctor, appearing as a bathrobe, urged
> the mother to slap the girl with her slippers then take her
> pulse. The girl had begun to growl which was upsetting
> the cats. The mother upped the dosage of bottle caps
> and added some baby Aspirin. The doctor suggested
> more conventional medication, the girl sounded bipolar
> and should be on a leash. What they didn't know
> was that the girl had collected enough stickers
> to reward the universe. She had a blanket and a bear.
> She had resolved that when she got up from the floor
> that last time, she'd be in another time zone
> with better tasting furniture and a door that closed.

This scene is out of time in significant ways. In "Lyric Poetry and the Problem of Time," David Baker states that "time is the fundamental subject of the lyric poem" (32). Marking the conventional division between narrative and lyric poetry, Baker tracks the ways in which the lyric has a different and fundamental relationship with the concept and experience of time itself. In Goyette's opening pages, time is deliberately fractured: we are situated in the present moment that is neither omniscient nor strictly memory. Here, the time of the poem takes place after the girl's death by overdose and yet it situates her—the sentient subject—as prescient. She knows there will be a last time, and she is ready. Meanwhile, the mother—isolated and defensive, allegorical even, hiding in the closet—calls the doctor. The doctor diagnoses via binoculars, which is close to the kinds of medical appointments that patients in the UK began experiencing well before 2020 (Smyth). It is possible to gloss over the disjunctured temporality: the girl is and is not dead, the mother is and is not hiding. The doctor has and has not yet made a proclamation on mental health. So, what is this investigative lyric up to?

    Omniscience, defamiliarization, metonymy, a touch of the phantasmagoric; each of these tools serve to both distance the singularity of the lyric *I* from an individual speaker and, somehow, to draw the reader closer to the bone. Not quite working in the realm of narrative poetry, Goyette has fiddled with lyric transmission and time. But whose bones are we drawn to? And for what purpose? I think a partial answer to this question lies in the title itself. A reincarnation is a rebirth of a soul into a new body. In Goyette's hands a girl is briefly reincarnated, yes, but there is something more happening here.

There is the reincarnation of catharsis as a tool for bringing about other kinds of communities of care. In "elevating the lyric," as Queyras puts it, and moving the reader through a connective acedia, Goyette positions poetry as an animator of intra-relation (Barad).

Between Feelings and Facts

In order to think through the ways in which Goyette elevates the lyric, it is necessary to frame the terms of the long poem's engagement. Riley's death was, as I have mentioned, headline news. Many of the headlines took a whodunnit angle, in which parents, physicians, and psychiatrist were put under a journalistic spotlight. The aim, it seems, was both to get to the so-called facts as well as to tell a good story. In a 2007 exposé titled "Who Killed Rebecca Riley?" Katie Couric interviewed the girl's mother, who was in prison awaiting trial. A transcript of the CBS-televised interview includes these excerpts:

> The toddler who could barely speak in full sentences was diagnosed with bipolar disorder after several sessions over eight months. She had just turned three. And she wasn't the only one in the family: her ten-year-old brother and four-year-old sister were already being treated for the same illness by the same doctor at Tufts-New England Medical Center. Rebecca was eventually prescribed three medications to stabilize her mood: Seroquel, an anti-psychotic; Depakote, an anti-seizure drug; and Clonidine, a blood pressure medication—medications that would ultimately prove fatal on Dec. 13th. (CBS)

Here, facts are placed in a tense relationship with story. Riley's age is named only after the observation of her speech development. The medicalization of her siblings is likewise offered after the observation that "she wasn't the only one in her family." The effect is subtle. The implication of culpability is couched in journalistic tone but objectivity slips. The interview then shifts to Couric asking Riley's mother questions about her daughter's treatment: "Did you ever think, 'Well, she's two and a half years old.' There's this thing called the terrible 2's. Did you think this could, in fact, be normal?" Couric asks. "Yes," Riley tells Couric. "The psychiatrist said that she thought that it was more than just normal" (CBS). In this complicated exchange, Riley's mother's capacity to know and to be a mother is placed in tension with the expertise of the child's psychiatrist. Rebecca's overdose was caused by her mother giving her an over-the-counter cough and cold medication, allegedly to help her sleep. While both parents were found guilty of first-degree murder, several jurors acknowledged that they were outraged at the failure to indict and try the prescribing doctor. Dr. Kayoko Kifuji's diagnosis and prescriptions were defended by the Tufts New England Medical Institute, and Dr. Kifuji agreed to testify only after receiving immunity from self-indictment. Dr. Kifuji has since been cleared of any wrongdoing and continues to practice child psychiatry (Wen).[3]

What can we do, nearly a decade hence, with this information? We can, I suppose, parse the ways in which physicians and psychiatrists are bound up in diagnostic practices that benefit from Big Pharma. We can certainly consider the significance of the fact that every single article on this tragedy emphasizes that Carolyn and Michael Riley were unemployed and on welfare. We might consider that most doctors do not follow up with patients about their adherence to prescriptions (Seaman). But I wager that none of these reflections repositions us in a more ethical and engaged relationship with this event, or with future similar events. For, as Couric notes in her interview, Dr. Kifuji's diagnosis and prescriptions are not out of line with current practices in the United States. Indeed, it is estimated that more than a million children Riley's age are currently on similar dosages with similar diagnoses (CBS). Why bother with this story when it is quotidian? I asked Goyette this in a conversation and she was thoughtful before responding. There is something about a call to witness, she reflected. Poetry leaves space for ellipses and perspective to do ethical work. The ordinariness of both biological and necropolitical forces are at work here. It seems to me that Goyette's feminist poetics are working to transform ethics at the level of the line break, metaphor, and personification. And so, it is to the ethical possibility of an elevated lyric poetry that I will return.

Poethical Relation

Brief Reincarnation moves from dream-state recollection to the courtroom, to the woods. The reader encounters first the girl, who is not yet ghost, but also already after-death. Recall that opening section, where the girl, clearly built on some or all of Riley's story, stands on her own, unnamed: "She had a blanket and a bear. She had resolved that when she got up from the floor that last time, she'd be in another time zone with better tasting furniture." The next actor in the chorus of voices making this text is the mother. Or rather, "the mother" who "sits in the closet. / Lights a candle, and locates the doctor with binoculars." For again, Goyette is careful not to appropriate story or voice. Mother is distanced from specificity and broadened into trope. Instead, the cast of voices is porous enough to be filled with our own readerly assumptions and associations. After the closet scene, where a mother—the girl's mother—is hiding from her child, we next meet her with the doctor. Here frank frustration with a preschool-aged child is fused with familiar practices associated with both surrealism and psychiatry:

> they were trying their hand at automatic writing. The doctor wrote *Chevrolet* and *hubcaps*. The mother wrote *she's driving me crazy*. The doctor discussed the dosage and they both agreed, given the century and the 24-hour drugstore, they could treat themselves to a chocolate bar and maybe a slurpee.

The doctor is a twenty-first-century professional, addicted to her prescription pad. The capacity to turn to prescription is aligned with the twenty-first-century reflex of checking a phone. The reader learns that the doctor is constantly interfacing with prescriptions rather than patients and that "she'd check it during meals with friends and they'd complain that her attention was elsewhere." Similarly, the lawyer is both specific and, on closer look, a trope: he is described as anxious, distracted, focused on finding the next parking spot. Meanwhile, the jury experiences feelings ubiquitous to sitting and listening to others. They are "hungry. They'd been promised croissants, a luxury, and had only got bagels without cream cheese." The father, on trial for his daughter's murder, is granted more particularity and, perhaps, a bit of lyric inference from the poet. He sits with a small fire burning in his crotch. Meanwhile, only the figures of the daycare teacher, the girl's own bear, and Poverty personified and allegorical, can see the ghost of the girl as she stalks the periphery of the courtroom sitting on laps, wishing for flowers, and wondering when next she can paint. We readers move from elevated perspective to the specificity of being *in medias mess* (Retallack 134). We are above time, and we are outside it, and we are in it, bellies growling and frustrated at the speaker's slowness and the lack of fancy snacks.

There's more. Through Goyette's elevated lyricism the reader is led through the anxious cacophony of the present, past adults ready to look away, and into something else. Not quite silence, we are led between the thickets of the anxious, absent, and overmedicated into a kind of community of witnesses. What are we witnessing? Not only a trial, which of course has both already happened, and has never happened this way. We are also witnessing a network of effects and affects, a network of failures in which system after system, structure after structure falters and a small girl falls a bit further. Yet, what *does not* falter is the sustained investigations of the lyric voice. Neither solitary in its interiority, nor perfectly omniscient, this lyric voice stretches across the entirety of the reincarnation. Queyras, again in conversation with Goyette, attends to the voice of the long poem this way: "How better to write of devastation than to project a point of view that is both inside the self and outside—at once looking down and out of the poet/body?" And after it is written? Then what? What happens to the readers, once we've read? What happens to that small girl and her roaring bear? What do we do with our sadness and stuplimity? How do we live with ourselves as witnesses of quotidian violences?

In Goyette's handling, we don't live with ourselves, in the solitude and siloing that suggests. We live alongside and with others. Here, "living with" figures as something akin to what performance theorist Elin Diamond calls the shudder of catharsis. Diamond draws on T.W. Adorno's now foundational postulation that "aesthetic behaviour might be defined as the ability to be horrified" (136). "The subject is lifeless except when it is able to shudder in response to the total spell," he writes, "and only the subject's shudder can transcend that spell" (48). For Diamond, the shudder of catharsis situates the subject on a precipice between feeling and seeing the other. The division between self and social being is one that Diamond suggests the shudder of catharsis can "heal and regulate" (154). As I will go on to demonstrate, Goyette's investigative lyric animates healing and regulation through intra-relations and response-ability (Barad).

Consider, for example, the relationship between the girl, her ghost, and her bear (to whom she also belongs). Readers first encounter the bear in the past tense:

> The mother had held the girl's bear up to her
> chest and it reported that the girl's heart was a bowl
> of oatmeal that may be a little too hot to eat
> but would soon be cool and just right. (Goyette)

Note the syntactical wobble between mother and girl—the "her" slips just enough to need the bear to clarify whose heart is heated. It is the bear who, when held to the girl's pulse, relays to her mother that her pulse "was sort of hibernating, it would soon / wake and be ferociously hungry." And it is the bear on the stand who bodies forth the ghost of the girl:

> The girl's ghost was not necessarily a ghost
> but more a representative of the girl's curiosity.
> She moved with an ease that belied her death
> and sat between her parents...
>
> The girl wanted her bear.
> She wanted to hold the bear to her heart and hear
> for herself. Why would she believe anything
> they told her? She could trust the bear. The times it insisted
> she was in a forest and would soon come to its edge.

Goyette's elevated lyricism opens the possibility to destabilize the "lyrical inference" of the individual, and even the human as the sole and central ego (Olson 24). The lyric is more than a set of poetic conventions, of course. To interrogate the lyric as a poetic form one must also interrogate binary oppositions of subject/object, human/inhuman, cultivated/wild, mother/father. The elevated and reoriented investigative lyric allows the poet to step aside, but not to be absent. The poet lives with the poetic act of witnessing but is removed from the centre of looking. Here, perhaps, is an example of what Joan Retallack calls the poethical: a move into a thickened poetics. For Retallack one's poethical work commences "when you no longer wish to shape materials (words, visual elements, sounds) into legitimate progeny of your own poetics. When you are released from filling in the delimiting forms...If you persist, patterns in your work may become more flexible, permeable, conversational, exploratory" (38). In *Brief Reincarnation* Goyette releases the lyric voice from the delimitations of the stable lyric *I*. Rather than testimony or defence we experience the silence-breaking work of voice itself. "There is something fierce, righteous, and deeply chlorophyllic about casting out into and losing sight of the land, of allowing voice to scythe or whisper a new way into silence, saying what it wants to say, not what I/we think it should," says Goyette to Queyras. And Queyras replies, "aren't we all famished in this moment?"

Response-ability in the Form of a Bear

Aren't we all famished in this moment for voices breaking silences? That's what Queyras and Goyette are discussing, and that is, I think, where *Brief Reincarnation* leaves us. As the trial draws to its gutting conclusions, language that is indecipherable to the readers as well as the adults in the text emerges and takes over. This begins when the doctor, the lawyer, and the father are discussing the ethics of using concentration to diagnose bipolar disorder in a two-year-old. Amidst this stupefying conversation "The ghost of the girl stood on a chair and roared." This roar is heard in the following section:

> The girl's bear heard the ghost of the girl's roar.
> …
> The ghost of the girl standing on the chair
> snarled back to the bear that the father had his rifle out
> and the bear was safer in its cave. The bear missed the girl's heart,
> the bear told the ghost of the girl, but so did the ghost of the girl.
> What was it like? the ghost of the girl asked, and the bear
> said it was like silver fish in a river, each beat sure and strong
> and swimming with the current. How did the bear find the girl?
> the ghost of the girl wanted to know. By smell, by the honey smell
> of the girl the bear had found the girl lying there that last time,
> on the floor without her heart.

Notice that the conversation takes place across time and space, and that it happens in snarls and growls and nudgings. Notice that the girl is not gone for the bear, it is only her heart they both miss. That little silver fish. And so, what do they do? They make new networks of care: "The bear had the ghost of the girl / in her arms when the judge came out / of his quarters." It is the bear, who holds the gaze of the judge, and the judge looks back, "The idea of justice hung between / them like flypaper." The bear looks law in the face, ignores Poverty and its vice-grip stories, and claims the girl as her own kin. "I claim this girl, she said. / The judge nodded. She's always been mine, / the bear said, and again, the judge nodded, bowing." After "snouting at the word *mother* like a carcass," the bear carries the ghost of her girl to the river and teaches her to catch her own heart.

"The queerness of phenomena unsettles the presumed separateness of questions of being-knowing-responding," observes Barad. "Responsibility,'" in her view, "is not about the right response, but a matter of inviting, welcoming, and enabling the response of the Other." Agency, meanwhile, is about "response-ability, about the possibilities of mutual response, which is not to deny but to attend to power imbalances. Agency is about possibilities for worldly re-configurings. So agency is not something possessed by humans, or non-humans for that matter. It is an enactment" (qtd. in Dolphijn and van der Tuin 55). Crucially, Barad underscores that agency "enlists 'non-humans' as well as 'humans.'" For her, response-ability indicates the possibility of intervention or irruption of power imbalances, where the action need not be only human. Barad's sense of response-ability locates agency in multiple potential places. What if, when "we" humans fail to intervene, what if when systems of care are lacking, what if there are other systems and networks of caring beings there, bearing witness? What if there are other systems bearing the emotional weight of living with one another? In *The Brief Reincarnation of a Girl* it is the bear who watches the girl, who claims her as her own kin, and who teaches her to feed her empty heart with fish. We, the readers, are moved from that lyric positionality of listener and confidant into the complicit collective of people and systems who failed. We fail, but we are changed in that failure. We leave changed by the story. We cannot unknow it, and the story of living with, in response-able networks of care don't end there. In her recent work Goyette has been photographing a century-old agave plant that bloomed for the first time in the summer of 2018. Having bloomed, it then died. It was not relocated to the greenhouse to winter. Each day Goyette went to visit the agave and photograph it. These photos were posted to social media. At first, they were accompanied with apt quotes from others. Later, though, there was an emergent elevated lyricism in the posts. The agave reaches to the pines. Goyettte watches the birds migrating. She holds the silence of women in her, a network of cellular intra-relation. Goyette's poethical wager is, for me, an ongoing and durational project of living with and across networks of care, and of inhabiting the exhausted lyric form in order to reanimate it with stories that demand attention and animate our capacity for response-ability.

Notes

1. I see connections between the questions I am asking here and those posed by Libe García Zarranz in her chapter "On Trans Aliveness as Feminist Praxis: Ivan Coyote's and Syrus Marcus Ware's Ordinary Archives." Ordinariness can, in certain circumstances, become a site for radical care as both García Zarranz here, and Susan Fraiman in her work *Extreme Domesticity: A View from the Margins* demonstrate. For example, Fraiman argues that while much literary criticism presents women as entrapped in domesticity, in some contexts where characters have experienced trauma the choice to document and write about the quotidian, especially in home spaces, becomes a practice of radical care.
2. I'm grateful to the vital work Erin Soros does in this collection and elsewhere in her work, which keeps company with the thinking I am attempting in a much more cursory fashion here.
3. I am again struck by the ways in which Soros addresses medicalization, diagnosis, and pathology in this volume.

Works Cited

Adorno, Theodor W. *Aesthetic Theory*. Translated by Christian Lenhardt. NYUP, 1984.

Ahmed, Sara. *The Cultural Politics of Emotion*. 2nd ed. Routledge, 2015.

Badiou, Alain. *Being and Event*. Bloomsbury, 2013.

Baker, David. "Lyric Poetry and the Problem of Time." *Literary Imagination*, vol. 9, no. 1, Jan. 2007, pp. 29–36.

Barad, Karen. *Meeting the Universe Halfway: Quantum Physics and the Entanglement of Matter and Meaning*. Duke UP, 2007.

Berlant, Lauren. *Cruel Optimism*. Duke UP, 2011.

CBS. "Katie Couric Reports: What Killed Rebecca Riley?" *CBS News*, 28 Sept. 2007. https://www.cbsnews.com/news/what-killed-rebecca-riley/.

Cvetkovich, Ann. *Depression: A Public Feeling*. Duke UP, 2012.

Diamond, Elin. "The Shudder of Catharsis in Twentieth-Century Performance." *Performativity and Performance*, edited by Andrew Parker and Eve Kosofsky Sedgwick, Routledge, 1995, pp. 152–172.

Dolphijn, Rick, and Iris van der Tuin. "'Matter Feels, Converses, Suffers, Desires, Yearns and Remembers': Interview with Karen Barad." *New Materialisms: Interviews & Cartographies*. Open Humanities Press, 2012. https://quod.lib.umich.edu/o/ohp/11515701.0001.001/1:4.3/--new-materialism-interviews-cartographies?rgn=div2;view=fulltext.

Fraiman, Susan. *Extreme Domesticity: A View from the Margins*. Columbia UP, 2019.

Goyette, Sue. *The Brief Reincarnation of a Girl*. Gaspereau Press, 2014.

Livesay, Dorothy. "The Documentary Poem: A Canadian Genre." *Contexts of Canadian Criticism*, edited by Eli Mandel, U of Chicago P, 1971, pp. 267–281.

Milne, Heather. *Poetry Matters: Neoliberalism, Affect, and the Posthuman in Twenty-First Century North American Feminist Poetics*. U of Iowa P, 2018.

Naylor, Paul. *Poetic Investigations: Singing the Holes in History.* Northwestern UP, 1999.

Ngai, Sianne. *Ugly Feelings.* Harvard UP, 2005.

Olson, Elder. *American Lyric Poems.* Appleton-Century, 1964.

Queyras, Sina. "Afterword: Lyric Conceptualism, A Manifesto in Progress." *Barking and Biting: The Poetry of Sina Queyras,* edited by Erin Wunker, Wilfrid Laurier UP, 2016, pp. 61–64.

Queyras, Sina. "Women, Epic, Live Wires: In Conversation with Sue Goyette." *Lemonhound 3.0* lemonhound.com, 12 Dec. 2017.

Retallack, Joan. *The Poethical Wager.* U of California P, 2003.

Seaman, Andrew M. "Doctors Need to Know If Patients Are Skipping Pills." *Reuters,* 11 May 2016. https://www.reuters.com/article/us-health-heart-medications/doctors-need-to-know-if-patients-are-skipping-pills-idUSKCN0Y22L5.

Smyth, Chris. "Millions of Patients to See Hospital Doctors by Skype under NHS Plan." *The Times,* 8 Jan. 2019. https://www.thetimes.co.uk/article/millions-of-patients-to-see-doctor-by-skype-under-nhs-plan-jj9fwmlk6.

Wen, Patricia. "Jurors Outraged by Psychiatrist's Conduct." *The Boston Globe,* 11 Feb. 2010. http://archive.boston.com/news/local/massachusetts/articles/2010/02/11/jurors_outraged_by_psychiatrists_conduct/.

5

Learning to "Live with" Death
Developing a Suicide-Affirmative Approach as an Ethics of "Living with" Suicidal People

ALEXANDRE BARIL

> NOTE: *I would like to warn the readers that this chapter deals with very sensitive topics, such as suicide and assisted suicide, and proposes a radical reconceptualization of how we theorize suicidality, and also of how we interact with suicidal people, including in our social movements. For some individuals, this discussion may trigger strong emotions. To this end, it is important to invite the readers to not remain isolated with their distress but to contact relatives/friends, as well as crisis and hotline services, for support if they are triggered by the discussion that follows. That being said, it is also crucial to remind the readers that, with very few exceptions, such as Trans LifeLine (a hotline dedicated to trans people discussed in this chapter) or Autisme Soutien (a chat service by and for autistic and neurodivergent people that officially endorses an anti-suicidist approach), all other suicide prevention services and hotlines in Canada might enable non-consensual rescues by tracing people's call and alerting emergency services (e.g., police, ambulance). As discussed below, the suicidist violence suicidal people experience, particularly when those individuals live at the intersection of multiple forms of oppression (e.g., racism, ableism, cisgenderism), such as forms of incarceration, institutionalization or forced treatments, often occur when non-consensual rescues are deployed. I believe it is important, for those experiencing suicidal ideations and distress, to know those facts in order to make informed decisions when it comes to contacting suicide prevention services and hotlines (and*

deciding which services best fit their needs). One final caveat: while my approach to suicide and assisted suicide is radically different from the current ones, it is not intended to encourage suicide. On the contrary, I am hopeful that my approach will help to reduce suicidal rates for marginalized groups.

A common idea in social justice culture is that if someone calls you out on being oppressive, you need to shut up, listen, put aside your automatic defensive reaction, and accept what they're saying, learn from it, and thank them. This is a useful ground rule, and it works for a lot of situations.
  —LEAH LAKSHMI PIEPZNA-SAMARASINHA,
    Care Work: Dreaming Disability Justice

Suicidal People Want to Speak Up: "Shut Up and Listen"
As a trans and disability scholar working in the field of critical suicidology—a discipline that insists on the sociopolitical aspects of suicidality (i.e., suicidal ideations, suicidal attempts, and completed suicides)—I subscribe to many listservs in which people exchange reflections, ideas, references, or forthcoming events pertaining to suicidality. When I started writing this chapter in January 2022, a headline (Wagner) regarding the cancellation of a play (*Right Before I Go*) about suicide that used actual suicide notes on an American university campus spurred debates and fraught discussions among several members of one listserv, with discussions echoing the disagreements elicited by the series *13 Reasons Why*, in which the main protagonist died by suicide (e.g., Krebs; Froese Sakal and Greensmith). On the one hand, some members believed that discussing suicidality frankly and publicly, as the screenwriter and playwriter Stan Zimmerman (best known for his series *Gilmore Girls*) intended to do in his play *Right Before I Go*, can open up crucial conversations about mental health, distress, and suicidal ideations—dialogues that might contribute to helping suicidal people connect with others and, as a result, save their lives. On the other hand, other members expressed concerns about the reception of such a play in a university setting at this particularly vulnerable time for students due to the pandemic and the neoliberal management of universities, which allocates very few resources to support students' mental health. Some listserv members working in the field of suicide prevention and sometimes

self-identifying as "suicide survivors"—namely, those who lost loved ones through suicide—agreed that talking about suicide could be helpful in some circumstances. Nevertheless, they also articulated fears about the unintended consequences that discussing suicidality publicly might have on distressed people and on the relatives of suicidal people, who might be triggered by suicide notes.

Those concerns are real, legitimate, and important to express. However, as a lifelong suicidal person—I have been experiencing suicidality since the age of twelve—I found myself quite disturbed after reading some of those exchanges. While the listserv members had no intention to make suicidal people feel worse about themselves and invalidate their discourses and final attempts to deliver key messages through suicide notes, reading those exchanges made me feel the way I often feel when expressing my reflections, concerns, needs, and claims as a suicidal person. This discourse seems to suggest that what should prevail over the voices of actively suicidal people who are often deemed too mentally ill or socially alienated to understand what is good for them, as well as over the voices of suicidal people through their suicide notes, is the *vision* of experts working in the field of suicide prevention, as well as of health care professionals, volunteers in suicide prevention organizations who have lost or almost lost someone they love due to suicide, or even *ex-suicidal* individuals who have now "recovered." It feels as though our voices, messages, and discourses as suicidal people are cast aside as risky and difficult to hear—and therefore unsuitable for being shared publicly with other people who need to be protected. Indeed, some scholars contend that "popularized and pathological suicide intervention and prevention frameworks...erase" suicidal people's narratives (Froese Sakal and Greensmith 45), and some suicidal people, such as Anna Mehler Paperny, in her memoir *Hello I Want to Die Please Fix Me*, testifies about the trauma she went through at the hands of people who thought they knew better than she what was best for her.

The voices of suicidal people are actively excluded from what I call the "preventionist script," a script comprised of values, approaches, discourses, attitudes, and practices regarding suicidality that is anchored in a prevention logic aiming at saving lives at all costs. In my book *Undoing Suicidism: A Trans, Queer, Crip Approach to Rethinking (Assisted) Suicide*, I contend that the preventionist script fails to truly connect with suicidal people. The literature demonstrates that suicidal people are afraid to reach out to prevention services because of the myriad mistreatments and forms of invalidation they experience through those services. Individuals who complete their suicide and leave notes behind, such as the ones in the play *Right Before I Go*, conceal their intentions and do not reach out to others or to prevention services, knowing that they will be *prevented* from acting upon their wishes (Fitzpatrick, "Epistemic Justice"; Stefan; Szasz; White). In other words, each person who does not reach out to suicide prevention services when they experience suicidality—such as Mehler Paperny the few times she attempted suicide—and each completed suicide are proof that the preventionist script does not work for many people, particularly *when someone is really determined to die*. Despite the support suicide prevention provides to some suicidal people who want to be helped, who want to continue to live, or who are ambivalent about dying, I believe that the preventionist script is failing a vast number of suicidal people, particularly those belonging to marginalized groups and those most determined to die. Those are the individuals who suicide prevention discourses and strategies desperately try to reach, without success, and many suicidal individuals, like me, Mehler Paperny, and Piepzna-Samarasinha, have testified about the failure of this outreach.

Although I am not discussing here the way suicide notes are portrayed in the play *Right Before I Go*, the conversations that the cancellation of the play elicited about the possibility, if not the necessity, for some people, to censor those suicide notes reminded me that those discourses, focused on the identification and management of suicidal risk, are still predominant today. The same can be said about the fears surrounding suicide contagion and the surveillance and censorship of some information that is perceived as causing or triggering suicide. These discourses come from individuals working from a traditional suicidology perspective, as well as from others who sometimes embrace critical suicidology, critical studies (e.g., feminist and gender studies, queer studies, trans studies, disability/crip/Mad studies, critical race studies), and from various activists in social movements. Those discourses that seek to ban suicide notes from the public sphere, or that overlook those left behind by suicidal people who are already too often forgotten or dismissed (Corriveau et al.; Furqan et al.; Perreault et al.) erase the voices of actively suicidal people who want to have frank, open, and honest discussions about suicidality. In the words of Jess Stohlmann-Rainey, a self-identified Mad, disabled, and fat person with a lived experience of suicidality, a lot of "safe messaging" stemming from suicide prevention has the effect of gaslighting suicidal people through forms of sanism. As I demonstrate in my work, the gaslighting experienced by suicidal people allows nonsuicidal people to frame them as irrational, insane, mad, or crazy (from a sanist medical/psychiatric perspective), or as alienated (from a sociopolitical perspective) (Baril, "Personnes suicidaires"; "Somatechnologies"; "Suicidism"; *Undoing Suicidism*). Furthermore, Stohlmann-Rainey argues that gaslighting suicidal people like her and I triggers us to doubt our experiences, thoughts, and interpretations of suicidality. Stohlmann-Rainey questions, in the end, who is protected and whose vulnerability is taken into consideration when people want to cancel or censor plays, series, or texts depicting suicidal stories:

> The illusory idea that we can control suicide by controlling the content a suicidal person is exposed to dominates these [prevention] guidelines. It begs the question—who is really being protected? The stories of suicidal people are being silenced. In the case of *13 Reasons Why*, the suicide is edited out, but not all of the rape, violence, and bullying leading up to it...Does this really protect suicidal people who might have shared experiences with the main character, or does it protect others from having to see the potential consequences of traumatic events?

Like Stohlmann-Rainey, I must admit that I regularly feel, in my personal life, as well as in my scholarly work on suicidality, gaslighted. This comes from well-meaning people working in the field of suicide prevention, from the relatives of suicidal people who want(ed) to prevent the death of their loved ones, and from scholars/activists with good intentions. The latter sometimes seem much more interested in eradicating suicidality at all costs and dismantling the oppressions that are believed to be the root causes of suicidality (e.g., sexism, heterosexism, racism, classism, cisgenderism, ableism), rather than trying to *learn from* suicidal people, alive or dead, for example through their suicide notes. However, as stated in the epigraph to this chapter by queer, disabled, non-binary femme disability/transformative justice activist Leah Lakshmi Piepzna-Samarasinha, a key lesson for social movements, when a group of marginalized people try to address the violence, discrimination, injustice, and mistreatment they face, is to "shut up and listen." While this lesson constitutes the basis on which scholars/activists have been trying to build a better world in critical scholarship and activism for those marginalized on the basis of sex/gender, race, class, religion, size, ability, to name only a few, the same principle seems elusive, almost unthinkable, when it comes to suicidal people expressing their worldviews, experiences, concerns, and needs. *For them, it is different*: what they have to say cannot be true, cannot be real, cannot be taken seriously, since it challenges what I conceptualize as "compulsory aliveness" and the "injunction to live and to futurity" too often endorsed by critical scholarship and activists themselves (Baril, "Somatechnologies"; "Suicidism"; *Undoing Suicidism*). In the spirit of Piepzna-Samarasinha's statement, I claim that when a marginalized group addresses critiques, concerns, and needs, scholars and activists should adopt a posture of humility, or, in other words, "shut up and listen." These critiques provide an opportunity to *learn about* suicidal people, their beliefs, values, needs, and lived experiences, and *learn with* suicidal people about how to transform discourses and practices to be more respectful and inclusive of their realities. Not only do I suggest that not listening to the voices of suicidal people represents a missed opportunity in terms of what we can *learn with* suicidal people and *about* suicidality, I also contend that this difficulty, or refusal to listen to suicidal people, constitutes a form of epistemic suicidist violence. As such, I coined the term *suicidism* to refer to "an oppressive system (stemming from non-suicidal perspectives) functioning at the normative, discursive, medical, legal, social, political, economic, and epistemic levels, a system in which suicidal people experience multiple forms of injustice and violence" (Baril, "Personnes suicidaires" 193; my translation).[1]

Building on the idea that suicidal people are oppressed and that their voices are silenced, and drawing on my queercrip model of suicidality and my suicide-affirmative approach (Baril, "Suicidism"; *Undoing Suicidism*), I propose to promote better recognition and respect of suicidal people. The discussion in the following pages focuses on how to reduce the epistemic violence of silencing suicidal people. To do so, the following section explores the epistemic violence suicidal people face, while the next one mobilizes two philosophical principles put forth by critical suicidologist Katrina Jaworski (597): wonder and generosity. I also suggest, following feminist care theorists such as Sophie Bourgault, using the notion of "attentive listening" in the various phases of care for suicidal people ("caring about," "taking care of," "care giving," and "care receiving"), as per Joan Tronto's canonical typology. Paired with wonder and generosity toward suicidality, attentive listening to suicidal people is crucial for building a world that is more inclusive, more respectful, and safer when expressing themselves. Then, in line with writer and trans activist Kai Cheng Thom's "nine-step guide to confronting the abuser in you, in me, in us all" (69), I suggest applying these steps to confront the suicidist abuser within ourselves in order to build bridges between suicidal people and those who are trying, not always successfully or respectfully, to support them. In the spirit of the transformative justice movement, instead of calling out and demonizing people who perpetuate suicidism, the goal is rather to critically examine how, even with the best of intentions, people can sometimes reproduce forms of oppression toward suicidal people and to suggest how to develop, in line with the wonder, generosity, attentive listening, or steps inspired by Thom, alternative ways of dealing with suicidality and suicidal people. I believe these principles and steps might help non-suicidal people, for whom suicide is often unilaterally negative, unacceptable, or incomprehensible, to *learn with* suicidal people about other ways to theorize and experience suicidality. Through that learning process, I wish to propose an ethics of "living with" suicidal people, both during their lives and, potentially, through the process of their death.

Suicidality and Epistemic Violence

In a blog post titled "Learning to Live with Wanting to Die," Cortez Wright, a self-identified Black fat non-binary queer femme, demonstrates how swiftly suicidal people learn how to lie and "shut up" about their suicidality to avoid harmful consequences, particularly when they belong to marginalized groups such as BIPOC communities, queer and trans communities, or disabled/Mad communities, a fact reiterated by numerous marginalized individuals (Dixon and Piepzna-Samarasinha; Piepzna-Samarasinha). They write, "I called a suicide-prevention hotline, not quite realizing that sometimes 'suicide prevention' looks like emergency vehicles and mandatory hospital stays when all you want, all you need, is to talk. Making mostly false promises of personal safety, I ended the phone call and learned to shut up about wanting to die." Like me and many other suicidal people who break the silence through online testimonials, documentaries, vlogs, or publications, such as Mehler Paperny in her memoir, Wright believes that what is more devastating than depression and suicidal ideations is the difficulty to speak out in the current context: "It's not the depression that threatens to kill us. It's the never getting to talk about it and release the emotions that build up inside." These testimonials are backed up by research (e.g., Rhodanthe et al.; Szasz; White; White and Morris) demonstrating how suicidal people, particularly those from marginalized groups and those determined to die, do not feel safe to reach out for help. For instance, in her interviews with suicidal people, Susan Stefan concludes that a majority of suicidal people do not discuss their wishes to die with anyone when they want to fulfil their objective: "Many people who kill themselves often plan their suicides carefully and conceal those plans with great success from the people who know them best, including friends and family. The people I interviewed were unanimous in saying that the more determined they were to kill themselves, the more they concealed their intentions from the people in their lives" (107–108). As I show in my work, suicidal people do not express themselves because when they do, they often experience the harmful effects of the preventionist script anchored in suicidist oppression.

Drawing upon concepts related to epistemic injustice from theorists such as Miranda Fricker, Kristie Dotson, and José Medina, my work demonstrates how suicidal people suffer from suicidist epistemic injustice in its various forms, such as testimonial injustice, which includes diverse forms of silencing, quieting, and smothering; along with hermeneutical injustice, hermeneutical marginalization, wilful hermeneutical ignorance, and even hermeneutical death (Baril, "Suicidism"; *Undoing Suicidism*). Building on the ideas of critical race and postcolonial feminists such as Gayatri Chakravorty Spivak's notion of epistemic violence, Dotson argues that this violence "damage[s] a given group's ability to speak and be heard" ("Tracking Epistemic Violence" 236). She describes epistemic oppression as based on "epistemic exclusions...that produce deficiencies in social knowledge. An *epistemic exclusion*...is an infringement on the epistemic agency of knowers that reduces her or his ability to participate in a given epistemic community" ("Cautionary Tale" 24). The epistemic oppression that suicidal people experience relates to their epistemic exclusion from knowledge-building on suicidality. Their experiential knowledge, values, and interpretations of suicidality when they contradict the preventionist script are either entirely forgotten, disregarded, or dismissed as "symptoms" of their mental illness or of the sociopolitical oppression that causes their distress.[2] This epistemic violence is part of a larger system of oppression, suicidism, that has to be dismantled and needs to be further acknowledged and theorized. Accordingly, I contend that embracing an ethics of care toward suicidal people, founded on wonder, generosity, and attentive listening, could represent a first step in the recognition of this structural violence too often invisible, even inside social movements.

An Ethics of Care toward Suicidal People: Wonder, Generosity, and Attentive Listening

In her innovative work on suicide, Jaworski (see also Jaworski and Scott) proposes an ethics based on the notion of wonder and generosity.[3] Her work, inspired by a Butlerian framework, aims to show that suicidality is performative and describes the relational agency and autonomy involved in suicide. I would like here to pay attention to her use of the philosophical principles of wonder and generosity, which are useful for developing a more complex, nuanced, and respectful response to suicidal people. According to Jaworski, wonder and generosity are attitudes to endorse in critical suicidology when we *speak with* suicidal people and when we *speak for* them once they are dead, an inevitable situation in the case of completed suicides. She suggests that these attitudes transform *how* we *speak with* and *for* them, in a way that honours the ethical aspects of suicide and the agency of suicidal people, and that does not moralize or pathologize suicidality. These attitudes, without falling into a simplistic relativist position, allow to contextualize knowledge and discourses on suicidality and avoid elevating some, such as those focused on absolute prevention, as "universal truths." Jaworski writes,

> Exercising wonder and generosity can be useful when we listen to people who survived their attempt. This kind of listening means that we respect their choices as their own, based on the meaning they attribute to it. It means we recognise their differences as first and foremost their own, rather than whether they fit a clinical category. In this sense, listening, vis-à-vis wonder and generosity, becomes "a form of ethical responsiveness," which is "located within specific contexts and networks of privilege and power" (Dreher and de Souza 2018, 22). I see this kind of responsiveness as crucial… for those who research suicide, especially since researchers are in the position of power to disseminate knowledge. (596)

Jaworski's ethics has deep resonance with feminist care ethics, especially in its insistence on the needs of marginalized and vulnerable individuals, the satisfaction of these needs, as well as the importance of being welcoming, attentive, and responsive to (different) voices (e.g., Gilligan; Paperman and Laugier; Tronto). Some care theorists, in the past few years, have insisted on the importance of active and attentive listening. For example, Bourgault, using a Weilian framework to interpret care ethics and politics, argues that listening is at the core of care. She notes that, surprisingly, scholars interested in the notion of listening have not linked their reflections to care ethics, and that care theorists, while conceptualizing similar notions such as attentiveness, rarely discuss the notion of listening explicitly. One of Bourgault's goals is to "convince the champions of care theory that what is at the heart of their ideal is listening" (314). She develops a notion of active and attentive listening as embodied and relational, a notion that I claim should be at the heart of attitudes toward suicidal people. Dismantling suicidism and its normative component of compulsory aliveness requires listening actively and attentively to suicidal people and their critiques about suicide prevention discourses and strategies. It also requires embracing attitudes of wonder and generosity toward what some suicidal people may want, such as access to assisted suicide or support throughout their suicide, which radically challenges the injunction to live taken for granted by many critical scholars and activists.

In my work, I develop a queercrip model of (assisted) suicide that comprises two components. The first one describes the existence of structural suicidism, its links to other oppressive systems from an intersectional lens, as well as its harmful consequences on suicidal people, particularly those belonging to marginalized groups. The second component, which is more normative than descriptive, proposes a political agenda to end this structural suicidist violence and thus a shift from a prevention logic to an accompaniment logic (*Undoing Suicidism*). I suggest working at multiple levels simultaneously: while scholars and activists need to tirelessly tackle the various -isms (e.g., sexism, heterosexism, cisgenderism, racism, colonialism, capitalism) that influence suicidality, they also need to develop assistance and support for suicidal people from an anti-suicidist perspective. The latter might sometimes include assisted suicide if this is what a suicidal person really needs after serious consideration and following an accompanied process in which they reflect on all the potential solutions to their problems. It is important to note that the form of assisted suicide I propose in my work is radically different than the forms of assisted death (e.g., euthanasia, medical assistance in dying) offered in various legal contexts and which I consider to be ableist, sanist, ageist, capitalist, and suicidist.

What I want to highlight here is the twofold response I usually receive to my queercrip model of (assisted) suicide and suicide-affirmative approach. On the one hand, reactions to the descriptive component are quite positive: scholars, activists, and practitioners often praise or adopt my comprehensive framework of suicidism and agree that there is a need to end the structural violence suicidal people experience. On the other hand, the same people often contest the possibility of supporting (assisted) suicide for suicidal people, and strong emotions arise when it comes to fully supporting someone they love in choosing death over life. For example, Grace Wedlake, who embraces suicidism as a framework, confesses that her emotions constitute barriers to supporting the right to die of people she loves, and that she experiences some forms of "discomfort with how to engage with [these] ideas in practice" (98). Instead of the curative logic at the root of the suicidist preventionist script, as well as the ableist/sanist/ageist logic of disposability central to current right-to-die discourses, which are not anchored, I believe, in care about/for suicidal people, the queercrip model of (assisted) suicide I propose posits positive rights for suicidal people and the possibility of assisted suicide. Support for suicidal people would be offered through what I call a suicide-affirmative approach (Baril, "Suicidism"; *Undoing Suicidism*): an approach inspired by trans-affirmative approaches and founded in anti-oppressive values such as bodily autonomy, self-determination, or informed consent, and driven by intersectionality and harm-reduction perspectives. My suicide-affirmative approach is both death-affirming *and* life-affirming.

A suicide-affirmative approach does not mean pushing suicidal people toward suicide. It means that instead of trying to cure suicidal people of their suicidality and eradicate their suicidality through a vast array of prevention measures like surveillance and control, institutions, community organizations, and practitioners should develop safer spaces in which to investigate, with suicidal people, their suicidality and desire for life *and* death. Such spaces also allow presenting and discussing a wide variety of options (including assisted suicide), instead of leaving suicidal individuals to fend for themselves and force them to not discuss their suicidality with anyone in order to fulfil their desire to die. This approach suggests a shift from prevention to accompaniment, a necessary turn in order to develop a more humane, caring, and respectful response to distressed and marginalized people. I contend that while my goal is to provide a better accompaniment for suicidal people instead of trying to save their lives at all costs (and sometimes against their will), as is the case in the preventionist script, my suicide-affirmative approach supporting assisted suicide for suicidal people could save more lives than current prevention strategies that are clearly failing those who complete their suicide and those who are not reaching out for support. In fact, the few peer-support initiatives that focus less on preventing suicidality and more on accompanying suicidal people show promising results (e.g., Rhodanthe et al.; Trans LifeLine).

In sum, the questions I raise on suicidism through my queercrip model of suicidality and suicide-affirmative approach invite rethinking what constitutes care in regard to suicidality. In Tronto's care language, suicidism as a framework allows me to ask the following questions: What does it mean to "care about" suicidality and suicidal people, to "take care of" suicidal people or to offer them "care giving"? I believe that an ethics of care founded on wonder, generosity, and attentive listening toward suicidal people can lead to a greater comprehension of some of the current forms of care offered in the name of suicide prevention as being more harmful and damaging than they are useful and helpful. The damaging aspect of suicide prevention is supported by the countless suicidal people who currently experience most suicide prevention interventions as forms of violent cure instead of care (e.g., Fitzpatrick, "Epistemic Justice"; Rhodanthe et al.; Stefan; Szasz; Trans LifeLine), as Mehler Paperny recounts. I argue that adding an anti-suicidist lens to analyze suicidality and intervention with suicidal people radically transforms the vision of what caring about and for suicidal people means.

A Process to Tackle the Suicidist "Abuser" within Ourselves

The transformative justice movement is led mostly by trans and queer people who self-identify as people of colour (often also disabled/Mad) and who hope to find better responses and solutions to forms of violence without counting on state institutions (e.g., police, prison, law) (Dixon and Piepzna-Samarasinha; Piepzna-Samarasinha). Similar to how I argue that suicide prevention and emergency services deployed to suicide crisis scenes often cause more harm than good, transformative justice activists argue that army, police, and prisons are "destructive and unnecessary" (Dixon and Piepzna-Samarasinha 7) ways to deal with violence and are particularly taxing for BIPOC, queer people, trans people, disabled/Mad people, poor people, and other marginalized individuals. These activists develop alternative ways to identify, denounce, and prevent violence, insisting on the fact that the dichotomy between perpetrators and victims of violence is too simplistic to represent the complexity of people's experiences. The transformative justice movement is not so much invested in calling out and blaming individuals' violent behaviours in order for them to be punished, as is the case with various legal systems. It is rather more interested in harm reduction, behaviour transformation, and healing both for "victims" and "abusers." It is in this spirit of transformative justice that Thom proposes a nine-step guide to help us recognize that we could all be abusers. This fundamental recognition helps to become more accountable for our actions and avoid reproducing violence and harm. While her guide to recognizing the abuser in us is not a panacea to solve all the problems of violence and abuse, I believe that her steps represent core attitudes that could be helpful when applying an ethics of care founded on wonder, generosity, and attentive listening toward suicidal people. *Although not intended for confronting the suicidist abuser in ourselves*, Thom's guide constitutes a step in the right direction to unpack and unmask the way each of us could reproduce violence such as suicidism.

As a first step, Thom suggests to "listen to the survivor." She insists on key features of this form of listening, "without becoming defensive…trying to…make excuses…minimizing or denying the extent of the harm…[or] trying to make oneself the center of the story being told" (70). Temptations are strong for those working from a preventionist script to engage in these problematic attitudes. Through their goal of helping, supporting, and saving suicidal people's lives, they might become defensive, minimize the negative consequences of their strategies (e.g., non-consensual rescues, forced institutionalization and treatments), or focus on *their* experience of suicidality of a loved one/a client, instead of on the traumas experienced by suicidal people themselves. In sum, it is important to put the emphasis on the people first concerned and listen carefully to their experiences, critiques, needs, and concerns without invalidating their voices. Thom additionally invites her readers to "take responsibility for the abuse" (71) and to become accountable for their actions. In the case of suicidality, can people working from a preventionist script who did and continue to do harm to suicidal people recognize the suicidist violence they reproduce and take responsibility for it? This is an important aspect in the transformation of suicidist behaviours toward the healing path sought by suicidal people.

Thom insists in her various steps that it is crucial to not feel guilt regarding our actions, but to recognize their impacts and mostly understand why we acted the way we did (72). In the case of people who reproduce suicidism, the reasons are numerous and understandable: it is their job and duty to prevent suicide, they want to help and support suicidal individuals, or they love the person who wants to die. Thom also points out the fact that being victims or survivors does not mean that we cannot simultaneously be abusers (73). For example, being a "survivor" of suicide, because of a past suicide attempt or because of the loss of someone we love by suicide, does not necessarily prevent us from reproducing suicidist violence toward suicidal people. In fact, sometimes those who are the most emotionally invested in suicidality are those who seem the most determined to impose their vision that life is worth living on everyone, and that suicide should never be an option. Another step suggested by Thom indicates that it is mostly the person who experienced the violence who should determine the healing process in order to leave them the space to testify and share their stories, emotions, and needs (73). This is exactly what should happen when it comes to suicidality: instead of designing suicide prevention strategies based on the perspectives of *ex-suicidal* people (often convinced that suicide attempts were mistakes) or on the perspectives of non-suicidal individuals, for whom suicide is incomprehensible, these strategies should focus on the perspectives of suicidal individuals and those of deceased individuals who left behind suicide notes. Initiatives by suicidal people such as peer-support projects (e.g., Rhodanthe et al.) propose very different strategies than those currently promoted in the majority of suicide prevention discourses.

As Thom mentions, because abusers are vilified, nobody wants to see themselves as such, hence why one of her steps is to "face the fear of accountability" (75). This fear prevents us from taking responsibility for our actions, a process that requires courage because of the potential negative consequences of doing so. In a world in which death is often seen as the ultimate loss, it could be frightening for those working from a preventionist script to imagine that the suicide prevention measures they put forth, instead of saving lives, could push people to complete their suicide by reinforcing their loneliness, powerlessness, and feeling that something is "wrong" with their suicidal thoughts. In her memoir, Mehler Paperny discusses worries when it comes to being transparent about her suicidality. She shares her experience of being brought by the police to the psychiatric ward against her will, being poorly treated during her hospitalization, and being restrained to her bed after suicide attempts. Like many suicidal people, Mehler Paperny had to lie her way out of the hospital with one goal in mind: going back home to complete her suicide. For people working in suicide prevention, facing the fear of being held accountable for suicides or suicide attempts they are trying to avoid could be difficult, but it is a necessary thing to do to start changing attitudes and practices toward suicidal people. While being accountable is crucial, Thom reminds of the importance of not confusing shame and guilt (76). While guilt is the normal outcome of being accountable and taking responsibility for our actions, shame about oneself is not helpful in transformative justice. The point is not, for those who are reproducing suicidism, to denigrate themselves but simply to recognize some of their questionable actions that may have harmed other people. Furthermore, Thom suggests to not "expect anyone to forgive you" (76). Hoping for forgiveness from suicidal people or from survivors of suicide attempts who have experienced harm through suicide prevention focuses on the person who committed the abuse, not on the person who suffers from it. The last step proposed by Thom is to "forgive yourself" (77). She claims that often we hurt and abuse other people because we are suffering ourselves. Suicidality confronts most of us: it places us in front of our own death, or the deaths of the people we love. Healing ourselves through forgiveness could be a step in the right direction to stop hurting others as a result of our own suffering related to death and suicidality. I believe that reconciliating ourselves with our complex relationship to death and suicidality would contribute to the way we treat other people's suicidality: instead of projecting our unresolved issues on others, we would be in a position of openness, listening, and welcoming the suicidal person with their thoughts and concerns. This process is not, by any means, a paint-by-numbers canvas providing all the answers to end structural suicidism. However, it constitutes a basis, in the spirit of transformative justice, to question suicidist assumptions, biases, attitudes, and practices, in an effort to build bridges with suicidal people. As Jennifer White reminds in her "ethics for suicide prevention," it is crucial to "not shy away from acknowledging and addressing our potential complicity with harm" (198). I think that this process could lead to better trust building between suicidal people and those who care about/for them.

Coda: An Ethics of "Living with" Suicidal People

The apparent oxymoron in the title of this chapter, "learning to 'live with' death," is rich in meaning. While life and death usually embody a radical dichotomy, from a queercrip perspective they need to be reconceptualized as intersecting and intertwined. Living with death, more specifically living with suicidality, is polysemic. Living with suicidality could mean, for non-suicidal people, living with the memory of a loved who died through suicide, living with the constant fear of the death of closed ones struggling with suicidality, or living through helping suicidal people. Living with suicidality, for ex-suicidal people, survivors of suicide attempts, or suicidal people who contemplate death as a potential solution could mean living with the memory of our own past struggles with distress and despair, living in constant fear that those obsessive thoughts of death will return at some point, living with the intense desire to end it all now, or learning to live with wanting to die, as Wright framed it. It could also mean supporting others with whom we share this pain through peer-support groups, lifelines, and other ways.

An ethics of "living with" suicidal people is thus not an oxymoron: while many suicidal people have died, and many continue to attempt suicide, the fact is that a majority of suicidal people, such as Wright, Piepzna-Samarasinha, Cortez, Mehler Paperny, or I, struggle to keep living and hope for better recognition, respect, and validation of our experiences with suicidality and suicide prevention services. Currently, for many of us, these services do not constitute care or a sustainable ethics of "living with" suicidal people. If the people working within social movements, (critical) suicidology, and suicide prevention want us alive, many of them need, to use Piepzna-Samarasinha's words, to "shut up and listen." What we have to say might not please them: it might clash with their conceptions of life, death, or suicidality, and with their agenda with regards to suicidality. However, listening to us represents one of their best chances for really understanding, for once, what we desperately need to perhaps decide to hang on to life for one more day, one more month, one more year, or beyond.

Notes

1. The limited space in this chapter prevents me from demonstrating the existence of suicidism. Readers interested in learning more about this structural suicidist violence are invited to read my work (see the works cited) in which I propose suicidism as a comprehensive framework to theorize the oppression of suicidal people.
2. About which suicidal stories circulate or not in the public sphere, see the work of Fitzpatrick.
3. Jaworski (594) builds on Marguerite La Caze's book *Wonder and Generosity*, a book inspired by a long tradition of philosophical reflections on those two notions.

Works Cited

Baril, Alexandre. "Les personnes suicidaires peuvent-elles parler? Théoriser l'oppression suicidiste à partir d'un modèle sociosubjectif du handicap." *Criminologie*, vol. 51, no. 2, 2018, pp. 189–212.

Baril, Alexandre. "The Somatechnologies of Canada's Medical Assistance in Dying Law: LGBTQ Discourses on Suicide and the Injunction to Live." *Somatechnics*, vol. 7, no. 2, 2017, pp. 201–217.

Baril, Alexandre. "Suicidism: A New Theoretical Framework to Conceptualize Suicide from an Anti-Oppressive Perspective." *Disability Studies Quarterly*, vol. 40, no. 3, 2020, pp. 1–40.

Baril, Alexandre. *Undoing Suicidism: A Trans, Queer, Crip Approach to Rethinking (Assisted) Suicide*. Temple UP, 2023. https://temple.manifoldapp.org/projects/undoing-suicidism

Bourgault, Sophie. "Attentive Listening and Care in a Neoliberal Era: Weilian Insights for Hurried Times." *Etica & Politica/Ethics & Politics*, vol. 18, no. 3, 2016, pp. 311–337.

Corriveau, Patrice, et al. "Créer et gérer une banque de données numérique: Les défis méthodologiques et éthiques de la construction et de la pérennité de la Plateforme d'analyse de la régulation sociale du suicide au Québec (PARSSQ)." *Bulletin de Méthodologie Sociologique*, vol. 150, 2021, pp. 28–50.

Dixon, Ejeris, and Leah Lakshmi Piepzna-Samarasinha, editors. *Beyond Survival: Strategies and Stories from the Transformative Justice Movement*. AK Press, 2020.

Dotson, Kristie. "A Cautionary Tale: On Limiting Epistemic Oppression." *Frontiers*, vol. 33, no. 1, 2012, pp. 24–47.

Dotson, Kristie. "Tracking Epistemic Violence, Tracking Practices of Silencing." *Hypatia*, vol. 26, no. 2, 2011, pp. 236–257.

Fitzpatrick, Scott J. "Epistemic Justice and the Struggle for Critical Suicide Literacy." *Social Epistemology*, vol. 34, no. 6, 2020, pp. 555–565.

Fitzpatrick, Scott J. "Ethical and Political Implications of the Turn to Stories in Suicide Prevention." *Philosophy, Psychiatry, & Psychology*, vol. 23, no. 3/4, 2016, pp. 265–276.

Fricker, Miranda. *Epistemic Injustice: Power and the Ethics of Knowing*. Oxford UP, 2007.

Froese Sakal, Jocelyn, and Cameron Greensmith. "Que(e)rying Youth Suicide: Unpacking Sexist and Racist Violence in *Skim* and *13 Reasons Why*." *Cultural Studies Review*, vol. 25, no. 2, 2019, pp. 31–51.

Furqan, Zainab, et al. "'I Can't Crack the Code': What Suicide Notes Teach Us about Experiences with Mental Illness and Mental Health Care." *Canadian Journal of Psychiatry*, vol. 64, no. 2, 2018, pp. 98–106.

Gilligan, Carol. *Une si grande différence*. Flammarion, 1986.

Jaworski, Katrina. "Towards Ethics of Wonder and Generosity in Critical Suicidology." *Social Epistemology*, vol. 34, no. 6, 2020, pp. 589–600.

Jaworski, Katrina, and Daniel G. Scott. "At the Limits of Suicide: The Bad Timing of the Gift." *Social Epistemology*, vol. 34, no. 6, 2020, pp. 577–588.

Krebs, Emily. "*13 Reasons Why* as a Vehicle for Public Understandings of Suicide." *Critical Studies in Media Communication*, vol. 37, no. 2, 2019, pp. 188–200.

Medina, José. *The Epistemology of Resistance: Gender and Racial Oppression, Epistemic Injustice, and Resistant Imaginations*. Oxford UP, 2013.

Mehler Paperny, Anna. *Hello I Want to Die Please Fix Me: Depression in the First Person*. Random House Canada, 2019.

Paperman, Patricia, and Sandra Laugier, editors. *Le souci des autres. Éthique et politique du care*. Éditions de l'École des hautes études en sciences sociales, 2005.

Perreault, Isabelle, et al. "While of Unsound Mind? Narratives of Responsibility in Suicide Notes from the Twentieth Century." *Histoire sociale*, vol. 49, no. 98, 2016, pp. 155–170.

Piepzna-Samarasinha, Leah Lakshmi. *Care Work: Dreaming Disability Justice*. Arsenal Pulp Press, 2018.

Rhodanthe, Leo, Emery Wishart, and Robyn Martin. *"All I Need Is Someone to Talk to": Evaluating DISCHARGED Suicide Peer Support*. Curtin University, 2019. https://www.transfolkofwa.org/wp-content/uploads/2020/01/Evaluating-DISCH%20ARGED-Suicide-Peer-Support.pdf.

Spivak, Gayatri Chakravorty. "Can the Subaltern Speak?" *Marxism and the Interpretation of Culture*, edited by Cary Nelson and Lawrence Grossberg, U of Illinois P, 1988, pp. 271–313.

Stefan, Susan. *Rational Suicide, Irrational Laws: Examining Current Approaches to Suicide in Policy and Law*. Oxford UP, 2016.

Stohlmann-Rainey, Jess. "How 'Safe Messaging' Gaslights Suicidal People." *Mad in America*, 4 Aug. 2019, https://www.madinamerica.com/2019/08/safe-messaging-gaslights-suicidal-people/.

Szasz, Thomas. *Fatal Freedom: The Ethics and Politics of Suicide*. Praeger Publishers, 1999.

Thom, Kai Cheng. "What to Do When You've Been Abusive." *Beyond Survival: Strategies and Stories from the Transformative Justice Movement*, edited by Ejeris Dixon and Leah Lakshmi Piepzna-Samarasinha, AK Press, 2020, pp. 67–77.

Trans Lifeline. "Why No Non-Consensual Active Rescue?" *Beyond Survival: Strategies and Stories from the Transformative Justice Movement*, edited by Ejeris Dixon and Leah Lakshmi Piepzna-Samarasinha, AK Press, 2020, pp. 135–139.

Tronto, Joan C. *Moral Boundaries: A Political Argument for an Ethic of Care*. Routledge, 1993.

Wagner, Tara Lynn. "Writer Speaks out after University Cancels Play Featuring Real Suicide Notes." *Spectrum News 1*, 27 Jan. 2022, https://spectrumnews1.com/ca/la-west/arts/2022/01/27/writer-speaks-out-after-university-cancels-play-featuring-real-suicide-notes?cid=share_clip.

Wedlake, Grace. "Complicating Theory through Practice: Affirming the Right to Die for Suicidal People." *Canadian Journal of Disability Studies*, vol. 9, no. 4, 2020, pp. 89–110.

White, Jennifer. "Hello Cruel World! Embracing a Collective Ethics for Suicide Prevention." *Suicide and Social Justice: New Perspectives on the Politics of Suicide and Suicide Prevention*, edited by Mark E. Button and Ian Marsh, Routledge, 2020, pp. 197–210.

White, Jennifer, and Jonathan Morris. "Re-thinking Ethics and Politics in Suicide Prevention: Bringing Narrative Ideas into Dialogue with Critical Suicide Studies." *International Journal of Environmental Research and Public Health*, vol. 16, no. 18, 2019, 3236.

Wright, Cortez. "Learning to Live with Wanting to Die." *The Body Is Not an Apology*, 10 June 2018, https://thebodyisnotanapology.com/magazine/learning-to-live-with-wanting-to-die/.

6
Here Is a Broken Word
Psychosis and Ethical Accompaniment

ERIN SOROS

> *Listening watches over the unexpected.*
> —ANNE DUFOURMANTELLE, *Power of Gentleness*

ETHICAL LONELINESS is a term that philosopher Jill Stauffer chooses to describe the painful state of suffering that fails to be witnessed. It is negation inside negation: "the experience of being abandoned by humanity compounded by the experience of not being heard" (9). The concentration camp victim is tortured and dehumanized, anguish unseen by a larger community, and then even on release from the camps, the full extent of the devastation that this prisoner confronted is not grasped by others, not with any profound attunement or political reckoning. The survivor of colonial genocide not only manages ongoing experiences of individual and collective loss, but faces the cynical and calculated diminishment of atrocity offered by tidy narratives of national reconciliation. To be ethically lonely is not just to be physically alone in one's pain, but to experience the protracted and erasing psychological isolation of aloneness with others: to look for some acknowledgement, to speak for some reckoning, and instead to experience a turning away from all you have endured.

    I have taken you to Stauffer's concept of ethical loneliness because here I want to consider its opposite: what follows will be a tender lesson emerging from a moment when I fell into madness, and a friend listened, took a step toward the threshold of what a mind cannot seem to bear. I will describe not a collapse of subjectivities—no one goes mad with me—but rather accompaniment through the personal nuance of historical atrocity: ethical accompaniment.

On the day I begin this essay, I read a newspaper article that addressed what the Canadian state invested to defend the killing of Pierre Coriolan, a Black man, diagnosed schizophrenic, living in subsidized housing in Montréal. His neighbours had heard him yelling and tearing apart the room from which he'd recently been evicted, and called 911 to complain. The police arrived and within minutes shot him dead. When I first heard this news, I felt an immediate kinship with this man—his desperation, the strewn objects speaking what his words cannot—yet I also knew my secure distance from any room he has occupied: even if I am confronted by police when I am in a state of mental delirium, even if the threat of male violence reverberates in terrifying ways when police throw me to the ground, my whiteness will keep me breathing. As a white, highly educated woman I have also known the extended benefits of therapeutic assistance that he may never have received, the kind offered not through the paperwork hurry of a general clinic but in the rarified retreat of a book-lined office, privileged spaces for psychotic people whose accomplishments mark their episodes and their prospects as different from those without education or without income, those with the wrong accents and the wrong kin.

Pierre Coriolan's family has tried to raise funds to fight for justice and has expressed a continuing wish that the police had used techniques to defuse the situation. I don't know if "defuse" was the family's word or the journalist's, a common enough term to encounter when another mad Black person is killed—as is the word *de-escalate*, or the term *mental health crisis*, as if the crisis belonged to the mad person and not to the one whose gun created death. Even as these terms lean toward an impossible longing for one specific life instead of its loss and even as they express a future yearning for practices that keep the next person alive, they leave people lonely. Words such as *defuse* and *de-escalate* limit the possible horizon of care, compassed as they are to violence. Psychosis is a "fuse," some danger, risk of explosion that only specialized training and timing and tools can prevent. Or psychosis is an "escalation," still the suggestion of threat. And the threat needs to be contained, averted, controlled. But what if we were to imagine speaking not against psychosis, but with it? What if psychosis trembles reference, expanding the very possibility of response? What if odd language and disconcerting gestures, the loops of a sentence, the mess of a room, have something to say?

At first I am alone. I fall, as if through an echoing chamber, as if from a skyscraper passing dim windows. It is confusing here yet there is clarity enough, like the distant pulsing glimmer cast by moving cars. Everything is moving, and I am still. Or everything is still, and I am moving. I walk back and forth in my unkempt apartment, signature of an unravelling mind, and I recall newspaper articles about a serial killer who is finally caught. Except *recall* is the wrong word. I am not in the present reflecting on a past. And it's not the newspaper I see, but a foot, in the form of a sock under the bed. The detritus I've left strewn across the floor, litter of living, has become a book without binding in a language no one would understand. Tonight it is for me to read. The sock is not a foot and it is a foot, both, at once.

I worked for a decade, from 1990 to 2000, in the Vancouver neighbourhood where this man located his victims. He was convicted of murdering six women. Twenty-six bodies were found in his farm. He confessed to killing forty-nine. Numbers for people, for sunshine that the dead won't see, rain they won't feel, laughter and welcome and song they will no longer hear. His name? A choosing, a colour, an animal, a town. I don't want to name him. If I name him, I fear my words will once again split apart. I won't describe how he killed the women, why I see their bodies in pieces. I can tell you that for years, at an epicenter of Canadian genocide, I heard from women on the night they had been raped. I listened on the crisis line and in the hospital. Seventeen-hour overnight shifts. Plastic chairs slick to thighs, jitter walk, sweaty palm and calluses, white paper on padded table, narrow medical instruments like a pen to write a wounded body, the cafeteria's boiled smell, chapped sips of bitter coffee, eyes a cry, words a broken wooden staircase, danger of slipping, memory in splinters, hovering sleeplessness, children waiting, click of quarter in a phone, chipped nail polish, trembling shoulders, tracks gnarled like tree roots, Kleenex knot of snot, a wailing in a bathroom stall as if metal could howl. These women were not my family, not lovers, not friends; their stories are their stories, extending far before and beyond the twilight of crisis on which we met. And the moments I shared with them are some of the most physically and emotionally intimate of my life.

I heard, of course, only from the ones who survived. They fought, or they kept strategically still and silent like the corpse they didn't want to become.

They endured. They escaped—perhaps from the serial killer or one of his buddies, perhaps from other men, so many men. I know some of the women went back to their labour on Hastings or Powell or Main. I don't know their names, but I did know their names, briefly, a familial grace or a street proxy they uttered to me and then I uttered to them, shibboleth in the stark noisy glare of Emergency. I don't know which of these women are still alive. He was targeting sex workers, Indigenous sex workers. These are the deaths that police do not investigate. These are the deaths counted, on the street, grieved, on the street, and as meaningless to those driving past as a high-top hanging from a telephone wire, neighbourhood code of where to find what a local needs to find. When I relayed to the police what the sex workers had told me—they had come to the rape crisis centre in a group, not sitting down but standing together in the hallway as if they did not belong in a counselor's room, as if they had something to say on the very edge of a therapeutic space, the words *serial killer*, the words *killing us*—the officers laughed.

"Probably partying in Alberta."

"She has four children. She wouldn't leave her children."

"Well, she did though, didn't she?"

Laugh. Laugh. Laugh.

Police officers always stand so sturdy, legs wide, boots owning the ground.

I moved away; I could move away, first from the crisis line, then from this city. As the decade turned—that apprehensive excitement of 2000, our millennium new and yet unharmed—I crossed the border to live on the east coast of the United States for graduate study and various writing fellowships. Then as another decade approached with its promise of change, I flew across the ocean to England to take the next fellowship and then to pursue a PHD. And no one around me ever spoke of the serial killer who was finally convicted in 2007, years after murder and more murder, each woman with a name someone had whispered, called, cried.

If these women were other than these women—the colour of their skin, the cold of their work, the toll of their habits—news would have travelled. But then the police knew that, didn't they? All those seasons they did not bother to hear, when a vulnerable community risked requesting the sustaining power granted by human witness, and instead the ethical loneliness created and maintained by the misogyny of settler colonialism continued to enable the kill.

When I was physically close to the women who were most at risk, I knew my distance: my relative safety, the whiteness of my nights. And the further away I travelled, the more that the collective loss felt like a home I didn't know how to leave.

One night in England, in the damp cramp of my medieval flat, rain sheeting windows I never did curtain, I called the Carnegie Centre, on Hastings Street, in Vancouver. On the precipice of psychosis I reached out to a hook the way a mountain climber manages to link a rope to the face of a mountain. I asked the man who answered the phone if I could speak to someone in charge of commemorating the murdered women.

He knew immediately who could hear me. He transferred me to her line.

"Did it happen?" I asked her.

I don't know how I oriented this stranger to my question, my words intersecting in cracking angles, but I do know I asked it and that she was able to answer. "Yes," she said. And then she said, "Who is with you right now? Is anyone there? Who can be with you?"

No one was with me.

I could always call the academic colleague who said colonialism brought some good things. They got the railroad, he said.

I was admitted to the hospital—such a word, *admitted*, as if something private has been finally disclosed, as if I were allowed to enter a privileged space whereas in these cases I am walking in handcuffs or I am walking in compliance to the threat of force. The call to the Carnegie Centre—I remember it; I gripped it—but this stranger was right: her one voice so distant was not enough.

Years later I returned to my country. Living not in my hometown of Vancouver, but in Toronto in a season of overwhelming news, the summer of 2017, I start again to fall. I want you to know where I am located when I am falling because these tellings are disorienting but some things are certain and it can be helpful to answer the question: where are you? I am finding a foot under my bed, finding blood in the sink. But this time, someone is with me: my friend L. stays on the phone.

This is what she did: she made space for me to speak, and I discharged bits and pieces of language rapidly, at first with no interruption, words stumbling, repeating, like the verbal panic of someone who has just left the scene of an accident. And she held the words, sometimes echoing back what I had expressed, or asking a question, sometimes elaborating on one of my statements—she was not explaining or interpreting them, but opening a word tenderly the way you would detangle a knot while brushing a daughter's hair. We were thousands of miles apart, but on the phone it was as if a mirror held us together in its silver dimension. She did not reciprocate with a story of her own, not in those hours. She gently grasped what I said. If I used a confusing image, she offered a glimpse into what it might mean to her. She provided a nearing, a nodding. Unlike the nurses or the psychiatrists who could make no sense of my descriptions, she knew Hastings Street, the lumps of clothes found or stolen and available for resale for the next twenty-dollar hit, the pink optimism of the neon pig above the meat store, the glass condos reaching like monsters to push people away from the concrete where they slept. I was talking about the women who walked this street, and crosses, white crosses. No crosses anywhere on this street, just graffiti, ragged red witnessing and warnings.

In the pomegranate juice lining my fridge, I could see blood. In the tangle of a t-shirt, I could see the whiteness of white crosses. My friend L. is an Indigenous woman who is not going to say anything chipper to me about getting the railroad. And her ethical and compassionate insight, even in my vulnerable state, I knew it, could feel it, could finally lean my frightened mind toward a soul who heard not gibberish, but testimony. Suffering broke words, and words broke forth suffering. She did not dismiss the violence or the negation of it. She did not pathologize my need to tell and retell. On this occasion she refrained from offering the perspective of a wider political frame but stayed with each detail I offered. She remained intricately attuned to each possible nuance of my meanings, the ones that led to historical facts and the ones that led away from them. Her voice calm, her words braced a reality of violence that *was* a reality even if not, in that moment, present in my apartment. I spoke of bodies. And we spoke too of my body, its living need for breath, food, sleep. Since she could not see me, she often asked where I was or what I was doing, and I sensed that this effort of spatial orientation was for my benefit as much as it was for hers, bringing me back into a physical world through the effort to narrate something sturdy in words that I could trust. We stayed on the phone, off and on, for two days.

In *Catch Them Before They Fall*, the psychoanalyst Christopher Bollas describes a renegade move: if he apprehends that one of his clients is nearing breakdown, he extends the time of his sessions. Vulnerability to breakdown is exhibited in the pattern and speed of speech, an inability for a client to contain her own mind. He will cancel his other appointments and let one client speak with him all day, and the next day again, and the next, from nine to six. Part of the meaning and containment of psychoanalysis arrives through the regular structure and limit of one's weekly hours: Bollas admits he has been criticized for his departure from the expected temporal frame. But he enacted this innovation because he sees such crisis moments as meaning-rich entrances into and through the unconscious, a potential for change that demands space and time and the engaged presence of another. He knows the alternate would be hospitalization, and the numbing, sedating use of drugs that would prevent any psychic unfolding. In these extended sessions, he does not offer interpretation. He does not interject his analyses of what the client says. Instead he listens in a state of reverie, letting the client's unconscious resonate with his own.

When I first read of the expansiveness of this technique, after I had begun experiencing psychosis and before I met my friend L., I envied Bollas's patients who were allowed to experience their interior plenitude. My own experience of listening occurs only after the crisis, when I am able to translate it in scheduled hours to professional ears that I pay to listen. But when I have most needed to be heard, my psychic processes had been stopped by force. The suffering I tried to narrate in the hospital was refused a witness—by the dimming of eyes, the turning away of a face, by an order to cuff my body to a bed within a closed box. I spoke to walls. I called to walls. What I experienced in and through psychiatric hospital's human machinery was not care but a protracted and brutal form of unlistening.

A high dose of antipsychotics left me still and quiet, asleep fourteen hours a day, and the other hours blank, dull, my slack face nothing but a toy with the batteries removed.

What was my tune? What was it that my consciousness tried to express? What had I tried to communicate to the hold of another's mind?

I believe now, after experiencing L.'s listening—the generosity of her hours that sustained me through a psychotic experience so that I was able to avoid, for the first time, an involuntary stay in the hospital—that the visions of terror kept returning because these needed to be heard by someone who could intimately understand. My friend had her own grasp of colonial atrocity and her own comprehension of the violent effect of settler negation and her own psychic map of ongoing loss, private fear different from mine—and this specific listening offered reverie that had never been available for me in clinical hours, no matter how many were scheduled.

On the day I am revising this chapter, Canada is recognizing women murdered. December 6th has for decades signified a collective act of memorial, the month and the number a shorthand, as September 11th has become internationally a shorthand. On December 6th in 1989, fourteen women, engineering students in Montréal, were shot by a man who announced he was targeting feminists. The date marks the horror and tragedy of this event but it has also come to mark the ongoing struggle to end violence against women. When I was in the psychiatric ward in the UK, I repeatedly referenced December 6th—perhaps trying to invoke what had happened to those university students, or perhaps communicating my fear of such violence taking place once more, or perhaps using this date as a metonym for the other deaths, the less prestigious deaths, the lives my country does not mourn. The women I recall in my psychotic state are not the ones whose names have become a collective scroll. No CBC announcer speaks of how old the women who walked Hastings Street would have been this year; no *Vancouver Sun* journalist ruminates on what they would have accomplished had they lived; no elite institution notes what kind of person they would have become. So this date, December 6th, each year, December 6th, functions simultaneously as a marker of ethical accompaniment and of ethical abandonment.

I can never determine precisely what I was trying to say in the hospital when I kept referring to December 6th, but I know the nurses did not engage with what the term could have meant, what it said and unsaid. Instead, in the sing-song voice usually reserved for a kindergarten child, they told me that the date we shared in that ward was not December 6th. "It's March 14th," they'd announce. "It's April 9th," the sing-song giving way to annoyance as I repeatedly failed to accept how easy the answer could be. The mistaken date did not need to be marked in my files. My utterance did not need to be considered with care, but dismissed, corrected, as if that's all I hoped to hear through my repetition—some clarity about which box to tick on a calendar.

Yet even if they had come to understand the basic Canadian understanding of the significance of December 6th, I suspect I might have continued with my repetition. I spoke toward another kind of listening, a framing significantly different from what they could have found on Wikipedia. The date had become both a gravestone and its absence, both the communal marker of loss and the marker for the very lack of such marking when the loss involves those who live in what we call "the margins," that part of the page where no words exist, as if their deaths marched invisibly in the blank space running alongside the newspaper articles on other women.

What is perhaps too neatly called "culturally competent care" provides something more profound than competence: healing involves not just a shared factual knowledge of specific social context—words, rituals, history, geography—but also relational commitment. By this I mean my friend's commitment to me, and mine to her, and ours toward a future only madness can see. I had something to tell her, to give her, trust with her, something to return. Such a bond is unlikely to be explained in a policy or handbook but it makes ethical accompaniment possible in multidimensional and unpredictable ways. What if we listened to those who experience psychosis as if their story helped complete our own? What if psychosis is not only a call for ethical accompaniment, but also itself an offering—*itself a way to accompany*? What if one's madness can be a witness?

Here is a shattered piece of word.   Here is another.

And there we were, my friend and I, far apart but together, our voices a vibration over the phone as we placed the fragments together, the broken and breaking enactment of unbearable witnessing that needed the two of us, our coordinating efforts hesitant and careful and then sometimes glinting sure. I recognize something. This happened.

There is no scale on which I can place another's mind, no data to prove what one unconscious offers that another cannot. I provide no stats, no quantitative charts or even qualitative interviews to be analyzed for themes. I am siding with mystery. I am remembering the idiosyncratic way I met L. on the day I marked the anniversary of my first psychotic experience by attending a Shabbat service in a synagogue where I noticed someone I wanted to know. I am pausing with chance and calling and finding: the moment one caring person accepts a difficult listening, the moment we recognize another as someone to witness a meaning that had before been refused. I am saying that in times of vulnerability we sometimes do locate our singular listeners, those whose unconscious offers a reverie beyond any institutional affiliation, and that in my psychotic state I have been able to find mine.

We might pause to wonder not just what someone in a delusionary state is trying to communicate from a disenfranchised past, but also what such speech tells of our own lives, what we have seen or refused to see.

L. offered a visceral awareness of how colonialism and sexual violence and policing intersect—that white tangle of death. She possessed an ethical commitment to fighting both the atrocity and the active repudiation. But she also knew a private longing—here I will be elliptical because I want to share my own vulnerability and not those of others. What I expressed to her was not just the violence I had vicariously witnessed and the police and state abandonment, but the recuperative fantasy that would somehow resolve these misogynist, colonial crimes—or make everything go away, my magical belief as instant as the hands a child holds over her face to make herself disappear. By expanding the hours of his listening, Bollas provides his clients the chance to prevent breakdown, and such prevention is ideal, but there is something uniquely healing when one can be heard, deeply and compassionately heard, from *within the psychotic realm itself.* Outside hospital settings, I have experienced psychoanalytic listening, and profound therapeutic attunement, these forms of sustaining care—deeply skilled and empathetic practitioners have provided me a fluency with threshold states I would otherwise not know to speak—but my dialogue with L. was a riskier and ultimately more intimate journey because she companioned me right through the long hours of psychotic trance, just as in my own strange way I accompanied her. It was as if instead of hearing my dream, she entered it with me, both the nightmare entrapment and the fantasy escape. Her unconscious longing and my unconscious longing, our distinct missings, somehow greeted each other the way two separate faces lock eyes in the same mirror.

We can say "she lost her mind," but madness also provides its findings. When I begin to descend through flickering images of horror, I land where no such fear exists: a wedding. Somewhere there is a wedding. And my groom is waiting. This expectation is the absurd wonderland of my falling, the floor on which I always eventually land, as if I could walk into my own romantic storyline on Netflix and run into the arms of its reassuring final scene, all the strains in the plot leading only to a happy resolution. Instead I walk outside where faces on the street expand and voices reverberate with secret destinations and professions of love. I now believe that this wedding fantasy corresponds to a desire, in a cascade of remembered violence and confusing isolation, for ethical accompaniment: he will be there, my beloved, my listener, and he will say yes.

With L.'s ethical companionship, I was for once not looking for him alone. I carried the phone with me as I walked the streets of Toronto searching for the ceremony in an ecstatic sense of imminent union. L. did not dissuade my belief, but nor did she enhance it. She did not step into the place of the beloved, this fantasy that drew me from what I needed to face, but still, as I searched she stepped beside me. At times she was silent. I knew it would seem to passersby that I wasn't mad if I was talking not to myself but to someone on the phone.

Are you there? Are you still there?

There is always a moment in the autumn, Alice Munro says in one of her stories, when you realize you can no longer hear the birds. They have flown away for the winter—they have been gone for days—but only now do you notice the absence of their call. The resolution of my psychotic experience, when I was finally given the chance to undergo this transition without the intervention of psychiatric drugs, felt something like that awareness.

I sat in the kitchen, on the phone with L. I had talked and walked my way freely through the fantasy that gave me an escape from fear. I had been allowed to speak as I have never before been accompanied. I had offered what I could, in the way I could. And here I was, back in my Toronto apartment, clothes on the floor, dishes in the sink, a sock that was after all just a sock, and it was safe to have a shower, safe to turn on the stove for a cup of tea—no one was getting killed, not here, not tonight. And I grasped—at the glimmering edge of fantasy—that my beloved is not looking for me. No one waits, no groom sees. He is not listening. The disappointment of this realization tore me, the kind of anguish you wake into when you have been dreaming of someone who is no longer alive and then the cut of consciousness greets you in the bitter unshuttered morning.

The numbing effect of neuroleptic drugs and the psychiatric refusal to listen—these entwined negations—had for years prevented my mind's journey, denying me the pain of this specific and necessary gift, this grief, rip in my chest.

The women were dead. No magical romantic resolution could be found for their loss.

Do you think you can sleep now? my friend L. asked.

And sleep, what psychosis had mimicked and yet refused, delivering only waking nightmares and walking dreams that tantalized with fantasy wholeness, this relief came to me then, without involuntary pill or forced injection, yet without consolation for those I knew were gone, sleep curving around the body of sadness.

Works Cited

Bollas, Christopher. *Catch Them Before They Fall: The Psychoanalysis of Breakdown*. Routledge, 2013.

Dufourmantelle, Anne. *Power of Gentleness: Meditation on the Risk of Living*. Fordham UP, 2018.

Munro, Alice. "Corrie." *Dear Life,* Knopf, 2012, pp.154–174.

Stauffer, Jill. *Ethical Loneliness: The Injustice of Not Being Heard*. Columbia UP, 2015.

7

Synergies of Solidarity
Un/Learning with Feminist Menopause Imaginaries in Canadian Writing

VERONIKA SCHUCHTER

"THE FUTURE IS MENOPAUSAL," writes Ann Neumann in her article of the same name in *Baffler* magazine. There, she traces the cultural and capitalist history of hormone replacement therapy (HRT), which was first introduced in the 1940s to treat the symptoms of menopause and is still used to this day.[1] HRT gained much of its popularity through gynecologist Robert A. Wilson's 1966 book *A New Life: The Quest and the Key...Feminine Forever*, in which he describes menopause as "a preventable and curable deficiency disease" (105). He adds that "the loss of estrogen," which he equates with the loss of hyperfeminine cis womanhood to be upheld at any cost, "is a supreme tragedy" (105–106) to be averted by HRT. This is one instance where pharmaceutical intervention is presented as the solution to not only eradicate the sometimes physically and mentally debilitating symptoms of the menopause but to make women continue to be "feminine once more and forever" (107) within the confines of the heteropatriarchal gender binary. "Pathetically little has improved for menopausal women since Wilson died in 1981," Neumann writes, and "Big Pharma's attention to menopausal women over the past fifty years has unsurprisingly better served the industry's own financial need than women's physical menopause symptoms." From a pharmaceutical standpoint, the future is indeed menopausal and it is estimated that by 2025, 1.1 billion people will be peri/menopausal. In most (Western) countries large-scale medical studies remain disproportionately underfunded and access to appropriate menopause health care is often challenging for those who want to seek help (Neumann). I note this rapid commercialization of women's aging and health and the resultant biomedical intervention as a way of situating my literary analysis. Both primary sources discussed in this chapter—the 2017 collection *Writing Menopause: An Anthology of Fiction, Poetry and Creative Non-fiction*, edited by Jane Cawthorne and E.D. Morin, and the 2020 graphic memoir *Kimiko Does Cancer: A Graphic Memoir* by Kimiko Tobimatsu and illustrated by Keet Geniza—are embedded in this violent machinery of medical misogyny, ageism, and pharmaceutical profit. They are also part of a growing body of literary and cultural engagements with the menopause. While representations of the menopause remain sparse overall in comparison to creative works addressing other issues of women's health (Manguso; Neumann; Steinke), there is a significant explosion of literary works centring menopause experiences since around 2015.

While most of these texts reflect the lives of white, cis gender, and heterosexual women, *Writing Menopause* and *Kimiko Does Cancer* are part of a more inclusive literary menopause corpus emerging as a necessary critical counter-narrative to the heteronormative and ageist rhetoric that surrounds much of the discourse on the menopause. Cawthorne and Morin, the editors of *Writing Menopause*, state in their introduction that the "book is different. It is not about what the menopause is, but about how it feels," and that its fifty-four contributors offer "points of views that [go] beyond women [because] menopause is experienced by non-binary people and trans men too" (1). Tobimatsu's graphic memoir traces the impact of the menopause as the result of illness and the destabilizing effects it has on her body as a young, queer, mixed-race woman even after the cancer is gone. Both texts are examples of the kind of life-writing that is deeply grounded in corporeal experiences, and through making visible stories about non-normative bodies, health, and illness they create moments of what I term synergies of solidarity that allow for connections through shared experiences between these sources and beyond. Through selected pieces from the anthology and the graphic memoir, this chapter also explores how the creative realm is a crucial space for the process of un/learning sexist, racist, and ageist perceptions of those experiencing menopause. It offers ethical and inclusive ways to write about late middle-age that other forms of discourse do not.

Accordingly, my approach to theorizing these synergies of solidarity is twofold. In a first step, I want to begin to think through my responsibilities as a feminist researcher who is not yet menopausal but engages with people's textual menopause testimonies. There is immense generosity in sharing this deeply personal, vulnerable, and stigmatized experience and receiving it requires care and accountability. This reflection also requires connecting responsibly with this deferred identity within a feminist framework. To think through some of the issues that arise when working at the intersection of gender, age, and health, I propose the concept of menopause futurity as a working tool that allows for a transgenerational and multidirectional feminist practice. In a second step, I show how *Writing Menopause* and *Kimiko Does Cancer* are examples of literary configurations whose trajectory is collective, collaborative, and community-oriented by sharing diverse menopause experiences across generational lines. Ultimately, I suggest that thinking with and toward menopause makes possible an inclusive feminist realm with transgenerational solidarity at its core.

Menopause Futurity and Researcher Responsibility

As a cultural and corporeal phenomenon, the menopause brings together several intersecting markers of identity such as gender, age, and disability that are arguably more in flux than other more stable markers of identity such as race or sexuality. As a universally experienced process and socially constructed categorization, age presents a unique axis of identity because old age may become an increasingly stigmatized part of a person's identity, both how they view themselves and how they are viewed by those around them (Jose et al., 116–117). This also means that a socially perceived old person may often be identified by others as old before their gender, race, sexual orientation, or disability is registered. In one of the major studies on perceptions of age, Chopik et al. explain that as "people age, they become increasingly closer to identifying with a stigmatized group (i.e., older adults) [and] engage in efforts to psychologically distance themselves from older adults" (5). This often subconscious distancing from those perceived to be older than oneself to avoid confronting one's own inevitable aging is arguably both a destructive and generative force within the feminist movement. Most commonly, Western feminist movements have conceptually been arranged along generational lines, relying on the analogy of the different "waves" that focus on the needs and demands of women at specific points in time. Those waves allegedly evolve as new generations of feminists formulate their own demands and build on the achievements of their elders while also rejecting some of the ideals of those who came before them. As such, as with other ideologies, feminism's evolutionary potential is often portrayed to be rooted in generational conflict. Anglo-American feminism especially has tended to equate generations with difference and has put forward a narrative of linear progression—that is, each succession of a generational wave heralds progressive change.

Since the early 2000s, resistance to this model has grown and scholars such as Iris van der Tuin ("'Jumping Generations'"), Clare Hemmings ("Generational Dilemmas"; *Why Stories Matter*), Victoria Browne, and Alex Martinis Roe (*To Become Two*) have argued for more nuanced approaches to feminist movements at different points in time. In the following, I continue to think alongside the work of Martinis Roe that offers practice-based suggestions in moving toward a transgenerational feminism. By tracing this feminist genealogy, I show that the oftentimes marginalized positioning of aging discourses in feminist academia may stem to some extent from a unilateral engagement with aging and old feminists. Accordingly, it is productive to consider the menopause as a cultural and embodied phenomenon that spans generations and presents a transition towards being socially considered "older" for those experiencing it. To think through these limiting generational barriers, I propose the concept of menopause futurity, which is, at its core, multidirectional and transgenerational and a feminist relational practice that allows caring for those who have come before while also embracing one's own futures and those of the next generation. I come to this concept via Neumann's claim—already mentioned in the introduction to this chapter—that "the future is menopausal" and Martinis Roe's work on transgenerational feminism and feminist genealogies ("'Solidarity-in-Difference'"; *To Become Two*; "Forging Feminist Futures"). By centring feminist collective practice, it rejects the conventional wave model on the grounds that "linear models of time belong to ways of understanding the world that don't account for complex entanglements, and they ultimately serve to hide the agency of what has come before in shaping what is to come" (Martinis Roe, "Forging Feminist Futures"). Martinis Roe identifies that what is to come as "the futures imagined by earlier generations...actually brought about through the actions of later generations as they respond to what has come before them" ("Forging Feminist Futures"). The affirmative relational mode of transgenerational feminist practice that Martinis Roe proposes has the concept of acknowledgement at its core and this "entails situating yourself in relation to those who came before, but also affirming, continuing, and doing the politics of difference they invented—not doing and being the same as them" ("'Solidarity-in-Difference'"). The relational mode of "acknowledgement" can be one way to exit discourses that equate "young" with narratives of progress and "old" with narratives of loss.

Along those lines, the concept of menopausal futurity builds on this affirmative acknowledgement as another way to resist an understanding of feminism's evolution purely through the generational wave model. I illustrate this by briefly highlighting two edited collections and their introductions that are helpful in circumscribing the polarized generational tensions arising from a unilateral mode of argumentation around discourses of aging in the feminist academy. Both collections—*Figuring Age: Women, Bodies, Generations*, edited by Kathleen Woodward, and *Age Matters: Re-aligning Feminist Thinking*, edited Toni M. Calasanti and Kathleen F. Slevin—are concerned with the status of old women and the feminist movement. Woodward's collection was especially groundbreaking when it was published in 1999 because it centred the physical, social, and cultural lives of old women and brought much-needed attention to ageism and feminism. In the introduction, she observes that "ageism is entrenched within feminism itself," a culture that she also denotes as "lethal" (xi). Similarly, Calasanti and Slevin note in 2006 that all contributors to their collection are "committed feminists [who] share a frustration that feminist scholarship has paid scant attention to ageism, age relations, and old age" (ix). Further, they claim that feminist scholars and activists are guilty of "engag[ing] in our own oppression" (1) and they too ask a crucial question: "Where are the old women in feminisms, or their advocates?" (9). However, while they broach key issues, both introductions limit feminist positionalities of aging to quite static relations; old women seem to be unilaterally condemned to be looking back, while younger feminists ought to look ahead and show support to but also tend to look away, with Woodward claiming that "younger people...have functioned as mirrors to older women, reflecting them back half their size" (xii). This tension is further reinforced by the frequent referencing of renowned white feminist writers and philosophers—Susan Sontag, Simone de Beauvoir, Germaine Greer, Betty Friedan—who have written on the subject of aging and about their experiences of being an old woman. This citational praxis is especially interesting considering both introductions' insistence on allyship from young feminists. Most of the famous writers cited who went on to write pieces about old women did so once they were considered old or noticed themselves aging, physically as well as culturally.[2] In addition, the contributors to the edited collection have tangible experiences with aging and being perceived as an old woman. Calasanti and Slevin observe that "a handful of scholars in their sixties have done important work on age oppression" and that feminist scholars have recently "expressed more concern about aging perhaps because [they] are more aware of their own aging" (2). While both edited collections have started a necessary conversation about a lack of allyship between differently aged feminists, they also perpetuate some comparativist patterns that do not fully account for the intersectional entanglements of age.

Drawing on and departing from Woodward's and Calasanti and Slevin's work is a crucial conceptual building block in the process of moving toward a feminist understanding of aging that is multidirectional and transgenerational. It is perhaps only human that we care about the causes that directly impact our lives or those dear to us in tangible ways, but one could ask to what extent these famous white writers and philosophers were showing the same kind of solidarity to their elders when they became culturally invisibilized that are expected from new generations of feminists. This is not to dismiss the discriminatory structures of ageism and its very tangible consequences, but instead it is an effort to uncover the hardened binary position of young versus old that seems to frequently structure feminist discourse on aging, such as when Woodward states that as "younger women turn these very prejudices against women older than themselves, they will in effect be turning against their very future selves as older women" (xiii). While feminists should not just care about injustices because they see versions of themselves reflected in those oppressed, as the quote above insinuates, this outlook can still be generative because it allows for menopause futurity by demanding an awareness of old age as a deferred identity. Instead of only arguing from a unilateral perspective through which younger feminist can only look ahead to their future selves and older feminist can only look back to seek support, I propose shifting the conversation to how we can move toward a model of transgenerational, multidirectional allyship in which an anticipation of aging as well as the memory of youth brings with it acts of solidarity.

As I develop my concept of menopause futurity as a transgenerational feminist praxis and navigate twenty-first-century textual representations of the menopause, I am currently only sure of one thing: this process must be collective, dialogical, and transgenerational.³ The study of narratives pertaining to aging and health can leave authors, especially those who are not white, cis gender, and able bodied, vulnerable even if they share their stories deliberately and consensually. This work, in turn, requires a particular form of ethical consideration on the part of the researcher. It is crucial that I acknowledge and account for my positionality as a white cis woman of reproductive age who has not yet but will experience perimenopause in the next ten to fifteen years. Accordingly, as part of my broader feminist praxis, I must further consider the ethical implications of writing about a gendered experience of aging as a person who is not yet considered old and address the need for researchers to be cautious and self-reflexive when engaging with textual representations of aging and health.

Carla Rice's detailed reflections on ethical feminist scholarship in "Imagining the Other? Ethical Challenges of Researching and Writing Women's Embodied Lives" are particularly pertinent to my scholarly process. While her considerations pertain predominantly to her fieldwork interviewing women about their body image and collating qualitative data, I nevertheless see useful parallels emerge for an ethical engagement with menopause life-writing. Rice identifies four key areas of ethical practices when engaging with the accounts of othered experiences, whether the researcher partially shares those experiences or not: the accountability, responsibility, advocacy, and reflexivity of the researcher (250). These four areas help define the ethical markers that frame my analysis of literary menopause imaginaries and testimonies. While these relational gestures remain largely invisible in the actual literary analysis, they are nevertheless crucial, both to commit to menopause futurity as a practice that has acknowledgement of old feminists' value and contributions at its centre and to use the space of this chapter to hold myself accountable. In my ensuing literary analysis, I do not mention my positionality as a premenopausal cis woman as a way of "decentring myself" (Rice 259) while still holding myself accountable by discussing it in this separate section. In my reading of *Kimiko Does Cancer* and *Writing Menopause*, I follow a genealogy of a "practice of relations" that is central to Martinis Roe's work in *To Become Two*, which she in turn borrows from Liberia delle donne di Milano, an Italian feminist collective, and which she understands as "working on relationships as political practice where the relationship starts from and values each other's difference" (158). This is a generative approach for literary scholars who work with texts that feature life-writing that shares potentially vulnerable stories of health and illness, which not only centres the piece of literary criticism as end product but also places emphasis on the ethical methodology surrounding it. It is also a useful tool in reading both primary sources as being in relation to one another in the context of menopause futurity, which operates transgenerationally to overcome feminist generational divides.

Synergies of Solidarity

I rely on two textual examples of menopause futurity as collective and transgenerational practice: *Kimiko Does Cancer: A Graphic Memoir*, written by Kimiko Tobimatsu and illustrated by Keet Geniza and *Writing Menopause: An Anthology of Fiction, Poetry, and Creative Non-fiction*, edited by Jane Cawthorne and E.D. Morin. Both feminist collaborative projects bring together a broad range of menopause narratives to avoid essentializing personal experiences as being exclusively tied to aging and cis womanhood. As I show throughout the literary analysis, the texts are also community-oriented since the creators express the desire to build on the legacy of menopause representation in the hope that more people encounter stories in which they can see their own bodies and experiences reflected.

Kimiko Does Cancer is an autobiographical graphic memoir that tells the story of Kimiko Tobimatsu, who is diagnosed with a rare form of breast cancer at the age of twenty-five. Because of the cancer treatment, Tobimatsu must undergo lifelong hormonal treatment that results in surgical menopause. This kind of menopause is often overlooked in the general discourse, which tends to focus on the majority of menopause experiences revolving around cis women during late middle-age.[4] This memoir, however, demands a reconceptualization of the menopause not as a natural part of aging but as a necessary biomedical intervention on a young person's body. In an interview, Tobimatsu and Geniza describe their collaborative process over three years and how much of it hinged on careful communication when navigating moments of vulnerability. Tobimatsu describes how "Keet was respectful of [her] boundaries," especially when she was struggling to communicate her feelings, a process she ultimately viewed as one of personal growth (Folkmarson Käll et al. 166). She also points to one moment in which Geniza reminded her that "Art is vulnerability," which seems indicative of the approach the illustrator took with the project, further stating that she "came at it from a mostly intuitive or emotional understanding" (161). As the artist bearing witness to Tobimatsu's story, Geniza understood that she had to approach their project with care for her collaborator's vulnerability, and that she also had an artistic responsibility to the graphic memoir. She explains that she "wanted to handle it as gently as possible" but sometimes felt "guilty" for seemingly "pushing [Tobimatsu] to share more than she was comfortable with" because she could not help but think "what about the art?" (166).

What about the art, indeed? The editors of *Writing Menopause* turn to literature as a way of giving space to menopause stories but also as a way of serving their community, describing how collecting these literary testimonies "reflected our experiences and the experiences of the people we knew" (1). The collection brings together pieces by fifty-four writers across fiction, poetry, and creative nonfiction, presenting a diverse cross-section of how the menopause impacts lives. For this chapter, I selected three pieces from the collection that I read together with Tobimatsu's memoir to illustrate how life-writing can help to un/learn ways to conceptualize the menopause beyond it being reduced to a health issue that can only be addressed by white, middle-class, cis gender, and heterosexual women. More generally, menopause is still conceptualized as a strongly cis gender experience, particularly in discourses around biological essentialism that seek to instrumentalize the menopause to reinforce ideas of cis womanhood. The consequent exclusion of those who are not cis women or do not identify as women has serious ramifications for menopause health provisions for queer and trans people.[5]

Writing Menopause highlights othered menopause experiences and thus provides modes of unlearning the established cis gendered perspective of the menopause. It does so, for example, by featuring an interview with filmmaker, speaker, and advocate Buck Angel, who talks about his menopause journey as a trans man. He remains a highly divisive figure within the trans community, particularly through, for example, his opposing views on the medical transition of children and his alignment with a transmedicalist frame of reference, which he frequently asserts on X (formerly Twitter) and YouTube.[6] I do not agree with these particular views. At the time of revising this essay (March 2023), the inclusion of this interview from 2017 remains one the most substantial pieces in Canadian menopause writing to highlight the hugely marginalized experience of menopause by trans men and Angel's contribution in this context is valuable. In "Man with a Vagina" he shares that he thinks "menopause is a real thing that many people in the trans world do not talk about" because it "has always been and is still associated with women [and] trans men want to move as far away from that identity as possible" (52). This statement illustrates one instance in which the strongly gendered discourse around the menopause can have grave consequences for menopause health provision for trans and non-binary people who might not be able to access or might not want to seek appropriate care because of it. Further, Angel also importantly notes that "people mostly only see [menopause] as an aging thing. But…it is also about hormone change and in the trans community…many younger people are going through the change at an early age and having hysterectomies. Talking about this could help people deal with the mental and physical changes that happen during menopause" (54). Angel's advocacy for more gender- and trans-inclusive practices around the menopause is paramount because it also opens up the framing of the menopause more generally. How can we conceptualize the menopause if it is not something that exclusively happens to cis women "of a certain age"? What happens to the framing of the menopause when it is not solely a health issue connected to aging, as is the case with induced or surgical menopause?

Kimiko Does Cancer explores some of these key questions. The graphic memoir utilizes different shades of grey throughout and plays with contrast to reflect the characters' moods. It heavily relies on dialogue, which is marked by prominent speech bubbles, and context is introduced by text placed in the top left corner of panels. When the protagonist Kimiko is first diagnosed with breast cancer in her early twenties, she feels betrayed by her body because it "was unnerving thinking about how long the lump had been there, growing inside of me" (14). This image is superimposed on a panel of cells of human tissue, marking a change in perspective from watching the protagonist check her lump through her skin in the preceding images further highlighting the alienation she feels. She soon discovers that her cancer is hormone sensitive and that she will require daily medication to keep her menopausal to prevent the cancer from recurring. Kimiko's struggle navigating the health care system, her cancer, and her menopause as a mixed-race, queer woman becomes most visible through her desire and failure to seek community in several instances. Feelings of isolation and unrelatability are common tropes in textual representations of the menopause and these texts can in turn function as communities by proxy by representing a breadth of different experiences. I have also termed this capacity *synergies of solidarity* to mark those moments in which writers share vulnerable health experiences in an effort to be in community with others. By sharing their own individual struggles around menopause, gender, and aging, the authors in the edited collection and the graphic memoir create a communal plane of experiences. *Kimiko Does Cancer*, for example, carefully illustrates the additional difficulties queer and gender-nonconforming people are confronted with when accessing health care. After the cancer diagnosis, Kimiko faces physicians' rigid expectations around gender and femininity when discussing reconstructive breast surgery. The prospect of losing her breasts is one of the rare instances of her cancer diagnosis in which the protagonist feels something akin to cautious excitement, thinking to herself perched on a chair in a waiting room, "Losing my breast wouldn't be the worst thing in the world. I wonder if I'd like the look. I could play with gender a bit more" (25). However, as the narrative progresses, it becomes evident that there is little space in the medical system for gender-nonconforming people such as the protagonist. In a series of five panels, the memoir depicts the exchange with the plastic surgeon who displays a cheerful smile throughout; while observing the unevenness of Kimiko's breasts, the surgeon suggests self-evidently to "plump up" not just one but both breasts "while [she's] there" (56) without consulting the protagonist's opinion or asking after her desired gender presentation. According to Kimiko's facial expression, she does not seem particularly phased by this interaction since as "a queer woman, [she] went into this whole experience with some distrust towards doctors, particularly around sexual and physical health" (26). Throughout, the protagonist feels let down in her quest to seek communities who share her experiences of cancer and menopause. As a mixed-race woman, she feels that the "mainstream cancer narrative was so white, feminized and apolitical; the peppiness seemed to gloss over the way cancer affected people differently based on race and class" (39). To illustrate Kimiko's discomfort, the reader encounters several panels of three white women with light hair or scarfs draped around their heads in exaggerated superhero poses shouting "We're survivors, fighters, warriors!...We kick cancer's butt...And look good while doing it...AND LIVE IN THE MOMENT" (38–39). Along similar lines, as a person in her twenties, the protagonist also feels let down by the solidarity formed around experiences of the menopause. In a panel titled "Menopausal women try to relate" (74), the reader watches Kimiko in front of a Christmas tree, in an apron, with a stern facial expression, her arms crossed, listening to three middle-aged women who cheerfully declare, "Hot flashes? Been there, done that, honey" (74). Even though her face is out of frame in the subsequent images as she cooks a meal, her increasing annoyance at the women's perceived misplaced solidarity is paired with physical act of chopping, pounding, and stabbing of the food she is preparing, accompanied by a verbalization of her irritation: "It's frustrating that they think they know how I feel. I know they're trying to be empathetic...still it's annoying. Maybe they deserve an explanation for why it bothers me. But why should I have to??" (74). This notion of failed solidarity is also one that extends to several pieces in *Writing Menopause*.

One particular text that stood out to me is "Threshold" by Jane Silcott, which explores the menopause from the seemingly most ordinary position of an educated, straight white cis woman. There, Silcott relays the moment when she first encountered being othered by the menopause:

> It began with a conversation with a man, an attractive man as it happens, but an academic conversation...We were talking about aging and then gender and so for me, the obvious topic of menopause came up...I thought it was safe to mention something personal, so I said I was menopausal. It's not as if he jumped back or anything. He didn't run. But there was something. A squinching, if you can call it that. A momentary tightening in his pupil...and I felt suddenly and overwhelmingly ashamed. Why was that? Why be ashamed over a completely common experience?...But in that moment when his pupil squinched, I understood—perhaps for the first time—what the meaning of menopause really is. (170)

The last sentence acts almost as an inversion of the introduction's resolve in that this contributor arrives at the meaning of the menopause through an intensely emotional experience. Here, the menopause figures as a disruptor of conversation and politeness in which an invisible line is suddenly crossed and as soon as the academic conversation is anchored in the author's lived experience, the aging female body becomes too burdensome for the male interlocutor. The perceived burden, however, is projected back onto the narrator where the shamefulness of aging and its corporeal processes collide—her shame associated with menopause has an external trigger and is not necessarily internalized. This moment of perceived safety to share intimate personal information also resonates with another contribution titled "Ugly Duckling Syndrome" by Carolyn Gage, in which the writer states that "As lesbians, we began our journey with our coming out. Those same tools that enabled us to resist the institutions of compulsory heterosexuality will stand us in good stead as we sort through the myths and lies about menopause" (146). In that same text, Gage also asks, "And what if that syndrome had one single cause: heteropatriarchy?" (144) and "Are these traumatic responses to a sudden paradigm shift, as the body throws off the last constraints of an artificially imposed identity?" (146). The writer of this text manages to extract and identify external factors of her menopause experience. She uses the same mechanism through which she is marginalized, her queerness, more generally within society, but also more specifically within much of menopause representation, as a set of tools to not only distance herself from the internalized shame and misogyny the narrator in the previous contribution experienced, but to also combat this additional othering later in life. The identification of the heteropatriarchy is also applicable to the process that brings shame on the narrator in the other passage above: the sudden realization that one has lost male desirability that disproportionately affects straight women. This perceived loss is also portrayed in *Kimiko Does Cancer* in the protagonist's ambivalence toward her own induced menopause as a condition that is debilitating in its day-to-day effects but simultaneously a necessary medical intervention that keeps the cancer from recurring. This, then, leaves Kimiko in a bind: while menopause is largely considered a natural occurrence, it is not in her case: "These changes make me wonder how I should identify—Do I have a chronic illness? A disability? Is it appropriate to use those terms if the discomfort is from medication and the medication is preventative?" (91). The menopause, be it natural or induced, changes a body's familiar hormonal makeup and with it brings a shift in identity for many menopausal people; be it coming to terms with a new body, the sudden perceived loss of male desirability, the potential exiting of rigid gender norms, or identifying as a newly disabled person. I read these kinds of overlaps as emblematic for the kinds of synergies of solidarity that arise across the collection as an additional layer of collective un/learning. The almost dialogical qualities that emerge between some contributions allow the reader to pause and reflect and apply different lenses to the vast array of experiences that invite rereading and reconsidering. In an almost clichéd framing, textual menopause testimonies are reminders that there are as many different experiences of the menopause as there are menopausal people.

Both sets of texts offer up one glimpse into a future that is menopausal. In the introduction, I framed *Writing Menopause* and *Kimiko Does Cancer* as projects that are collective, collaborative, and community-oriented. In the literary analysis, I showed that they reveal their feminist menopause potentiality along these three axes and across generational lines. *Writing Menopause*, as an edited collection, is by design a collective and collaborative endeavour. The assemblage of diverse menopause experience into a collection achieves a shift from a predominantly solitary experience to a chorus of individual voices that keep each other company. This dynamic companionship emerges through reading the pieces together and forms the basis of what I term synergies of solidarity. The desire for solidarity and community is what binds together both the contributions within the collection but also extends to *Kimiko Does Cancer*, which intersects at various points with the experiences of the other contributors. The graphic memoir is also a feminist collaborative project between author and illustrator and implodes mainstream menopause narratives by challenging vectors of age, illness, race, and queerness. Moreover, I read the act of publishing and making oneself potentially vulnerable as a generous act of feminist solidarity through which menopausal people build community for others.

I suggest that the menopause, both as a tangible health issue as well as conceptual building block, is a useful tool to work toward modes of transgenerational feminist alliance. As briefly outlined, the generational and ageist divides within feminism can often be attributed to a unilateral positioning of young and old feminists in which the former are said to be dismissing the latter who in turn are seemingly unable to look ahead anymore. Thinking with menopause futurity allows for multidirectional modes of care and acknowledgement (Martinis Roe, "'Solidarity-in-Difference'") across generations; a relational practice in which acknowledging, including, and caring for those who have come before us is also embracing our own futures and the ones of those who will come after us. There is room for ambiguity and, instead of a hardened binary (young versus old), for a move towards a transgenerational practice of relations in which the anticipation of old age and the memory of youth leads to acts of feminist solidarity. Centring menopause and its many configurations is one way to challenge, even one's own, ideas of womanhood, ageism, sexism, hostile medical establishments, as well as feminist practice. "Every day I unlearn," writes Jane Silcott in *Writing Menopause*, highlighting the urgency of the ongoing, collective endeavour of un/learning.

Notes

1. Throughout this chapter, I use the terms *menopause* and *menopausal* as they are most commonly used to signify what in medical terms would be termed *perimenopause*—the process eventually leading to *menopause*. Strictly speaking, menopause only lasts one day and marks one year since the last period, after which a person is considered "postmenopausal."

2. *Age Matters* also features an article on Betty Friedan's *The Fountain of Age*, of which the editors note in the introduction, "In chapter 2, Ruth Ray explores the role of ageism and age relations within feminisms by reference to the work of Betty Friedan. Looking through an age lens at Friedan's career, Ray shows, first, that like so many feminists, Friedan does not focus on aging until she herself becomes old" (9). Susan Sontag was forty-two when "The Double Standard of Ageing" was published in 1972; Simone de Beauvoir was sixty-two when *La Viellesse* came out also in 1972, later translated in 1972 as *Old Age* (UK) and *The Coming of Age* (US); Germaine Greer was fifty-two at the initial publication of *Women, Aging and the Menopause* and seventy-nine at the publication of its fully update version in 2018; Betty Friedan was seventy-two when she published *The Fountain of Age* in 1993.

3. Much of our scholarly endeavours in literary studies revolves around individual thought and work, required to get jobs and promotions within academia. In line with this collection's focus of "learning with," I would like to open up my solitary contribution (though indebted to a genealogy of brilliant feminist thinkers) to conversations with its readers. If you are reading this chapter and some of the ideas and questions resonate with you, please get in touch—you can find me on X (formerly Twitter) @V_Schuchter.

4. Two recent literary examples that centre experiences of induced menopause include "Surgical Menopause—in Ten Postures" by Susan Merrill Squier and Shelley L. Wall, in *Menopause: A Comic Treatment*, edited by MK Czerwiec, and *Surgical Menopause: Not Your Typical Menopause*, edited by Helen Kemp, featuring twelve stories of those directly affected by surgical menopause.

5. Two excellent examples of inclusive practices around the menopause are the Queer Menopause Project founded by Tania Glyde, a psychotherapist and counsellor working with LGBTQI+ clientele, and the Queer Menopause Collective (www.queermenopause.com); and the first book about the menopause using gender-neutral language, *What*

Fresh Hell Is This? Perimenopause, Menopause, Other Indignities, and You, by Heather Corinna.

6. His X account is @BuckAngel. His YouTube Account @BuckAngelOfficial (last accessed March 2023), from 2022 onwards, contains video interviews with titles such as "Gay Man Would've MISTAKENLY Transitioned In Today's World," "Mom Loses Child Custody Thanks to Trans Cult," "Non-Binary Is NOT Trans," "Dangers of Medically Transitioning Children," frequently platforming the stories of individuals who have detransitioned and purposefully formulating controversial clickbait video titles.

Works Cited

Browne, Victoria. *Feminism, Time, and Nonlinear History*. Palgrave Macmillan, 2014.

Calasanti, Toni M., and Kathleen F. Slevin, editors. *Age Matters: Re-Aligning Feminist Thinking*. 2006. Routledge, 2013.

Cawthorne, Jane, and E.D. Morin, editors. *Writing Menopause: An Anthology of Fiction, Poetry and Creative Non-fiction*. Inanna Press and Education, 2017.

Chopik, William J., et al. "Age Differences in Age Perceptions and Developmental Transitions." *Frontiers in Psychology*, vol. 9, 2018.

Corinna, Heather. *What Fresh Hell Is This? Perimenopause, Menopause, Other Indignities, and You*. Hachette Go, 2021.

Czerwiec, MK, editor. *Menopause: A Comic Treatment*. Pennsylvania State UP, 2020.

de Beauvoir, Simone. *Old Age*. Translated by Patrick O'Brian, Penguin Books, 1977.

Folkmarson Käll, Lisa, et al. "Kimiko Does Cancer." *Lambda Nordica*, vol. 27, no. 2–3, 2021, pp. 158–73.

Friedan, Betty. *The Fountain of Age*. Vintage, 1994.

Greer, Germaine. *The Change: Women, Aging and the Menopause*. Fully revised and updated, Bloomsbury, 2019.

Hemmings, Clare. "Generational Dilemmas: A Response to Iris van der Tuin's "'Jumping Generations": On Second- and Third-Wave Feminist Epistemology.'" *Australian Feminist Studies*, vol. 24, no. 59, Mar. 2009, pp. 33–37.

Hemmings, Clare. *Why Stories Matter: The Political Grammar of Feminist Theory*. Duke UP, 2011.

Jose, Justin P., et al. "Age Identity and Social Exclusion of Older Persons: A Psychosocial Perspective." *Ageing International*, vol. 47, 2022, pp. 115–133.

Kemp, Helen, editor. *Surgical Menopause: Not Your Typical Menopause*. Self-published, 2021.

Manguso, Sarah. "Where Are All the Books about Menopause?" *The New Yorker*, 24 June 2019, https://www.newyorker.com/magazine/2019/06/24/where-are-all-the-books-about-menopause.

Martinis Roe, Alex. "Forging Feminist Futures: An Interview with Alex Martinis Roe." *EuropeNow*, 16 Jan. 2020, https://www.europenowjournal.org/2020/01/15/forging-feminist-futures-an-interview-with-alex-martinis-roe/.

Martinis Roe, Alex. "'Solidarity-in-Difference' and the Politics of Transgenerational Feminism: A Conversation with Alex Martinis Roe." *AQNB*, 8 May 2017, https://www.aqnb.com/2017/05/08/solidarity-in-difference-and-the-politics-of-transgenerational-feminism-a-conversation-with-alex-martinis-roe/.

Martinis Roe, Alex. *To Become Two: Propositions for Feminist Collective Practice*. Archive Books, 2018.

Morin, E.D. "Man with a Vagina—E.D. Morin interviews Buck Angel." Cawthorne and Morin, pp. 50–54.

Neumann, Ann. "The Future Is Menopausal: Post-Reproductive Women and the New Feminism." *The Baffler*, no. 48, Nov. 2019, https://thebaffler.com/salvos/the-future-is-menopausal-neumann.

Rice, Carla. "Imagining the Other? Ethical Challenges of Researching and Writing Women's Embodied Lives." *Feminism & Psychology*, vol. 19, no. 2, May 2009, pp. 245–266.

Steinke, Darcey. "The Postmenopausal Novel." *The Paris Review*, 17 June 2019, https://www.theparisreview.org/blog/2019/06/17/the-post-menopausal-novel/.

Tobimatsu, Kimiko. *Kimiko Does Cancer: A Graphic Memoir*. Arsenal Pulp Press, 2020.

van der Tuin, Iris, et al. "Generational Feminism, Continental Philosophy, and New Materialism: Interview with Iris van der Tuin." *Figure/Ground*, 28 Dec. 2014. https://figureground.org/interview-with-iris-van-der-tuin/.

van der Tuin, Iris. "'Jumping Generations': On Second- and Third-Wave Feminist Epistemology." *Australian Feminist Studies*, vol. 24, no. 59, Mar. 2009, pp. 17–31.

Wilson, Robert A. *A New Life: The Quest and the Key...Feminine Forever*. W.H. Allen, 1966.

Woodward, Kathleen, editor. *Figuring Age: Women, Bodies, Generations*. Indiana UP, 1999.

8

Learning with Jovette Marchessault's Decolonial Feminist Critique through Her Autobiographical Relations

ÉLISE COUTURE-GRONDIN

> *We as feminists must be aware of our history on this continent.*
> —PAULA GUNN ALLEN, *The Sacred Hoop*

> *La critique est un travail sérieux : lire un livre pour en parler est pour moi un exercice autant intellectuel que spirituel. Je pense qu'on se livre à cet exercice pour soi-même d'abord et ensuite pour le bien de sa collectivité.*
> —JOVETTE MARCHESSAULT, "Entrevue"[1]

BORN IN MONTRÉAL, autodidact artist, writer, and playwright Jovette Marchessault (1938–2012) was a unique voice in Québec's feminist literary circles.[2] When she started to write, she won the prestigious France-Québec prize for *Comme une enfant de la terre 1: Le crachat solaire* published in 1975.[3] First of a trilogy, this autobiography situates Marchaussault's autobiographical self,[4] Jovette, in the larger historical context of "la terre amérindienne" (the Native American land) (59, 61, 117), moving from the narrator's cosmic birth to her rebirth in her thirties, when she travels around the Americas to find herself as a woman and reconnect with her Indigenous heritage. Following up in 1980, *La mère des herbes* presents a more lineal chronology from Jovette's childhood to her decision to become a writer in the 1970s. This second volume, which is the focus of this chapter, highlights the narrator's intimate connection to her grandmother whose mother was Innu—"Montagnaise" in the text—and whose father was a settler from Normandy. Jovette reflects on how she learned from her elder's sense of creativity, willfulness, and understanding of relationships. In interviews, the author confirms the deep influence her grandmother had on her decision to become an artist and writer ("Entrevue" 58; *Les terribles vivantes*), and on her feminist conception of the world: "Les histoires de ma grand-mère, à mon tour je les transmets et c'est ce que les femmes font depuis le commencement du monde" (Marchessault, "Jovette Marchessault" 54).[5] The grandmother's stories in *La mère des herbes* push Jovette to develop a critical perspective on the oppressive environment of the 1930s and 1940s, which includes an analysis of settler colonial history in the metropole, the province of Québec, and the whole continent. The text denounces, among others, the evangelization of Indigenous girls, Catholic dogma, as well as how settler colonialism is imbricated with violence against women, children, and land.

The text develops these critiques notably through the inclusion of a play, set in the seventeenth century during the early colonization of Québec, written and performed by the teenage girls of the narrator's neighbourhood. Featuring the life story of Kateri Tekakwitha, Marie de l'Incarnation, and Jeanne Mance, among others, "in a constant effort of transfiguration based on our national heroines" (*Mother of the Grass* 62),[6] the play participates in reconsidering Québec's nationalism through a decolonial lens. Referring to the Kanien'kehá:ka Saint Kateri Tekakwitha, Marchessault asserts, "En m'attachant à elle, encore une fois c'est l'histoire des femmes que j'écris, vue par une femme. Et cela donne une tout autre version parce que en tant que féministe, je décode. Je démens la version officielle et truquée" ("Jovette Marchessault" 54).[7] The transfiguration of women's life stories, including her own, is at the centre of Marchessault's literary practice and resonates with Laguna Pueblo feminist Paula Gunn Allen's injunction—initially made in 1986—that "we as feminists must be aware of our history of this continent" (214). Through her creative nonfiction, Marchessault was one of the few to address the history of settler colonialism from a feminist perspective in her time, and her writing significantly highlights the fact that "everyone…has a relationship to settler colonialism" (Arvin et al. 9).

Feminist critics received her literary works with interest, noting that they "participent à un projet utopique féministe" (participate in a feminist utopian project) (Godard, "En mémoire de l'avenir" 101) that is also ecofeminist in how it never puts humans above animals or nature (Orenstein 257). In the trilogy, particularly the first two volumes, the close relationship to the grandmother, named Louisa, appears as a symbol of this alternative relationality. Although it seems to be vital for Marchessault to assert her Indigenous heritage from her paternal grandmother and grandfather, she does not use it to position herself as an Indigenous author,[8] having been raised in the city with no apparent contact with the Innu community. For instance, Marie Vautier, while omitting the importance of decolonization in Marchessault's writing—notices the critics' difficulty to acknowledge both Marchessault's Indigenous heritage with "the absence of a self/other (Québécois/Amerindian) dichotomy," and the fact that she "writes from deeply *within* a feminist perspective *and* a complex Québécois/Amerindian identity" (108, emphasis in original). In other literary analyses of Marchessault's writing—almost all in French despite most of her literary works now having been translated to English—critics barely mention the author's Indigenous heritage and completely overlook her critique of settler colonialism and anti-racist position. I believe this disregard highlights a deep ignorance about and denial of the settler colonial context in Québec. It surely says more about the critical readership than the author herself. Accordingly, reading *Mother of the Grass* more than forty years after its publication, how can I, as a settler feminist critic, emphasize the decolonial and critical aspect of her literary creations through engaged and ethical reading practices?

In her creative writing, Marchessault did not theorize the entanglements of patriarchy and settler colonialism as much as she depicted their effects on the subject. Moreover, if Marchessault's autobiographical texts offer alternative historical narratives, they do not follow the standards set by the discipline of history. Her writing is dense, saturated with images and lyrical musings—what Marie-Claire Blais calls "ses excès d'image" (her excess of images) (27)—inviting multiple interpretations from the readers, whom she places in a unique affective relationship with the texts. Feeling "profondément rattachée" (deeply attached) ("Entrevue" 223) to each of the women's stories that she includes in her writing ("Jovette Marchessault" 57), she even explained, in an interview, that for her literary criticism is an exercise that we do for ourselves first and then for the collective good ("Entrevue" 220).

The act of reading is crucial to understanding how Marchessault's writing mobilizes and situates feminist criticism as a "gesture of self-inscription" (Godard, "Becoming My Hero" 112). As Godard states, "Readers actively and continuously participate in the creation of meanings in texts by bringing their own life and literary experiences to bear upon texts" ("Becoming My Hero" 113). Similarly, life-writing scholars Sidonie Smith and Julia Watson explain that the "intersubjective truth…emerg[ing] in autobiographical acts… require[s] the care and active engagement of both readers and writers" (18). They understand the particular power of autobiographies in rewriting history as coming from "the densities of rhetorical, literary, ethical, political, and cultural dimensions" (13). For them, autobiographical texts cannot be simply read as "history" because their literariness involves the reader's response to it: "The complexity of autobiographical texts requires reading practices that engage the narrative tropes, sociocultural contexts, rhetorical aims, and narrative shifts within the historical or chronological trajectory of the text" (13).

As I think about my praxis, reading (with) Marchessault means inscribing myself in the history of settler colonialism in Québec to resist its ongoing reproduction. I propose a feminist reading practice of *Mother of the Grass* that highlights the trope of the "Native American Land," the urban sociocultural context in which the narrator was raised, the rhetorical strategies used to destabilize the readers' conventional ideas about the history of Québec and the continent, and the distinct narrative transition between the protagonist's life and the play inserted in the text. The gesture of self-inscription in a settler colonial context, through this reading practice, helps develop, I contend, a decolonial feminist critique of Québec history rooted in subjective and collective awareness.

Self-Inscribing in/as Relational Critique

I came across Jovette Marchessault's books in the first years of my PHD, when I was working on positioning myself as a feminist settler scholar from Québec and starting my research in the field of Indigenous literatures. I was particularly interested in the 1970s and 1980s contexts and more specifically in the emergence of both feminist and Indigenous voices in literature and organized movements.⁹ Yet, as I read texts by Indigenous women who did not position as feminists and by settler feminists who did not stand against past and present colonial structures, the absence of an effective solidarity between these two movements became clear. I also learned—through Corrie Scott's and Julie Burelle's scholarship, as well as through my literary analysis of Laure Morali's 2008 edited collection *Aimititau! Parlons-nous!*— about the historical and ongoing unease, for a majority of people in Québec, to acknowledge their position as colonizers in relation to First Peoples when the focus of liberation for them/us has been the history of conquest by the English.

At the time Marchessault is writing, feminist movements in Québec did not have a strong decolonial awareness (Chung; Maillé). Even relatively recently, the editors of the 2017 special issue *Femmes autochtones en mouvement: Fragments de décolonisation* in the journal *Recherches féministes* denounced the continuous exclusion of Indigenous women from francophone academic circles and the fact that the imbrication of gender and colonialism has never become central in feminist studies (Léger and Morales Hudon 3–4; see also Perrault). Nevertheless, important texts by Indigenous women such as Jane (Willis) Pachano (Cree), An Antane Kapesh (Innu), and Éléonore Sioui (Wendat) illuminate the settler colonial context in the territory we now call Québec. Moreover, Indigenous writers such as Lee Maracle (Stó:lō) and Jeannette Armstrong (Syilx Okanagan) were also making space for Indigenous women's voices in feminist literary circles by attending academic events—all outside of Québec—that aimed at addressing issues of racism and voice appropriation in literature.[10]

There is no trace of Marchessault participating directly in these conversations and her writing cannot be easily positioned in Indigenous literature. If her literary project differs greatly from those by the Indigenous women writers I just mentioned, her work nevertheless includes important decolonial aspects. I find it curious that Marchessault's work was not included in any of the francophone anthologies or bibliographies of Indigenous literatures in Québec (Boudreau; Dezutter et al.; Gatti), but that it appears in two anthologies of Indigenous literatures in English Canada. In 1990 the first chapter of *Mother of the Grass* was included in the anthology *All My Relations*, and, in 2004, her short story "The Moon of the Dancing Suns," on the impact of First Peoples' participation in the Second World War, came out in the anthology *Our Story: Aboriginal Voices on Canada's Past*. It could be, as Isabelle

St-Amand argued in 2010, that Indigenous literatures have a longer and stronger publishing history in English Canada (30). In fact, Indigenous literatures in French became recognized particularly in the following decade, the 2010s, with the creation of a first Indigenous press, Hannenorak, and the organization of the first Indigenous book fair, which became Kwahiatonhk!, both providing an institutional framework for the promotion of Indigenous authors.

That being said, my goal in analyzing Marchessault's work is not to research her biographical life or comment on her Indigenous identity to situate her work as and in Indigenous literature. Rather, it is to look at her literary strategies and the ways in which she constructs her voice to articulate a critique of colonialism from her singular position as a feminist lesbian Québécoise with Indigenous heritage.[11] In line with Marchessault's self-identification, this position should be nuanced by her claim: "Je me sens comme une âme qui écrit sur d'autres âmes" ("Entrevue" 226).[12] In what follows, I underline how, in *Mother of the Grass*, the grandmother's teachings bring Jovette to a process of self-discovery that is much more significant for her than putting forward specific identity markers.

Mother of the Grass: A Grandmother's Stories as a Way to Withstand

Marchessault explains that the title *Mother of the Grass* comes from the expression her grandmother used to describe the moon. It also represents her childhood, which she cherished for the knowledge she learned from the women of the family: "Quelle chance! Grandir au bord du fleuve, dans un univers de femmes où j'ai été choyée, aimée, où j'ai appris le respect des choses vivantes, que ce soient des herbes ou des animaux!" (Marchessault, "Jovette Marchessault" 55).[13] The first three chapters (she calls them songs) feature Jovette's upbringing in the rural west end of Montréal in the early 1940s, in a house beside the river. Every summer, the surrounding areas fill with families on vacation, allowing young Jovette to witness the authoritarian nature of Catholic education and the violence of parents towards their children. Living close to the river prepares Jovette "to withstand" (8) the harsher urban environment, as Jovette's family is forced to move to Saint-Henri, a Montréal neighbourhood historically associated with the working class and poor living conditions after the Second World War. Songs four to seven recount her life in this oppressive urban "Enorm-ality" (l'Énorme-normal) (46, 159). Growing up, she feels the burden of institutions wanting to erase any mode of existence that differs from their dominant social norms: the clergy, the family, the school, and the workplace all push women to silence and "bow" their heads, leaving "no energy for the route leading to self-discovery" (122). Self-discovery is a central theme of the autobiographical narrative: learned from her grandmother, it is a form of personal affirmation made possible by her critical outlook on oppressive social structures, the relationship with nature, and the subversive use of language.

First, Jovette learns from Louisa how she withstood social and religious normativity, notably through developing her own interpretation of the Little Catechism. In her version, when Adam and Eve are expulsed from Eden, they are "ashamed of the Father" rather than ashamed of themselves: "They left and never returned, each of them with his or her own strength and with a clear comprehension of desire in their bodies" (57). The grandmother's understanding of the creation story gives strength back to women and is an important model for Jovette, who sees how girls in Catholic families are supposed to repress their desires. In the grandmother's tale, God and the father at the head of the family are the same; the Devil is deemed "a spirit in revolt" (121); and the Serpent, presented as a leader who "rose up against God" and "against the supreme oppressor" (55), "always had another interpretation. A real complainer. He was always against whatever. He was anti-father and anti-family" (120). These interpretations are paramount for Jovette as she experiences the weight of religious constraints, particularly as a young lesbian. Significantly, it is when Marchessault writes about her grandmother's influence on her art in *Mother of the Grass* that she does her coming out in her writing.

Second, the text links the grandmother's comprehension of relationships to the environment, particularly the river and forest, spaces beyond the Church's influence: "But while waiting, waiting for them to teach us about the length and breadth of Hell, Grandmother took us with her—and going with her was not a fall but a passionate spring space, a march forward which provided blood, scent, and identity to everything on earth or in the skies" (47). The grandmother teaches that everything not only has an identity, but a body and senses—"blood" and "scent"—and a place in this world: "Grandmother was harvesting…Each life had its own name, its own identity, its own place atop an unmoving stone" (48). As she brings Jovette and her friend Maurice in the forest, she encourages them to "take the time to leave... individual roads to observe these beautiful living things" (48). The narrator does not highlight Louisa's knowledge of plants in particular as much as the possibility to learn from relating to nature. Jovette asserts, "living beside a river teaches you one thing at least—to withstand" (8). In the grandmother's vision, all lives—human and non-human—have value and knowledge: "What she knew and understood about each and every thing was a recognition which was life-giving, which injected vitality. Listening to her was for me to listen to the collective voice of every living thing" (18). The knowledge she transmits opposes and challenges the Catholic Great Chain of Being that dictates the hierarchy between humans and places the non-human (animals, plants, the natural world) at the bottom, justifying and naturalizing systems of oppression.

The grandmother also contests colonial structures more explicitly, using two coercive symbols of Québec nationalism: "No hydro dam or police barricade can indefinitely contain [the grandmother's] lunary words, this world-water-spirit in motion" (19). These allusions to the opposition to the construction of hydro dams on Indigenous land and the police efforts to end the resistance against colonial encroachment come with no further explanation yet situate the grandmother's alternative interpretation of the dominant narrative in a decolonial frame, one that also follows an entirely different type of relationality and changes the nature of her "lunary words." The grandmother's predominant relational frame is a rhetorical strategy that offers readers an alternative version of Catholic and colonial history and prevents approaching Marchessault's autobiography as relying on identity politics, a particular definable Indigenous identity from which to lay a decolonial discourse. Hasty connections between the earth and Indigenous Peoples turns Indigenous identity into an empty vessel that everyone may appropriate all the while obfuscating the complexity of lived lives. Janice Gould's (Koyangk'auwi Maidu) explains,

> My mother taught us kids to love and respect the earth from the time we were little. She never called it the Indian way. It seemed to be her way. Without a living cultural system available to lodge these values in, it is hard to know whether these are Indian beliefs or not. I wish I could claim my love of the earth, and other values, as Indian, as Maidu, with absolute certainty. But for a mixed-blood like myself, that is not possible. (85–86)

Similarly, the alternative relationality learned by Jovette is not grounded in a specific cultural system sustained by community. As they walk "in the woods of the Chapel of the Atonement" (48), Jovette and Maurice discover the different elements of the forest as well as who they are: "we altered our identities along the way…Who were we? Who were we really? Were we emeralds in their rocky wombs or explorers or gold prospectors cast out from the hard, sharp matter of a great American city? Or were we children of the earth in search of a universal Mother?" (49). Jovette's grandmother inspires her to see the world differently and take the place she wants.

The influential knowledge and positions of Jovette's grandmother, along with her subversive use of words, form the heritage that the author weaves in her own writing, further stressing how vital it is to acknowledge her Indigenous identity while also making clear that it does not fully determine who she is. As I argue above, beyond identifying with her Indigenous roots, Marchessault offers her own relation to settler colonialism through a rewriting of historical narratives. This rewriting appears more explicitly in the play that somehow interrupts, as well as epitomizes, the narration of Jovette's childhood.

Rewriting Colonial History: Women's Voices against Patriarchal and Colonial Violence

In song three, the teenage girls on vacation in the west end find a way to escape parental discipline by creating "a deranged play, a play that was dangerous for everyone" (61), which they perform for their families at the end of the summer. Told from the perspective of Jovette, who is younger and impressed, the play addresses the relationships between settlers and Indigenous Peoples "in a constant effort of transfiguration based on our national heroines" (62). The inclusion of a dramatic creation in the text further emphasizes the role of art and language to challenge oppressive systems: "They knew that the text would be spoken out loud, proclaimed before an audience of a hundred witnesses…the words would become rockets and incantations in an August night" (62). The performance mobilizes the same spirit of contestation that the young Jovette has learned from her grandmother, which the audience receives as too subversive.

Everyone except for Jovette and Maurice's grandmothers is "bothered, somewhat confounded" that so many Indigenous people are saved by Kanien'kehá:ka Saint Kateri Tekakwitha's miracle and that settlers are "being held up to ridicule" (69). In the play, Lambert Closse, an early settler remembered for fighting Indigenous Peoples, warns of an imminent attack and focuses on describing Algonquins and Iroquois war practices.[14] Marie de l'Incarnation, Jeanne Mance, Madeleine de Verchère, and Marguerite Bourgeois, who listen to Closse's account, feel shocked, nevertheless, because they learn from him that one of the priests used violent tactics, torturing one of the Indigenous individuals. The women ask, "Are not the crucifix, prayers, and threat of eternal fire and epidemics enough for them any more?" (64). They continue with their critique of settler Catholic violence, nuancing Closse's statements: "Though [the Iroquois] tortured its captives by fire, they never raped women or humiliated corpses" (65). The dialogues insist on the gendered and sexual violence at the heart of the Catholic colonization and evangelization. Furthermore, when the Bishop of Laval tells Marie de l'Incarnation that she should spend all her time converting Indigenous girls, she answers that the Iroquois are "too proud and independent a spirit to submit to the yoke of French civilization" (63), adding that, in the meantime, "soldiers of that very same king, the colonists of that very same king, and every jailbird in the colony raped them, abusing them at their pleasure with violence and lust" (63). In the play, the settler women emphasize the violence of their own people.

Moreover, these dramatized figures contextualize Indigenous Peoples' seeming acts of violence as a response to land theft: "Oh, the Iroquois's cry of vengeance, their cry of rage against those who had stolen their country" (66). In the unfolding of the play, it is often hard to separate between Jovette's thoughts about the performance and the play's dialogues and scenes. However, just after acknowledging the Indigenous land in the previous passage, the text gives voice to "the Iroquois tribes" (*sic*) through direct speech: "Our country…is filled with fish and venison…Our voices will dissipate the clouds in the air and then you can see that our hearts and your hearts are not hidden in any way…We would like to be your friends but we hear your arquebuses and your canons whistling on every side" (66). In addition to introducing readers and audience members to an Indigenous perspective, this passage makes clear that the settlers are the ones who initiated violence to this land.

On the verge of war, the protagonists of the play seek the help of Kateri Tekakwitha to avoid any more deaths. Kateri appears as a model for Jovette who expresses her preference for this character: "We children liked this one best of all because it did not slowly peter out but exploded with the force of a stick of dynamite" (67). Kateri is presented as fearless, fleeing in the forest to escape her uncle, surviving accusations of witchery, and choosing a non-normative life because she is "alone, having rejected a fiancé, a husband, and children" (67). Through her choices, "Kateri had displeased everyone," even "her own people" (67), and yet she symbolizes the possibility to live independently and passionately: "Such was Kateri Tekakwitha in her long-house, mistress at her own fireside" (67). Thinking back on this description of Kateri's life, the narrator links the capacity to rewrite history with the desire to live free from the constraints of social norms. These women, and the young playwrights who perform their life stories, offer a subversive relationship to colonial history:

> These sainted women, for they were saints since our Holy Mother the Church, through the ejaculatory voice of her husband, the Holy Father, had affirmed they were for some decades now, these sainted women, then, had made a little free with the history of Canada, the official, truthful history, the history taught in our convents, collèges classiques, and our elementary schools which serves Enorm-ality. (69)

This ironic passage insists on how family as a patriarchal structure serves not only to transmit heteronormative values but a one-sided historical narrative that mostly benefits and maintains white men in position of power.

Throughout the book, especially in the second part, Marchessault connects seventeenth-century settler colonial history to her lived experience, proposing that the violence with which settlers and the Catholic Church undertook colonization still predominates in institutions such as school, workplace, and family in the Montréal of the 1940s. In the small Saint-Henri apartment, in a situation of "abject poverty" (73), the young narrator witnesses children being continuously beaten, women isolated in their naturalized role of caregiver for their families: "We were far apart from one another, each woman wrapped in the aura of her own incomprehensible world" (74). In the city, the women of the family are no longer models for Jovette, who thinks, "Mama, mommies, why didn't you speak up more?" (83). Defeated, Jovette tries to kill herself. This desperate act paradoxically allows the expression of shared despair through a common language with her grandmother who saves her, and her mother. The latter understands Jovette's attempt because "it coincided with something that had long been within her" (99). This form of silent language reinforces sorority and underlines the difficulty to speak up and write about the shared experience of self-erasure.

As a lesbian teenager, Jovette denounces the persistent influence of the Little Catechism and the Devil (118) by using the image of the pen as a phallic symbol, stressing the erasure of women's voice, particularly that of lesbians, who appear as "inconceivable to one and all" (144): "It is long like a lead pencil. It writes history, holy scripture, and sword-and-buckler romances. There is a penis in every grammatical rule, in every word in the dictionary" (141–142). The phallic metaphor resonates with the "ejaculatory voice" of the "Holy Father" affirming "the official, truthful history" in the passage of the play. For Jovette, it seems that in order to write history freely and truthfully one needs to be critical of heteronormative and patriarchal structures. Drawing on her feminist perspective, the author strategically connects colonial violence with violence against women and avoids idealizing Indigenous Peoples, explaining in an interview that being "visionary" peoples does not prevent them from being "phallocrates" (male chauvinist) (Marchessault, "Jovette Marchessault" 54). The way Marchessault conceives of her location as "géographiquement parlant, socialement parlant, sexuellement parlant, textuellement parlant...dans la marge" (geographically speaking, socially speaking, sexually speaking, textually speaking...I'm in the margin) ("Entrevue" 222) further resonates with the figure of Kateri Tekakwitha who, in the text, displeases everyone—even her own people.

The ending of *Mother of the Grass* returns to the grandmother's influence on Jovette, who is ready to become a writer. When Jovette learns about her death, she is shaken and calls her boss to quit. For the first and only time in the whole trilogy, readers learn the narrator's full name: "Hello, Grosslot, this is Jovette Marchessault and I will not be back today, or tomorrow, or the day after. It is over" (173). This crucial moment emphasizes the power of the autobiographical act and the process of self-discovery acquired from her grandmother, which also developed her creativity. The narrator takes a firm stance "to withstand" what oppresses her, using her grandmother's phrase "world-water-spirit in motion," which she claims are her "only inheritance...[her] most precious possession" (173). In this part of the text where the narrator and the author are the closest, readers can see how the play, "a deranged" text, a text "that [is] dangerous for everyone" (61), echoes the power of the autobiographical text *Mother of the Grass*. And just as with the play, seen by the learning eyes of young Jovette, the reaction of the audience to Marchessault's text is of primary importance to learn about and withstand past and ongoing forms of patriarchal and colonial oppression as well as engage in another form of relationality based on creativity rather than normativity.

Learning with Marchessault's Autobiographical Relations

The subject of Marchessault's autobiography resists social norms by engaging in self-discovery. She is a subject in expansion, in relation, full of desires, and the "I" in the autobiography certainly defies expectations in many ways. Marchessault explains,

> Le "je" de la trilogie…n'est pas le composant socio-biologique que l'on comprend habituellement en "je," "moi" et il n'est pas non plus identifiable avec les fonctions du corps ou enfermé dans des formes sociales et culturelles…le "je" tente de s'imprégner d'une nouvelle conception des relations humaines et des liens qui nous unissent au monde animal, végétal et minéral…Ce "je" qui est aussi celui de l'humanité. ("Entrevue" 225)[15]

Marchessault asserts her humanity, explaining that what matters to her is to write what she feels: "J'écris avec toute l'énergie qui m'habite; voilà ce que je fais" ("Entrevue" 221).[16] The vitality of Marchessault's speech reflects the grandmother's intensity, portrayed in the book as a "visceral need she had to speak to [Jovette] about her desires, her hopes, her irrational self. She had the gift of being able wholly to involve herself in her words, to incarnate herself in flesh and blood in her subject matter" (18). In the midst of the historical and systemic violences described throughout the book, the grandmother's relationship to words offers possibilities of resistance: "Women's words which fill up the aqueducts of your ears and the blood channels of your body from head to toe during the nine months when every human being, without regard to race, sex, or social class, is aquatic within the tender surfaces of the womb" (19). Learning a different language made of women's words by her grandmother allows the narrator, Jovette, to denounce "what was done to [her]" (159) and do the work of rediscovering herself. This intimate yet collective journey is irremediably political as her struggle is one against historical, social, and cultural structures that maintain the invisibility of minoritized groups.

I doubt that *Mother of the Grass* encouraged solidarity between a majority of white settler feminists and Indigenous women. However, by addressing herself particularly to the feminist cultural milieu in Québec, having lived herself in a French Catholic community, Marchessault pushes readers to question how Québécois culture is rooted in colonial and patriarchal violence. For her, writing and reading are acts of self-discovery, a personal and spiritual exercise. This text resonated with me for the force of its writing, its originality, and being one of the few to articulate a decolonial critique from a Québécois feminist position at the time. Despite the vitality of Marchessault's writing, *Mother of the Grass* is hard to read, and I often felt overwhelmed by the systems of oppression that attempt to suppress women's desires, actions, and experiences. This reading experience taught me to reflect on my position as a woman as irremediably linked to the historical trajectory of settler colonialism, and it taught me to avoid considering the latter from a distance, as if only of the past or only affecting others. As a white settler feminist Québécoise reader, writer, and critical thinker, I find that Marchessault's rich contribution, which is unlike other feminist discourses at the time, offers an invaluable description of how the colonial project is inextricably linked to the history of the continent, the province of Québec, and the city of Montréal, and continues to mark today's relations. Learning with her and others who today undertake this task of revisiting historical narratives, such as Virginia Pésémapéo Bordeleau, Natasha Kanapé Fontaine, Marie-Andrée Gill, to name just a few, what type of feminist criticism can we propose to include all voices and subjectivities? What could a relational feminist ethics, inspired by Marchessault's complex relationality, mean for a decolonial and intersectional approach to literary criticism today?

Notes

1. Critique is serious work: reading a book and talking about it is, for me, as much an intellectual exercise as it is a spiritual one. I think we do it first for ourselves and then for the collective good. All translations by the author.
2. In the documentary *Les terribles vivantes*, she sits beside Nicole Brossard and Louky Bersianik.
3. The English translation, *Like a Child of the Earth*, was published in 1988.
4. From now on, I use "Jovette" to refer to the autobiographical self, which is the narrator and protagonist of the story, and to mark the difference with the author, Marchessault.

5. Now I take my turn transmitting my grandmother's stories, following what women have done since the beginning of the world.
6. All quotes from *La mère des herbes* come from the English translation, *Mother of the Grass*, translated by Yvonne M. Klein. From now on, I will refer to the book by its English title.
7. By focusing on her, I'm once again writing a woman's story, from the perspective of a woman. And it gives a whole new version because, as a feminist, I decode. I deny the official and false version.
8. See Gatti for his definition of an Indigenous author as one that self-identifies as such, and for the nuances he brings when authors refuse to locate themselves through cultural locations.
9. For Isabelle Boisclair, 1975 is the "acte de naissance officiel de la littérature féministe au Québec" (official birth of feminist literature in Québec) (162) due to the creation of the first feminist publisher in Québec, the Éditions de la Pleine Lune, and the significant increase of titles published by women. At the time, literary texts by Indigenous women were overlooked and not considered feminist. This period also saw the creation of new social organizations defending the rights of women, such as La Fédération des Femmes du Québec in 1966 and Femmes Autochtones du Québec in 1968. Although there were alliances between these groups over the years, deep and lasting changes in the relationships between Indigenous and settler women and in the latter's decolonial awareness have been, and are, slow to materialize (Léger and Morales Hudon 8).
10. Held in Vancouver, the 1983 conference Women and Words / Les femmes et les mots was the first to bring together women from diverse communities in Canada to address issues of racism: francophone, anglophone, women of colour, and white women (Dybikowski et al.; Marlatt 15–16). In 1988 the conference Telling It: Women and Language across Cultures followed up on these discussions by bringing this group of women together once again. Lee Maracle, Jeannette Armstrong, Lenore Keeshig-Tobias, and Beatrice Culleton-Mosionier attended these conferences that were meant to address differences within the feminist movement.
11. I feel unease with some who questioned her Indigenous heritage: Louis Hamelin and Pol Pelletier suggest, for different reasons, that despite Marchessault's Indigenous heritage, she cannot be considered an Indigenous author and playwright.
12. I feel like a soul writing about other souls.
13. What luck! To grow up at the river's edge, in a women's universe where I have been pampered, loved, and where I have learned to respect all living things, be it the grass or the animals.
14. The text uses the colonial terms *Algonquins* and *Iroquois*, words taught in my history classes that perpetuate a disregard for Indigenous Peoples' self-identification, traditional territories, and perspectives. The "Algonquins" may prefer the term *Anishinaabe*, among other ways of self-identifying. With now nine communities in Québec, their traditional territory spans from the northwest of Montréal to Abitibi-Témiscamingue and Ontario.

The "Iroquois" call themselves the Haudenosaunee and comprise five nations from east to west, in Québec, Ontario, and the United States: the Mohawks, the Oneidas, the Onondagas, the Cayugas, and the Senecas, whose traditional territories are along the St. Lawrence River.

15. The trilogy's "I"...is not the socio-biological component that we usually understand as "I," "me," and it's not either recognizable by the body's functions or by the social and cultural norms...The "I" aims at impregnating itself with a new conception of human relationships and with the bonds that link us to the animal, vegetal, and mineral realms... This "I" is also that of humanity.
16. I write with the whole energy that lives in me; this is what I do.

Works Cited

Arvin, Maile, et al. "Decolonizing Feminism: Challenging Connections between Settler Colonialism and Heteropatriarchy." *Feminist Formations,* vol. 25, no. 1, 2013, pp. 8–34.

Blais, Marie-Claire. "Retour à *Comme une enfant de la terre (Livre I)*." *De l'invisible au visible: L'imaginaire de Jovette Marchessault*, edited by Roseanna Dufault and Celita Lamar, Éditions du remue-ménage, 2012, pp. 27–33.

Boisclair, Isabelle. "Ouvrir la voie/x." *Trajectoires au féminin dans la littérature Québécoise (1960–1990)*, edited by Lucie Joubert, Les Éditions Nota Bene, 2000, pp. 157–172.

Boudreau, Diane. *Histoire de la littérature amérindienne au Québec: Oralité et écriture.* L'Hexagone, 1993.

Burelle, Julie. *Encounters on Contested Lands: Indigenous Performances of Sovereignty and Nationhood in Québec.* Northwestern UP, 2019.

Chung, Ryoa. "Les défis du féminisme autochtone. Entretien avec Widia Larivière." *Nouveaux Cahiers du socialisme*, no. 19, 2018, pp. 200–202.

Dezutter, Olivier, et al. *Tracer un chemin / Meshkanatsheu: Écrits des premiers peuples.* Éditions Hannenorak, 2017.

Dybikowski, Ann, et al., editors. *In the Feminine: Women and Words / Les femmes et les mots. Conference Proceedings 1983.* Longspoon Press, 1985.

Gatti, Maurizio. *Littérature amérindienne du Québec: Écrits de langue française.* Éditions Hurtubise, 2004.

Godard, Barbara. "Becoming My Hero, Becoming Myself: Notes towards a Feminist Theory of Reading." *Language in Her Eye: Views on Writing and Gender by Canadian Women Writing in English*, edited by Libby Scheier, Sarah Sheard, and Eleanor Wachtel, Coach House, 1990, pp. 112–122.

Godard, Barbara. "En mémoire de l'avenir: Les stratégies de transformation dans la narration de Jovette Marchessault." *Voix et images*, vol. 17, no. 1, 1991, pp. 100–115.

Gould, Janice. "The Problem of Being 'Indian': One Mixed-Blood's Dilemma." *De/Colonizing the Subject: The Politics of Gender in Women's Autobiography*, edited by Sidonie Smith and Julia Watson, U of Minnesota P, 1988, pp. 81–87.

Gunn Allen, Paula. *The Sacred Hoop: Recovering the Feminine in American Indian Traditions*. 1986. Beacon Press, 1992.

Hamelin, Louis. "Les temps superposés: Chronique d'un non-liseur de poésie." *Le Devoir*, 12 Jan. 2013.

Kapesh, An Antane. *Eukuan nin matshi-manitu Innushkueu / Je suis une maudite sauvagesse*. 1976. Mémoire d'encrier, 2019.

Léger, Marie, and Anahi Morales Hudon. "Femmes autochtones en mouvement: Fragments de décolonisation." *Recherches féministes*, vol. 30, no. 1, 2017, pp. 3–13.

Les terribles vivantes: Louky Bersianik, Jovette Marchessault, Nicole Brossard. Directed by Dorothy Todd Hénaut, ONF, 1986.

Maillé, Chantal. "Réception de la théorie postcoloniale dans le féminisme québécois." *Recherches féministes*, vol. 20, no. 2, 2007, pp. 91–111.

Maracle, Lee. *Memory Serves: Oratories*. NeWest Press, 2015.

Marchessault, Jovette. *Comme une enfant de la terre 1: Le crachat solaire*. Leméac Éditeur, 1975.

Marchessault, Jovette. Interview by Claudine Potvin. "Entrevue avec Jovette Marchessault." *Voix et images*, vol. 16, no. 2, 1991, pp. 218–229.

Marchessault, Jovette. Interview by Donald Smith. "Jovette Marchessault: De la femme tellurique à la démythification sociale." *Lettres québécoises*, no. 27, 1982, pp. 52–58.

Marchessault, Jovette. *Like a Child of the Earth*. Translated by Y.M. Klein, Talonbooks, 1988.

Marchessault, Jovette. *La mère des herbes*. Quinze, 1980.

Marchessault, Jovette. "The Moon of the Dancing Suns." *Our Story: Aboriginal Voices on Canada's Past*, edited by Thomas King, Anchor Canada, 2004, pp. 129–153.

Marchessault, Jovette. *Mother of the Grass*. Translated by Y.M. Klein, Talonbooks, 1989.

Marchessault, Jovette. "Song One: The Riverside." *All My Relations: An Anthology of Contemporary Canadian Native Fiction*, edited by Thomas King, U of Oklahoma P, 1992.

Marlatt, Daphne. "Introduction: Meeting on Fractured Margins." *Telling It: Women and Language across Cultures: The Transformation of a Conference*, edited by The Telling It Book Collective, Press Gang Publishers, 1990, pp. 9–18.

Morali, Laure. *Aimititau! Parlons-nous!* Mémoire d'encrier, 2008.

Orenstein, Gloria F. "Les voyages visionnaires de trois créatrices féministes-matristiques: Emily Carr, Jovette Marchessault et Gloria Oreinstein." *Voix et images*, vol. 16, no. 2, 1991, pp. 253–261.

Pachano (Willis), Jane. *Geniesh: An Indian Girlhood*. New Press, 1973.

Pelletier, Pol. "En temps de COVID, tout est permis? NON! Pol prend soin de Jovette disparue." *Jeu: Revue de Théâtre*, 22 Jan. 2021.

Perrault, Julie. "La violence intersectionnelle dans la pensée féministe autochtone contemporaine." *Recherches féministes*, vol. 28, no. 2, 2015, pp. 33–52.

Scott, Corrie. *De Groulx à Laferrière: Un parcours de la race dans la littérature québécoise*. Les éditions XYZ, 2014.

Sioui, Éléonore. *Andatha*. Éditions Hyperborée, 1985.

Sioui, Éléonore. "Éducation: Le droit d'être." *Recherches amérindiennes du Québec,* vol. 2, no. 4–5, 1972.

Smith, Sidonie, and Julia Watson. *Reading Autobiography: A Guide for Interpreting Life Narratives*, 2nd ed., U of Minnesota P, 2010.

St-Amand, Isabelle. "Discours critiques pour l'étude de la littérature autochtone dans l'espace francophone du Québec." *SCL/ELC*, vol. 35, no. 2, 2010, pp. 30–52.

Vautier, Marie. *New World Myth: Postmodernism and Postcolonialism in Canadian Fiction*, McGill-Queen's UP, 1990.

9
The Poethical Tao
Chinese Canadian Situated Solidarities on Turtle Island

LARISSA LAI

IN THIS CHAPTER, I lay out the concept of the poethical tao in order to illustrate my current thinking on creative and critical practice in a Chinese Canadian vein, with implications for Asian Canadian feminist literary production more broadly. Specifically, I propose a poetics for writing, criticism, and community building, which are the three main practices that comprise my work. So much contemporary thought, creation, and activism has been predicated on a Marxist model that depends on the dialectic first proposed by Hegel and turned on its head by Marx. Such a model presupposes a ruling class and a proletariat, a colonizer and a colonized, a centre and periphery. The Marxist inheritances that drive much contemporary activist work, while productive for getting a place at the table, now need to be repositioned if that place at the table is to be habitable. What I'm proposing here is a mode of thought and action that can be taken up from a specifically Chinese Canadian location, one that doesn't so much throw dialectical tools out the window as offer a way of thinking about when to use them and when to use other modes. It's not so much a method as a poetics, or rather, a poethics. Let me explain.

I begin this essay with Dorothy Christian and Rita Wong's notion of the "un/settler" as they use it in *Downstream*, and expand it through a reading of Lisa Lowe's *Intimacies of Four Continents* to locate the Chinese Canadian both as a figure and as a subjective site from which thought and action can be deployed, though of course, even for someone who looks like me, it is not the only site from which to think and act. A particularly difficult term for Chinese Canadians is the term *sovereignty*, which I believe we must embrace as a matter of solidarity with Indigenous struggles around land and Black assertions of Black life.[1] If there's a difficult gift that Chinese Canadians might have to offer in relation to the term *sovereignty*, however, it is that not all sovereignties are desirable. Lowe's work on "the intimacies of four continents" is helpful for thinking how race is produced through land and body sovereignties as the economics of colonial capital unfold in the Americas. I'll explain this through Dionne Brand's *At the Full and Change of the Moon* and Paul Yee's *A Superior Man*, with a detour through one of Yee's books for children, *Ghost Train*.

Through the notion of the poethical wager as articulated by Fred Wah, Erín Moure, and Joan Retallack, I propose an embrace of gambling in radical coalition across fields of incommensurate and ever-shifting difference in the service of dreams for which there cannot be blueprints. In the embrace of dreams without blueprints, I turn to the utopian/speculative fiction theorist Tom Moylan, who suggests that the right fictions can offer us visions for the way through. Ursula LeGuin's notion of the literary experiment helps me elaborate. With her, I take up the I Ching, particularly as Stephen Karcher reads it, as a tool not so much of divination as for returning to earth through attention to the specificities of the moment. I claim Chinese Canadianness as a poethical, speculative fictional, literary site that emphasizes both the critical and the creative, embracing the possibilities of language and the imagination.

| Rita Wong uses the term *un/settler* to address her responsibilities on Turtle Island in the edited collection *Downstream* (2), particularly in relation to her activist work on water, enacted in collaboration with the Secwepemc filmmaker Dorothy Christian. I take up the slash because it offers the term as a field of contradiction, simultaneously both "settler" and "unsettler." I think it's important from Asian locations to claim the term *settler* because it is through the processes of state citizenship that we've struggled for and gained access to both human and civil rights within the democratic nation-state structure. Especially now, in the wake of the Russian attack on Ukraine, the passing of the national security law in Hong Kong, and current tensions between Taiwan and the People's Republic of China, I value those rights. I don't, however, wish to accede to the settler position as though it were

something devised for me and embraced by me unproblematically. Nor do I want to accede to understandings of rights and democracy as though they were solely Western concepts; rather, I think of them as collectively though unevenly produced in the complex international crucible of modernity. *Un/settler* is a helpful spelling of the term because it creates room to refuse,[2] modify, or undo the settler condition when the opportunity arises. For indeed, the painful thing to accept is that those rights and the ideals that bring them into being are predicated on land theft, slavery, and indentureship, which are the racialized conditions of liberal modernity, as Lowe teaches us in *The Intimacies of Four Continents*:

> To observe that the genealogy of modern liberalism is simultaneously a genealogy of colonial divisions of humanity is a project of tracking the ways in which race, geography, nation, caste, religion, gender, sexuality and other social differences become elaborated as normative categories for governance under the rubrics of liberty and sovereignty…The operations that pronounce colonial divisions of humanity—settler seizure and native removal, slavery and racial dispossession, and racialized expropriations of many kinds—are imbricated processes, not sequential events; they are ongoing and continuous in our contemporary moment, not temporally distinct or as yet concluded. (7)

Lowe's work helps me see the paradox that the regime of rights into which Asian Canadians are supplementally included are predicated on an originary dispossession of those rights *avant la lettre* in order to create them first for the normative Euro-descended citizen-subject. Consider, for instance, the ways in which Chinese immigration to Canada was restricted by the Head Tax, and then excluded through the Chinese Immigration Act, all the way up until 1947, when we finally gained the right to citizenship. In other words, there is no such thing as a Chinese Canadian until after white Canadians are created through the exploitation and exclusion of Chinese people as one condition among many that found the Canadian state. Only then can "Chinese Canadians" be added, supplementally, to "regular" Canadians and offered the rights of citizenship that were designed for white (or whitened) Canadians in the first instance. However, it is important to recognize that our exclusion, as one prior condition of their founding, paradoxically gives us a stake in their production.

But Chinese Canadians are far from the only ones undone by the racial dispossession that founds modern liberalism, and certainly not the first. To recognize the erasure of Indigenous people through the concept of terra nullius for the purposes of land expropriation is to recognize the production of the category "Indigenous" at precisely the point of (attempted) erasure. Once we can see this clearly, it's easy to understand why so many of the Indigenous people of Turtle Island prefer to be called by the names of their nations. These affirm who they were and who they are, prior to and in excess of genocidal state designations. At a quarter turn, the category of Blackness comes into being through the violent dispossession of people from land in Africa and the particular project of slavery in the Americas for the purposes of land expropriation and capital production. The conversion of living Indigenous land into capitalist property through white, Black, and Asian labour is the project that produces race as we currently understand and inhabit it.

I find Dara Culhane's reading of John Locke's labour theory of property useful to articulate how Blackness, Asianness, and Indigeneity are produced in the colonial context. Locke explains the Western legal logic through which land becomes real estate: "Whatsoever then he removes out of the state that nature hath provided, and left it in, he hath mixed his labour with, and joined to something that is his own, and thereby makes it property" (27). Culhane recognizes that this magic works only in the Americas and only with regards to white men's labour. According to Locke, Indigenous people have property rights only to "the fruit they gather, the deer they catch and the corn they pick" (qtd. in Culhane 53). If the conversion of sacred land to real estate is the project of colonialism through capitalization, or what we currently call monetization, white labour is the magic substance that accomplishes this legal transubstantiation. It would make sense, from a colonizing point of view, to want to extend the capacity of that labour as far as possible, by, for instance rendering white those not previously deemed so—Irish, Italians, and Ukranians, for instance—and using other forms of non-Indigenous, racialized labour to extend the white man's labouring arm. The logic of slavery becomes eminently more clear and more reprehensible understood in this way. If human beings can be rendered non-human, and then rendered (white) property, then their labour can extend white property-making labour without their white masters owing them anything (at least not within the terms of colonial logic).[3]

And if the point comes, which it did, in which the moral and ethical horror of materializing such logic is such that it cannot be sustained, which was what happened, then it would make sense to find a supplemental substitute for that form of labour. This is how indentureship comes into being. Lowe is eminently clear on how these forms of labour are racialized, with the consequence of tremendous suffering and the denial not just of citizenship but of full human subjectivity for Indigenous, Black, and Asian peoples. She is clear too on the strategies used by the colonial system to ensure that Black and Asian people would resent rather than support one another, through the production of racialized characteristics that rendered each abject in the eyes of the other.

It is fully possible to read this unfolding in a bounded, nation-state context, but to see these conditions most clearly, it's more productive to read globally, which the ever-prescient novelist Dionne Brand did in her 1999 novel *At the Full and Change of the Moon*. That novel begins with the poisoning of a rebellious contingent of slaves called the Sans Peur on a fictional plantation in Trinidad called Mon Chagrin. The poisoner is herself one of the Sans Peur, a medicine woman called Marie Ursule, whom Brand describes as "queen of rebels, queen of evenings, queen of malingerings and sabotage, queen of ruin" (5). Pointedly, Marie Ursule uses a poison called woorara, also known as curare, which she knows about because the Indigenous Carib people of the island have taught her. Prior to poisoning the Sans Peur, Marie Ursule attempted to kill the slaveholder de Lambert, but was betrayed by a traitor, and punished by having her leg placed in irons and her ear cut off. She resorts to poisoning, not because she wishes to harm the men of the Sans Peur for the sake of harming them, but because, unable to kill him, she wants to deprive de Lambert of his property and livelihood. There is a wrenching contradiction at heart of her actions—she must destroy herself and those she loves in order get revenge against the one she hates, and in so doing put a stop to the violence of slavery at least at Mon Chagrin. Brand suggests, further, that de Lambert is not personally a racist monster within the terms of the time and place; he has in fact married a mixed-race woman. But if there is any such thing as solidarity or open-mindedness present in such a marriage, it is very limited. Both de Lambert and his mixed-race wife own slaves. It is the logic of slavery that is monstrous and none of those caught up in it can escape it, or the way it poisons their souls. Whatever potential for decency de Lambert might hold, that decency is severely curtailed because he lives by a land and human destroying system and can only make judgements within its own frame.[4] For the slaves, however, there is no escape except by exiting life itself. The only person Marie Ursule saves from this mass suicide is her daughter Bola, who goes on to mother many descendants, including, generations later, a descendant named after her, who is born in Toronto and returns to Culebra Bay.

As Marie Ursule and her descendants rebel against the production and reproduction of human beings as property, the land too seems to rebel against its production as property, even against the slaves who extend the property-making arm of de Lambert. It grows the woorara that poisons them, killing them but also freeing them from the imperative to grow the plantation's commercial crop, cacao. One might read the woorara as a generous but difficult gift from the land in a specifically tailored return for the cultivation of cacao with Black slave labour. The land plays with Kamena, the father of Marie Ursule's child, too, looking for the fictional maroon colony of Terre Bouillante, that is "boiling earth," the place he hopes to take Bola in refuge. He leaves Bola in a lively, village-swallowing swamp to seek it, finds it, goes back for her, but can never find it again, as though it actively hides from him. It is as though the land itself offers him a glimpse of the freedom he longs for before closing the door to that freedom and consigning him to a life of longing.

Through Brand's acknowledgement of the source of woorara, the figure of the second Bola, the contemporary, Toronto-born woman, and Marie Ursule's other descendants who move into other global territories including Venezuela, Curaçao, New York, Amsterdam, and Toronto, Brand connects Marie Ursule's story to our lives and stories in contemporary Canada and shows us how we are still related to her. Through these connections, Brand relationally connects Marie Ursule and the necropolitical logic of the plantation to other Indigenous spaces and places.[5] She sees that land theft and body theft produce further injustices and ongoing psychic unrest.[6] Kim Green, in "'Hold This for Me': Counter Memory and Trauma in Dionne Brand's *At the Full and Change of the Moon*," articulates this unrest (reading Avery Gordon) as haunting, asking, "What happens when the people who have to contend with the 'traumatic ghosts' of slavery actively choose to forget or try to forget?" (181) Green's piece is powerful for its articulations of how trauma reappears. I'd like to note further that, in the international settings of the novel, the descendants of Marie Ursule struggle with spirituality, anger, poisons, and the problem of the body as property.

The system of indentureship that replaced the system of slavery in the Americas was actively used on the West Coast of Canada in the service of building the railway, among other nation-building activities. This is a known history that Lowe articulates in some detail. The territories of indentureship do not mirror exactly the territories of slavery, and yet the two forms of labour, which are simultaneously racial forms are intimately bound together.[7] Though most of the Chinese workers who came to Canada/Turtle Island in the late nineteenth and early twentieth centuries came as sojourners, rather than as potential citizens, their labour too extended the labouring arm of the white man, converting sacred land into property. In the opening up of the West, and the connecting of British Columbia to the Ottawa Valley and Georgian Bay lines, it was instrumental in the settlement and development of Western Canada, after the decimation of the buffalo. In nationalist terms, Chinese workers have been hailed as heroes for doing the back-breaking work of nation-building. In the wake of the Truth and Reconciliation Commission, however, (if we were not aware before) it seems to me that we ought to be claiming the nation as a matter of accountability. Chinese Canadians have participated in land theft, as a matter of survival, perhaps, but participated nonetheless.

I have argued elsewhere ("Bone to Bone, Spirit to Spirit" 241) that in the logic of racialized settlement, the loh wah kiu who worked on the railway in the late nineteenth century functioned as prosthetic to the white bodies whose Lockean labour turned sacred land into property. In so doing they functioned as disembodied "arms" to the Canadian state in order to extend the whole and complete property-making bodies of white men, not, in the end, to own property, but rather to make money to send back to China in the form of remittances. Here, I wish to extend that argument through a reading of Paul Yee's work, specifically one of his children's books, *Ghost Train*, created in collaboration with the illustrator Harvey Chan, and his more recent novel for adults, *A Superior Man*. Both address the railway building period and Asian-Indigenous relations.

Published in 1996, *Ghost Train* tells the story of a South Chinese peasant girl called Choon-yi who has lost an arm, but who, with the remaining arm, paints magical pictures of such accuracy that they seem more than real: "The flowers she coloured seemed to give off fragrance. The animals she sketched seemed to breathe and move." Choon-yi's family is poor and starving. To make money, her father travels to Gold Mountain—in other words, Canada—to work on the railway, enduring the danger and loneliness that have been well documented as the lot of the sojourner uncles. One day, he sends for her, but when she arrives after a long journey by ship, she learns from the railway foreman that he is already dead. In a dream, her father visits her and asks her to paint the train, or what he calls the "fire-car." She has no idea what a fire-car is like and goes to great lengths to find and arrange a ride on one for herself. She is bewildered by the experience, until she paints it, and only then does it seem real. She dreams again of her father, who asks her to take the painting to the real train tracks the next day, lay it on the tracks, and light incense. When she does so, her dead father appears to her, lifelike and fleshy, though only as long as she doesn't touch him. Together they ride the train and see all the sojourners who died building the railway. She falls asleep one last time, and in the dream, her father tells her to take the painting back to China, climb a high hill, and burn it at the top. The smoke's ascent to the heavens will enable the sojourners' ghosts to go home.

The story is astonishing in its layout and handling of a range of psychic states—waking consciousness, painting, dreaming, and the magical awake state in which the dead father returns alive. Arguably, there exists in addition the spirit state of all the dead sojourners who might return to China if Choon-yi manages to get back and burn the painting on the mountaintop.

I'm particularly struck by the figuration of Choon-yi as missing an arm.[8] In light of what I said earlier about Chinese labourers as extending the white, property-making arms of white labourers, there is a sense in which the lost father is the lost arm of the dreaming girl—an arm given over, and ultimately destroyed by the state in order to wrench the land away from its being for itself and its relationship to the original inhabitants. The property-making magic of the dead sojourners' whitened labour is only a first step, which is followed by the magic of painting that Choon-yi does with her remaining arm, which brings the dead father back to life, at least, in a waking dream. There are two metaphors at work in my reading: The father is alive in Choon-yi's remaining arm, but dead in the missing arm. And the Chinese worker is the colonial state's property-making phantom limb. The dream needs to be imagined and imprinted on consciousness to become real. In many ways, this magic is like the economic magic of real estate—imagined, laboured for, and thus made legally material.[9]

Though Yee does not delve too deeply into questions of land relations and Asian-Indigenous relations in *Ghost Train* (though they are implicitly still present), he takes these issues up overtly in his 2015 novel for adults, *A Superior Man*. The railway worker father in *Ghost Train* is figured somewhat romantically, as an unsung national hero, a nation-building martyr scorned by the racist nation. Lindsay Diehl has argued that much of Yee's early work claims the narrative that focuses

> on restoring the lost manhood of Chinese men…[by modifying] the heroic journey motif of white settler nation building myths to claim a sense of Chinese Canadian belonging…The primary objective is not necessarily to debunk these myths, so much as to modify them and point out what is presumably "missing"—the "major role" that Chinese Canadian men have played in shaping, clearing and cultivating the land. The narratives substitute "Gold Mountain heroes" for "Great White men" as embodiments of the nation. (42)

The Chinese worker in *A Superior Man*, published nineteen years after *Ghost Train*, however, is not heroic; rather the novel's flawed protagonist, Yang Hok, is a selfish, prideful, unpleasant fellow, albeit one who has suffered greatly and witnessed unspeakable horrors as part of a land-clearing team for the Canadian Pacific Railway. In the years between *Ghost Train* and *A Superior Man*, Yee has recognized, along with many other Chinese Canadian writers, scholars, and activists, the debts we owe and the profound responsibilities we hold towards both Black and Indigenous communities and towards the land. For a The Insurgent Architects' (TIA) House blog titled "Justice Aesthetics," Yee writes,

> Today Chinese Canadians proudly see the Chinese coolies who worked on the Canadian Pacific Railway as our contribution to nation building.
> They don't see that the iron road was the main device that brought settlers to the Canadian west. The greatest impact of those settlers was the destruction of the culture and communities of Canada's Aboriginal People. Even today, that dark legacy lives on.

In humanizing the sojourner character by showing him to be selfish and prideful, Yee writes with humility;[10] it's a humility that does our communities a service also, by allowing us our flaws, oversights and missteps—our human complexity, while at the same time as recognizing our accountability to Indigenous people and the land.

Yee's figuration of Yang Hok as a "coolie" or indentured worker is helpful in terms of making visible the historical condition that Lowe calls "the intimacies of four continents." Yee, in fact, offers a note on the term as front matter, before the novel even begins, in which he explains his use of the term in nineteenth-century Canada to describe Chinese railway workers. He also acknowledges workers brought from India to the Caribbean and South America to replace Black slave labour in the same period, though oddly, he doesn't recognize the Chinese indentured workers in the same spaces, though Lowe does. This disconnect is likely a symptom of how deeply racial positions have been segregated historically and shows the need to draw connections.

As the novel opens, Yang Hok is working as a bouncer for a Chinese gambling hall in Victoria, British Columbia, as he prepares to return to China with his savings. He is looking forward to being able to show off his money there and give substance to his own earlier hyperbolic bragging. Before he can board his ship, he is visited by his former lover, Mary, a Nlaka'pamux woman from Lytton, who comes to him with their three-year-old son, Peter, in tow. Mary wants Yang Hok to take Peter and wants money from him too. Yang Hok attempts to flee, but Mary leaves Peter at Yang Hok's boarding house, and Yang Hok is forced to take guardianship. Yang Hok's boat is sailing for China the next day. He wants to leave Peter at the mission school but learns it will cost fifty dollars. "Fifty dollars?" Yang Hok says. "That's a man's life!" (30). Indeed, fifty dollars in 1885 was the price of the Chinese Head Tax implemented in that very year, four years after the completion of the Canadian Pacific Railway, which is also the year Yee's novel is set. Would-be indentured workers would have had to borrow this money to come to Canada to work and would not be free until that fifty dollars was paid off. If it never was, then his life would be, in a sense, bought and sold.

One of his compatriots says, "My money is my blood," a sentiment that Yang Hok shares. Peter, of course, is also Yang Hok's blood, but Yang Hok is too racist against Indigenous people to accept this: "I was going home to get married," he says. "My children would be Chinese, not mix-blood" (23). He plans to dump the boy with Mary's people, forge the papers to make it look legal, and go back to China as planned (33–34). Yang Hok is not a very nice guy!

However unpleasant a fellow Yang Hok is, it's clear that his social condition is a major contributing factor towards his unpleasantness. Yee, in fact, brilliantly thematizes this problem in the novel's title, *A Superior Man*, which reflects on how Yang Hok can possibly become a good man in Confucian terms, that is in terms of even his own cultural ideals, when as a survivor of his village's destruction, as a former bandit, and then as an exploited coolie, survival and making money have been the only possible and barely achievable ideals. But, by the same token, other men, specifically Sam Bing, who have suffered as profoundly are able to care for other people, including young Peter, with grace and humility. Does our suffering ever excuse our incapacities to act well?

When Yang Hok's compatriot says "My money is my blood," the metaphor is closely tied to the referent it stands in for. In the long flashback sections of the novel, Yee painstakingly shows us the gallons of Chinese blood spilled laying the track bed for the railway. The novel, in fact, reads as a litany of the varieties of Chinese death—men crushed beneath falling trees, men hit by flying rock, men blasted out of half-complete tunnels, all the time pursued by fear of killing airs and memories of banditry and ill deeds of their own in China. Once the soothing romance of national heroism is lifted, we find a community of desperate, vicious, frightened men, living lives of peril, mistrust, suffering, and also sometimes an ugly bravado, that however, as Yee seems to suggest through the presence of more noble characters, is not a foregone conclusion. Yee details this in stark realism, capturing in English the flavour and rhythm of South Chinese working men's speech in its crisp short syllables. The novel is beautiful in its starkness—to have Yang Hok's point of view gives us the humanness of an experience that outside of Yee's work and that of a few other loh wah kiu descendants has been little documented.

There are two metaphorical bodies at work in *A Superior Man*. Earlier, I talked about the Chinese indentured labourer as a prosthetic "arm" to the white national labouring body. This metaphor implicitly still holds in *A Superior Man*. But Yee's overt metaphor, "My money is my blood," refers to a different body—the body of the Chinese indentured labourer, not imagined in 1885 as a national body at all, but in fact, a body to be returned to China as soon as possible. Though the labour can be nationalized, the blood that flows through the labouring arm is not national—it's for this reason that the nation and its representatives can be so cavalier about spilling it. When sacred land is converted into real estate on Turtle Island, the medium of conversion is Chinese blood.

What's interesting is the way that that blood returns in the finance capital of Chinese oligarchs and business tycoons to purchase the land in the form of real estate, if one thinks, for instance of the famous Li Ka Shing purchase of the former Expo lands in Vancouver, using capital acquired through the deployment of Chinese labour in the People's Republic of China and Hong Kong.

What I hope I've illustrated here is the relationship of Black labour to Asian labour in the expropriation of Indigenous land in a Turtle Island and global context. While Black people were forcibly displaced from Africa and made into property, Asian people were not. Articulated as "free labour" in the aftermath of slavery by the former slave-holding classes, Chinese people at the turn of the last century also worked under brutal, though different, conditions. However, what the distinction between slavery and indentureship did most pointedly was foreclose solidarity. Lowe notes that, in Trinidad, white slaveholders were clear about wanting a non-Black racialized group as a cushion between themselves and their former slaves (24). East Asian and South Asian labour in the aftermath of slavery functioned as an early prototype for scab labour, replacing slavery and thus diminishing the leverage that newly freed Black workers might otherwise have had to push for concessions or even different economic forms from their former white masters. This was a condition particularly acute in Trinidad, as Lowe explains. On the West Coast of Canada, curiously, low-cost Chinese labour and low-cost Chinese life were understood as undercutting white working-class labour. This antipathy was the source of much racial rage, not to mention the 1907 anti-Asian riots in Vancouver, and the overt relationship between Chinese labour and white union labour. To read the production of race through the economics of land expropriation helps us see how colonial management was racial management,[11] and how it produced a politics of divide and conquer.

This recognition is helpful in the present to keep us on guard against the ever-evolving forms of state management that seek to contain us in the present, most pointedly in this moment, state multiculturalism, which dehistoricizes racial positions as they were produced through labour and land expropriation. It newly places differently racialized people in equally weighted positions in relation to the state, which is still normatively white in spite of all of its supplemental attempts at inclusion. It places the state at the centre of any cross-racial communication.

These are the unbearable conditions under which liberal democratic state sovereignty is produced, which we participate in when we struggle for and gain rights. There is no question but that it is painful to face, and indeed I'd like to take a moment now to pause and do so. The work of critique can be dangerous in its seemingly neutral affect, and I want to be clear that I don't feel neutral at all about this state of affairs.[12] I'd like to acknowledge here the affects that might be flowing through me and you, dear reader, perhaps grief, perhaps rage, as a way of bringing our contemporary bodies into presence on the page.

I'd also like to recognize, however, that other contemporary forms of government, including state socialism and communism with Chinese characteristics, are neither cleaner nor better; in fact, I value democratic ideals above many that people strive for in the contemporary moment, not absolutely, but passionately and contingently, with the recognition that these ideals have international roots, and that they may also evolve and transform. Further, I feel that as Chinese Canadians we have responsibilities to Black and Indigenous people through the state, and that to jettison the state would be to elide those responsibilities. It is important to recognize, however, that we have relationships to Black and Indigenous people in excess of the state. I seek solidarities both through and around the state; these take radically different forms, some of which might be ideal, but many of which, because they come out of history, cannot be.

While state processes tend to want to seek resolutions to contradictions, I suggest that this is not movement in a meaningful direction. Projects such as Pierre Trudeau's 1969 White Paper, for instance, sought to do exactly that, by drawing Indigenous Peoples into Canadian citizenship as a way to extinguish existing rights not yet fully named or articulated in state terms. Indigenous people are rightly suspicious that the Truth and Reconciliation Commission could be used for the same goals, which is why many insist that the Calls to Action must be a beginning and not an end. State Multiculturalism is in fact another such form, one that covers over and contains more complex histories while holding Québec at bay.

If attempts at closure produce colonial hegemony as usual, I want to articulate an ethics of engagement in the service of productive openings. I do so from a specifically Chinese Canadian location, recognizing, as I have above, that different ethics are called for depending how we are situated.

Rather than seeking the resolution of contradictions, I turn to recent developments in speculative fiction and utopian thought, as well as to recent developments in contemporary poetics to find ways of inhabiting that don't aim for an easy resolution, containment, or forgetting of the complicated and often violent and unjust processes that have brought us to this point, but rather a way of living imaginatively to be among others in the best way possible. I embrace a practice of poethics in order, as Donna Haraway would put it, to stay with the trouble.

I propose a notion of speculative Taoist poethics, a practice I imagine, enact, and further develop in a lived, relational way. It is not a religious practice, or even necessarily a spiritual one. Rather, I think of it as an inhabited poetic practice, hence, "poethics." In particular, I draw upon Fred Wah's notion of "ethnic poetics" when in his essay collection *Faking It*, he writes, "ethics is what surrounds you like your house it's where you live" (57). Though he never uses the term *poethics* as such, he speaks of poetics as "the tools designed or located by writers and artists to initiate movement change" (51). I pull Wah's ideas close to Joan Retallack's notion of the poethical wager, particularly when she finds, with her alter ego, Quinta Slef, that ethical agency is embedded in a complex world and the ways—both direct and indirect—that ethical agency is entangled with complex and interlocking phenomena (24). As I have just shown, the entanglements are complicated, and to build relationships from Asian locations to Black, Indigenous, white, and land-based locations, one must attend to the complexities of the entanglements. Dialectic opposition might sometimes be the answer, but often, it's not. I don't want to throw dialectic strategies out the window; there are times when they are necessary, or at least useful. But the real question is when to use them, and when to take up other kinds of action. I turn to the tao, and particularly the I Ching to do this. From my own position, the I Ching offers a metaphysics of relation from my own culture, one that might productively step into conversation with the Medicine Wheel and the Sun Wheel, which I have been taught a little bit about by the Cree and Blackfoot Elders with whom I have been working at the Insurgent Architects' House for Creative Writing. To take up the I Ching is a way of entering into conversation with at least some Indigenous people without appropriating their ways of knowing. It is also a way of thinking beside Blackness without taking up the same cultural space.

I understand the I Ching as both an oracle and as a mode of attention. I take it up because it offers a kind of poethical techne to understand where we truly are. What I particularly like about it is that, through its system of whole and broken lines, it makes room for binaries, it makes room for a range of interlocking dialectics to impinge upon one another in surprising ways. It allows me to think across a range of fields—racial, economic, ecological, spiritual, and more—all simultaneously. Speaking of the spiritual, it makes room as well for that way of being with others that the late Lee Maracle called "spirit-to-spirit" relations, as a matriarchal mode of responding to the call for nation-to-nation relations by Glenn Coulthard and others. Maracle writes, "In a society governed first and foremost by spirit-to-spirit relationships to all beings, memory serves much differently than in a society in which property possession determines importance" (*Memory Serves* 2). The I Ching makes room for the Marxist inheritance of activist work without being ruled by it; it doesn't throw out the dialectic, since to reject is itself a binary action. Rejection, as Frantz Fanon has taught us, always entails an embrace. Famously, he writes, "For not only must the black man be black; he must be black in relation to the white man" (110). The I Ching helps me see patterns of opposition in relation to one another, and to see how the patterns of opposition might play out to offer a range of possible outcomes.

But even what constitutes "outcome," or as I'd prefer, "emergence" depends on the questioner's understanding of what matters, since no moment is eternal, and all moments invariably slip away. The capacity to register the right emergence, to claim an endpoint, constitutes a kind of utopianism: "this is my moment of arrival." Arrival might be a successful revolution, the return of a lost homeland, or the granting of citizenship in a new one. But it might also be something much more ephemeral, and harder to see.

The danger of claiming the moment, of course, is that one might claim the wrong one. Wayde Compton shows us this in his incredible cycle of short stories *The Outer Harbour*, in which "Arrival" is the name of a condominium high-rise on the fictional Pauline Johnson Island that has erupted in the middle of the Georgia Strait, named after the mid-twentieth-century Mohawk poet. When the promise of new land becomes the promise of real estate and capital wealth, the only utopia we arrive at is that tired old utopia of Western settlement, which we already know is no utopia at all. Though Compton is too generous to point a finger at Asian speculation, this is part of the dynamic that drives the real estate situation in Vancouver, as to some extent, Toronto. But Compton offers us a speculation of a different kind—the speculation of speculative fiction, in which "Arrival" passes into another moment, perhaps a more utopian one in spite of initial appearances. At the end of the book, the building becomes a carceral institution, but one that doesn't function well as the "composites," that is, new digital humans, whom the state attempts to contain there walk freely through its walls, and in fact sometimes glitch from one location to another without any apparent linear movement from one location to the next. The condo building turned detention centre becomes a site of refuge. It is not exactly a utopia in the sense of Thomas Moore's original coinage—the good place that is no place. Rather, it is an insurgent utopia of the type that offers us an unexpected, newly embodied community still working out its issues, as I've described in "Insurgent Utopias: How to Recognize the Knock at the Door."

I'll close with another example of such a space, in the early work of Lee Maracle, which is the Chinese Canadian café called "the 4-Star" in "Polka Partners, Uptown Indians and White Folks." The 4-Star is located in downtown Vancouver, near Pigeon Park, which, the narrator, Stacey, tells us, is "the skids for white folks." She says, "for us, it was just a village, not really part of Vancouver" (286). The 4-Star, she tells us, is no different from any one of a number of Chinese Canadian cafés, including the Silver Grill in Kamloops, or, I suggest, the Diamond Grill in Nelson, BC, given to us in such loving detail by the poet Fred Wah. The 4-Star is where Stacey and her friends Mose and Tony hang out, served by Jimmy, a Chinese Canadian waiter who likes them and sometimes puts his own money towards their bill if they are short (287), so that the manager, who doesn't like them, won't kick them out. This is the place where Stacey, Mose, and Tony gather to laugh, dance, and hook up, until a man whom Stacey describes as an "uptown Indian" and dubs "Polka Boy" (289) arrives and organizes a proper community centre for them. Stacey and other urban Indigenous people living in the area throw themselves body and soul into the building of the community centre. A clinic is soon added to the project. But then one day the clinic's funding is cut. Polka Boy tells her, "The city couldn't justify funding a racially segregated clinic" (298), a remark that points to one of the greatest hypocrisies of the white liberalism—that's it's perfectly happy to have white enclaves without remarking on them or protesting them, but balks as soon as affirmative action strategies are embraced by Indigenous people. He plans to move the whole project uptown. Stacey and her friends are devastated—let down by the project that seemed in some ways more pure, but turned out to be less reliable than the 4-Star. The story closes with Stacey looking in on Jimmy, alone in the 4-Star, drumming on the counter with his fingers, bored (303). She tells herself she will look in on him later, though we are not given that scene in the story. There's a wistfulness in her look back, and a recognition of something utopian about the restaurant, registered only in hindsight.[13]

The time spent at the 4-Star never did, in the moment of experiencing it, register as an arrival, yet Stacey sees it as one when she looks back. It illustrates for us an instance of the intimacy of four continents in which Asian-Indigenous relations are foregrounded without triangulation through a white intermediary. To hold up such a moment is also to take a gamble, for there is no guarantee that the moment will produce further such moments, and indeed no guarantee that such moments might not give way in a later moment to strained relations, as when, for instance, Asian Canadians speculate on real estate in Vancouver's False Creek, which was once the Squamish village of Snauq ("Goodbye Snauq" 14). Maracle's characteristic generosity is at work in her understanding of the Li Ka Shing land purchase. She leaves her reading of it for us as a kind of gift, and helps me now in my articulation of what movement along the wheel of the I Ching might offer in terms of the ways we do critical work in the present moment, and perhaps the ways some of us might engage our organizing for activist work also. It offers an important hinge between the work of criticism and the work of community building, practices that, to my mind, must mutually produce one another.

This essay lays out the concept of the poethical tao through a critical-creative uptake of the I Ching. It does so for the purposes offering relational possibilities across Indigenous, Black, and Asian locations as they might be enacted from a specifically Chinese Canadian location. Through careful readings of Dionne Brand's *At the Full and Change of the Moon*, two books by Paul Yee, *Ghost Train* and *A Superior Man*, Wayde Compton's *The Outer Harbour*, and Lee Maracle's "Polka Partners, Uptown Indians and White Folks," I've considered how racial positions have been historically produced through colonial land expropriation and the strange and violent economic magic that converts both land and human beings into property, and how this violence has ongoing reverberations in the present. I've illustrated the ways in which Chinese Canadian bodies are fragmented in this process, but also the specific historical ways in which we are implicated in and therefore responsible for the ongoing violence of the colonial project. Through the poethical tao, specifically in response to Maracle's call for spirit-to-spirit relations, I've offered possibilities for meaningful engagement that might sometimes be oppositional, but sometimes might be adjacent, parallel, or at right angles to the stances and actions of others. In so doing, I hope I've deepened the range of possibilities available to readers, writers, critics, activists, artists, and organizers to engage the work of living with others—in the aftermath and ongoingness of unbearable history—in complex, generous, and productive ways that might move us in the direction of a better world, however circuitously and contingently.

Notes

1. Please see Nadine Chambers's "Sometimes Clocks Turn Back for Us to Move Forward: Reflections on Black and Indigenous Geographies" and Tavleen Purewal's "Port Rupture(s) and, Cross-Racial Kinships in Dionne Brand and Lee Maracle."
2. My thinking on refusal considers the important work that unfolds in *Refuse: CanLit in Ruins*, edited by Hannah McGregor, Julie Rak, and Erin Wunker. In this essay, I consider refusal as one strategy among many to be taken up when the moment calls for it.
3. I discuss these issues in more detail in "Bone to Bone, Spirit to Spirit: Sovereign Matriarchy, Asian/Indigenous Relations, and the Work of Directed Remembering." See also Rinaldo Walcott's *On Property*.
4. For more on the cruel intimacies of slavery, please see Christina Sharpe's *Monstrous Intimacies: Making Post-Slavery Subjects*. While Sharpe writes largely of the violent non-consensual sexual intimacies between white men and Black women and their consequences for contemporary Black subjectivities, clearly the monstrous institution of slavery creates difficult intimacies among Black people that would not otherwise exist, including the intimacy of Marie Ursule's helping the Sans Peur men to their deaths.
5. Alicia Elliott addresses in some detail a different but connected necropolitical logic affecting Indigenous people on Turtle Island in her talk "The Colonialism-Depression Link" given at the Poetics and Ethics of "Learning With" conference at Norwegian University of Science and Technology (NTNU) in 2021, in which she draws the specific connection between systemic racism and depression, and shows the ways in which the ongoingness of colonization systemically undermines Indigenous life by cutting Indigenous people off from clean water, safe housing, child-care supports, and the general wealth created by colonial production on stolen land.
6. Erin Soros's essay in this volume beautifully and painfully details what such unrest might look like for a contemporary person.

7. I note that in fact the district of North Vancouver in British Columbia's Lower Mainland has a strong economic underpinning in slavery. The families that founded it amassed their fortunes in the transatlantic slave trade. See Richter for more. My gratitude to Nadine Chambers for sharing this history with me.
8. There are implications here too in disability studies, which might query the figuration of the disabled character, Choon-yi, as having magical abilities.
9. Though it would take this chapter in a different direction, I'm interested in Choon-yi's missing arm in relation to the arm that rises from the grave of the dead girl child (66–67) in Sara Ahmed's *Living a Feminist Life*. For Ahmed, the arm is curiously both an appendage and a full embodiment of the willful feminist killjoy who insists on fighting back against the powers that be. Choon-yi's missing arm cannot fight back—it has been cut off and made to serve the Canadian state. Her magic arm doesn't fight back either, but it does create. There is powerful feminist agency in her magic arm. I might suggest that Choon-yi offers us a different kind of activist figure, that of the imaginative builder rather than the willful fighter. Our movements need both. The questions our moment calls for are: What ought one fight? What ought one build? The answers to these questions are more complex than they might first appear, hence my interest in poethics, which I lay out in what follows.
10. One might understand the humility embraced by Yee here in Warren Cariou's sense, when, in his essay "On Critical Humility," he suggests that critical humility might be less argument based and more story based. In offering Yang Hok as a kind of negative example, albeit one in a position of considerable suffering, Yee offers a humble critique of the Gold Mountain hero as a figure to be lauded.
11. Colonial management was also gender and sexuality management, if one thinks, for instance, of how the Chinese sojourners were mostly men, and how women were largely left in China to keep the family going there. See Yuen-Fong Woon's *The Excluded Wife* for more. Denise Chong's *The Concubine's Children* documents the life of one Chinese woman—the author's grandmother—who did come to Canada in the early part of the twentieth century. To understand formations of queerness under this system, see Richard Fung's 1996 single-channel video *Dirty Laundry*, as well as Suzette Mayr's recent novel *The Sleeping Car Porter*.
12. My recent poetry book *Iron Goddess of Mercy* takes on the fullest range of affects that I'm able to embody in relation to these conditions as a kind of temporary inhabitation or possession. Both Erin Soros's and Erin Wunker's chapters in this volume discuss at length the affective modes that necessarily emerge from the conditions I'm describing.
13. One might read this wistfulness in relation to the longing explored by Dionne Brand in *What We All Long For*, and also the epigraph to Adrienne Rich's *Dark Fields of the Republic*, which comes from F. Scott Fitzgerald's *The Great Gatsby*: "He had come a long way to this blue lawn, and his dream must have seemed so close that he could hardly fail to grasp it. He did not know that it was already behind him, somewhere back in that vast obscurity

beyond the city, where the dark fields of the republic rolled on under the night." I recognize, in keeping with some traditional temporalities that embrace time as circular, that the past is always there in the present. Such thinking opens the possibility for a kind of "return" that depends on the work of directed remembering (4), as Maracle articulates in *Memory Serves*.

Works Cited

Ahmed, Sara. *Living a Feminist Life*. Duke UP, 2016.

Brand, Dionne. *At the Full and Change of the Moon*. Knopf, 1999.

Brand, Dionne. *What We All Long For*. Knopf, 2005.

Cariou, Warren. "On Critical Humility." *Studies in American Indian Literatures*, vol. 32, no. 3–4, 2020, pp.1–12.

Chambers, Nadine. "Sometimes Clocks Turn Back for Us to Move Forward: Reflections on Black and Indigenous Geographies." *Counterclockwise*, special issue of *Canada and Beyond*, vol. 8, no. 1, Dec. 2019, pp. 23–39.

Christian, Dorothy, and Rita Wong, editors. *Downstream: Reimagining Water*. Wilfrid Laurier UP, 2017.

Chong, Denise. *The Concubine's Children: Portrait of a Family Divided*. Penguin, 2006.

Compton, Wayde. *The Outer Harbour*. Arsenal Pulp Press, 2015.

Coulthard, Glenn. *Red Skins, White Masks*. U of Minnesota P, 2014.

Culhane, Dara. *The Pleasure of the Crown: Anthropology, Law and First Nations*. Talonbooks, 1998.

Diehl, Lindsay. "'Want to Be a Superior Man?' The Production of Chinese Canadian Masculinities in Paul Yee's Writing." *Counterclockwise*, special issue of *Canada and Beyond*, vol. 8, 2019, pp. 42–50.

Elliott, Alicia. "The Colonialism-Depression Link: A Talk with Alicia Elliott." 27 Jan. 2021. *The Poetics and Ethics of 'Learning With' Indigenous, Canadian, Québécois Feminist Production Today*, https://ntnu.cloud.panopto.eu/Panopto/Pages/Viewer.aspx?id=77dee96c-859a-4500-a3e9-acbd01534079.

Fanon, Frantz. *Black Skin, White Masks*. Grove, 1967.

Fung, Richard. *Dirty Laundry*. 1996. Dist. Vtape.

Green, Kim. "'Hold This for Me': Counter Memory and Trauma in Dionne Brand's *At the Full and Change of the Moon*." *American Review of Canadian Studies*, vol. 50, no. 2, 2020, pp. 180–193.

Haraway, Donna J. *Staying with the Trouble: Making Kin in the Chthulucene*. Duke UP, 2016.

Karcher, Stephen. *Total I Ching*. Piatkus, 2009.

Lai, Larissa. "Bone to Bone, Spirit to Spirit: Sovereign Matriarchy, Asian/Indigenous Relations and the Work of Directed Re-membering." *Ideology in Postcolonial Texts and Contexts*, edited by Katja Sarkowsky and Mark U. Stein, Brill Rodopi, 2021, pp. 223–258.

Lai, Larissa. "Insurgent Utopias: How to Recognize the Knock at the Door." *Exploring the Fantastic*, edited by Ina Batzke, et al. Transcript Verlag, 2018, pp. 91–113.

Lai, Larissa. *Iron Goddess of Mercy*. Arsenal Pulp, 2021.

Locke, John. *Second Treatise of Civil Government*. 1690. University of Adelaide Library, 2014.

Lowe, Lisa. *The Intimacies of Four Continents*. Duke UP, 2015.

McGregor, Hannah et al., editors. *Refuse: CanLit in Ruins*. Book*hug, 2018.

Maracle, Lee. "Goodbye Snauq." *First Wives Club: Coast Salish Style*, Theytus Books, 2010, pp. 13–26.

Maracle, Lee. *Memory Serves: Oratories*. NeWest, 2015.

Maracle, Lee. "Polka Partners, Uptown Indians and White Folks." *Sojourners and Sundogs*, Press Gang, 1999. pp. 286–304.

Mayr, Suzette. *The Sleeping Car Porter*. Coach House, 2022.

Moylan, Tom. *Demand the Impossible*. Methuen, 1986.

Purewal, Tavleen. "Port Ruptures(s) and Cross-Racial Kinships in Dionne Brand and Lee Maracle." *Counterclockwise*, special issue of *Canada and Beyond*, vol. 8, no. 1, Dec. 2019, pp. 52–60.

Retallack, Joan. *The Poethical Wager*. U of California P, 2004.

Rich, Adrienne. *The Dark Fields of the Republic*. Norton, 1995.

Richter, Brent. "North Vancouver Built on Profits from the Slave Trade, Founding Family Says." *North Shore News*, 22 Feb. 2022, https://www.nsnews.com/local-news/north-vancouver-built-on-profits-from-the-slave-trade-founding-family-says-5080781.

Sharpe, Christina. *Monstrous Intimacies: Making Post-Slavery Subjects*. Duke UP, 2010.

Wah, Fred. *Diamond Grill*. NeWest, 1996.

Wah, Fred. *Faking It: Poetics and Hybridity*. NeWest, 2000.

Walcott, Rinaldo. *On Property*. Biblioasis, 2021.

Woon, Yuen-Fong. *The Excluded Wife*. McGill-Queen's UP, 1998.

Yee, Paul. *Ghost Train*. Groundwood, 1996.

Yee, Paul. "Justice Aesthetics: Paul Yee on A Superior Man." *The Insurgent Architects' House for Creative Writing* blog, 3 Apr. 2016, https://www.tiahouse.ca/justice-aesthetics-paul-yee-superior-man/.

Yee, Paul. *A Superior Man*. Arsenal Pulp Press, 2015.

10
On Trans Aliveness as Feminist Praxis
Ivan Coyote's and Syrus Marcus Ware's Ordinary Archives

LIBE GARCÍA ZARRANZ

COVID-19 and its aftermath has facilitated a profound encounter with the ordinariness of death, accentuating pre-existing social, economic, and political inequities that extend to the artistic realm. In the words of Danielle Peers, Canada Research Chair in Disability and Movement Cultures, "this pandemic has made clear that eugenics, white supremacy, and colonialism are alive and well-intertwined." The ongoing global pandemic continues to hypervisibilize the uneven regulation of life and death, together with "the contemporary conditions of ordinary brutality" that Christina Sharpe denounces (*Monstrous* 20). At the same time, this historical juncture has also borne witness to the resurgence of social justice movements led by Black, trans, and other minoritized peoples. I seek to conceptualize these spaces of resistance as complex instances of the ordinary. In such a paradoxical context, it is also key to emphasize that growing anti-Black and anti-trans violence co-exists with a higher visibility for Black and trans peoples (Gossett et al.) and with the abundance of published Black and trans literary and artistic productions in settler Canada, where I situate this research.

The written and visual worlds of Ivan Coyote and Syrus Marcus Ware, which will be the focus of this chapter, contest pervasive necropolitical impulses while cultivating what trans studies scholar Hil Malatino calls "arts of living" (5).

In the collection *Care Of: Letters, Connections, Cures*, Coyote assembles and responds to twenty-one intimate notes and messages they received from strangers over the years. By weaving their own personal stories into this tapestry of voices, Coyote experiments with the complexities and paradoxes of the ordinary as a site of care for trans life from their experience as a white non-binary trans storyteller. In the second part of the chapter, I propose to learn with Ware's participatory performance *Activist Love Letters* (2012–) and the various iterations of the *Activist Portrait Series* (2016–). In these collective projects, Ware seeks to "relate across difference" ("Art" 00:22:00) by inviting strangers to write love letters to activists they admire, collecting the responses, and drawing very large-scale portraits of them. By positioning himself as a Black trans queer artist, Ware, with his durational transmedia projects, urges viewers to act as collectors of the ordinary in ways that counter individualistic and cis-centric impulses. Coyote's and Ware's ordinary archives, I claim, propose a poetics and aesthetics of trans aliveness with deep implications for feminist praxis. I will further reflect on this point in the last part of my essay. This final section takes the form of a letter, addressed to Coyote, in which I situate myself as a cis feminist educator and researcher of queer and transnational orientations who resists conceptualizing trans as a supplement to the feminist project and instead thinks *with* trans knowledges and artistic practices as instances of feminist world making. As Dominique Hétu and I contend in the introductory remarks to this collection, living and learning with these contradictions, paradoxes, and possibilities is vital for the advancement of any kind of feminist intervention that prides itself on sustaining ethics and social justice as driving forces.

For those readers unfamiliar with the artists in this essay, Ivan Coyote is a celebrated storyteller, performer, musician, filmmaker, and award-winning writer from Whitehorse in Canada's Yukon territory. They have created four films, seven stage shows, and three albums that combine storytelling with music. Coyote is also an experienced educator who has toured public schools around the world for two decades, speaking to youth, teachers, and administrators and encouraging dialogue and action to foster safety and social justice for everyone. *Care Of: Letters, Connections, and Cures* is their thirteenth book and was a finalist for the 2021 Governor General's Literary Award for English-language nonfiction. In their introduction to *Care Of*, Coyote's words engulf readers in a world where storytelling is embodied, performative, and always changing: "The two things all of my bones know best is telling stories on a stage, and the feeling of wheels or wings and road rolling under me" (1). When the COVID-19 pandemic hit the world in March 2020, Coyote found the time and space to stop, retrieve, and reread all those emails, handwritten notes, as well as social media messages received over the years and still waiting for a response. In Coyote's words, the letters contained "stories and souls and substance" (4) and the people who wrote them became "a lifeline…an antidote, a cure" to the "sudden stillness" of the world (5). Coyote responded to these notes, longings, and calls by weaving their own personal stories, memories, and songs into them, creating a collective archive of voices that move, at least this reader, at every line. As Coyote intimates, "I answered each letter with a story that the original letter shook loose from my ribcage" (3). The collection assembles stories about death, friendship, motherhood, disability, mentorship, and allyship; a feminist archive of the ordinary, if you will, where trans lives and kinship are given central space.

In *Care Of*, these themes and longings are often told in fragmented and discontinued form, which creates an intended sense of disorientation in the book. Adonastare, one of the letter writers, comments on this aspect: "I have to apologize, I didn't have direction in this email. I never do. But I'm starting to realize if I let a lack of direction stop me from writing, I'll never write anything" (222). The conjunction "but" is deeply meaningful here, as it signals a determination to find meaning in directionlessness; to experiment with storytelling in queer ways that resist chrononormativity (Freeman), which designates the normative uses of time. Adonastare's letter thus breaks with these social scripts by resisting to follow the expectations of linear writing and practicing instead a form of deviant temporal framework. In another note to Coyote, this time written in 2017, Melinda reflects on the paradoxes of categorization: "I wanted to say thank you for providing those words, that widening of options beyond gender, and empathy for, and non-dismissal of faith, and the immediate acceptance that being queer, feminist and faithful is not an oxymoron" (99). Melinda identifies herself with others situated at the "messy cross-sections of things a society and family says can't exist" (99), thus showing awareness of the potential of queer mess to be a source of joy instead of shame. In this regard, Melinda's choice of words to describe her thank you note as "messy and discombobulated" (99) seems intentional, offering a queer map where disorientation is rendered ordinary. In my view, Adonastare's and Melinda's letters resonate with Sara Ahmed's queer affective work that teaches us, feminist readers, how "a mess can be a queer map" and how orientations towards and disorientations away from minoritized bodies, objects, times, and spaces matter.

These ordinary disorientations and reorientations in Coyote's collection are deeply grounded in the textures of everyday trans life, what Malatino describes as "the rhythms of the trans mundane" (5). In *Trans Care*, Malatino reformulates the notion of care outside cis-centric models, insisting on the fact that "care isn't abstract, but only ever manifested through practice—action, labor, work—it is integral to our ways of doing" (41). Grounded in collective relations, Malatino's care ethics resonate with Coyote's extensive experience practicing care as a doing in their continued activist pedagogies in schools.[1] In my view, the intertwined narratives of joy, trauma, loss, and love in Coyote's collection constitute a site of trans aliveness and care that is collectively made and that endures. The letters thus begin to offer some answers to Malatino's pertinent questions: "What ethos—what practice of living otherwise—might enable more liberatory forms of trans existence? What practices of care might ensure trans flourishing?" (5). The emphasis here on aliveness deeply resonates with Coyote's work and how it resists the lingering on the necropolitical or what Eric Stanley has termed "overkill" (9). Responding to ordinary acts of violence targeting queer and trans Black bodies, Stanley intimates as follows: "I feel in the fleshiness of the everyday like a kind of near life or a death-in-waiting. Catastrophically, this imminent threat constitutes for the queer that which is the sign of vitality itself" (1). At the face of anti-queer violence, Stanley asks, "What then becomes of the possibility of queer *life*, if queerness is produced always and only through the negativity of forced death and at the threshold of obliteration?" (1, emphasis in original). Historically speaking, endurance and resistance are integral to queer lives, something that Coyote's letters testify to. In their response to Darach, a trans man studying at the University of British Columbia in Vancouver, Coyote explains how "most days it's hard not to feel like we are thrust into a constant battle, just by being. By insisting to exist" (162). It is this act of repetition, this determination to demand one's existence that becomes a force against the systematic attempts at regulating trans subjects and communities.

Insisting on trans existence thus allows for spaces of unruliness and ungovernability in Coyote's ordinary archives. Isabel González-Díaz discusses Coyote's collections *One in Every Crowd* (2012) and *Tomboy Survival Guide* (2016) as "an archive for transgender children and youth" (418) that confronts rigid and oppressive social norms. Coyote's archival work, in my view, further enacts a feminist practice of care by challenging heteronormative ideals while opening up spaces of resistance for queer and trans youth. I would argue that *Care Of* continues this care labour by worlding a collective site of trans aliveness that resists regulatory systems and discriminatory practices, thus signalling a strong feminist impulse. In one of the letters in the collection, Ace, a fifty-nine-year-old disabled binary trans man reflects on his experiences being discriminated against by younger non-binary trans folks and assumptions from women about men's misogyny. Coyote ponders about age in their response, confessing to feeling "like a historian" most days (10). The choice of words is significant here, especially in relation to considering Coyote's letters as archival work that traces histories that have been erased or left untold, stories that need unlearning or re-seeing. Responding to Ace, Coyote explains their profound sense of feminist accountability: "My work these days is taking everything I know about masculinity and turning it over, and then over again…to check myself and change myself so I am not standing even accidentally in the way of all women and girls moving into their rightful power and place in this world" (12). This turning over and away from hegemonic masculinities unravels through letter writing and responding, a genre that Coyote has learned through their grandmother (240), also making alliances—such as intergenerational ones—key constitutors of these undoings.[2]

Misogyny and the pernicious effects of toxic masculinity are central to many of the stories shared in *Care Of*. Melinda, who introduces herself as "a cisgender female, mostly closeted bisexual…raised in a conservative Christian home and school" (97), thanks Coyote for their words on how emotions are often reduced or dismissed based on their historically feminine—and thus stereotypically diminished—value. Again, the urgent plea to unlearn and unsee is vital to fight received normative constructions of gender and sexuality. In their response to Adonastare, Coyote confesses how they are continuously thinking about "how to build and embody a better masculine being in this deeply misogynist society and world" (226). This goal is also central to Coyote's 2019 nonfiction collection *Rebent Sinner*, in which they describe various encounters with youth as part of their performances in schools. For example, a sixteen-year-old kid tells Coyote about his abusive father and how he grew up learning that tears are a sign of weakness (118). As Coyote laments in *Care Of*, "one of the most valuable things this culture steals from our men is their tears" (105). The act of crying is, to Coyote, "inextricably linked to living" (*Care* 105); an event where the quotidian and the ordinary become acts of world making.³ Coyote's and Ware's activism and artistic practices enact these ordinary worldings by recentring and reframing trans care, trans life, and trans stories.

Drawing from Leah Lakshmi Piepzna-Samarasinha's revolutionary work on disability justice, Malatino calls for the sustenance of a queer and trans care web that "coheres through consistently foregrounding the realities of burnout and the gendered, raced, and classed dynamics that result in the differential distribution of care—for those receiving it as well as those giving it" (2). A reciprocal care web only functions, Malatino further claims, "when the work that composes it isn't exploitative, appropriative, or alienated" (2). I would argue that queer and trans care webs also emerge when the labour involved is not regulated by ableist chrononormative forces, as is the case with Syrus Marcus Ware's visual worlds, to which I now turn. Ware is a visual artist, scholar, community activist, and educator. He is a co-founder of Black Lives Matter Toronto and Toronto's Prison Justice Action Committee, as well as a member of the Performance Disability Art Collective. Ware is currently an assistant professor in the School of the Arts at McMaster University, in Hamilton, Ontario. For twelve years, he was the coordinator of the Art Gallery of Ontario Youth Program. He is the illustrator of Catherine Hernandez's picture book *I Promise*, published by Arsenal Pulp Press in 2019, and the author of *Abolition Is Love* (2023), among other books.

Ware's participatory performance *Activist Love Letters* and the *Activist Portrait Series* experiment with the capacious complexities of the ordinary while theorizing an aesthetics of aliveness (Quashie 10) as world making. In the multiple iterations of these interconnected projects, the artist asks strangers to write love letters to activists whom they admire: "If you could reach out to one person who moves you by what they do, who would it be? What would you say?" (*Activist Love*). Then, Ware mails the letters, collects the replies, and draws the portraits of some of these activists to then exhibit these transmedia materials in galleries and educational spaces across Canada. In Ware's words, the portraits become "an act of reverence; a celebration of life and choice and of action(s)" (*Activist Portrait*). Honouring the Black epistolary tradition of James Baldwin (Ware, "Love") and the Black feminist activism of Audre Lorde, these joint projects urge audiences to consider difference as an ordinary site of aliveness; to highlight the potential

FIGURE 10.1 *Activist Portrait Series*, Robert McLaughlin Gallery, Oshawa, Ontario. (Photo courtesy of Syrus Marcus Ware.)

of activism to counter the "everyday terrors" (Sharpe, *Monstrous* 9) that Black people are subject to and to forge worlds and futures otherwise. Ware's portraits were also part of his project *Baby, Don't Worry, You Know That We've Got You*, which was part of the 2017 exhibition *Every.Now.Then: Reframing Nationhood* at the Art Gallery of Ontario. Co-curated by Andrew Hunter and Anique Jordan, the exhibition showcased artworks offering untold counternarratives of the nation at a moment when the Canada 150 celebrations were peaking.

As shown in Figure 10.1, these portraits are large-scale, which is an intended strategy to reinvent the tradition of portraiture by recentring those Black bodies, trans bodies, and disabled bodies that are systematically hyper-regulated while also rendered disposable or erased from public life. Echoing Coyote's insistence on trans existence, Ware's portrait series allows for "unintelligible bodies—those on the margins" to re-enter the frame, as he claims in his artist's statement (*Activist Portrait Series*). In doing so, I would argue that the letters and the portrait series become an ungovernable archive of aliveness that turns collective activism into an act of world making.

I here draw from Kevin Quashie's work on Black "aliveness" as "a quality of being, a term of habitat, a manner and aesthetic, a feeling—or many of them, circuits in an atmosphere" (14). Quashie unravels what he calls a poetics of Black aliveness in the following terms: "In a black world, the case of our lives is aliveness; not death, not even death's vitality, but aliveness. We are alive, we are alive, or, as a poet once put it, 'This is the urgency: Live!' Such aliveness is relational and it moves one into other habitats of (one's) being, into and toward more" (12). This urgent call for the relationality of aliveness, with its "radiant moments of ordinariness made like art" (Brand 19), to honour the words of the poet Dionne Brand, stands at the core of Ware's *Activist Love Letters* and the *Activist Portrait Series*, in my view.

In Ware's durational artistic practices, relationality traverses time and space, challenging chrononormative frameworks, resonating with some of the letters in Coyote's collection. Existing outside prescriptive temporal and spatial frameworks is already a precondition for minoritized communities. According to Ware, "as Black queer people, as Black queer disabled people we [are] always already out of normative space/place and time" ("The Black" 160). Hence, Ware explores the possibilities of imagining futures otherwise by transforming the genre of portraiture into a durational practice, rethinking time and space in capacious ways. Some of Ware's portraits, as seen in Figure 10.2, are also central to the exhibition *2068: Touch Change*, curated by Vanessa Kwan in 2018.

Situated fifty years into the future and inspired by Octavia Butler's fictions, this exhibition is described as an "archive" and a "speculation" that invites audiences "to consider change as a constant, and hope as an ever-expanding network of relations." In my view, Ware's unregulated archive is populated by what Christina Sharpe refers to as "ordinary notes of care" ("And to Survive" 173). Writing about her previous work, Sharpe opens her article with the question "Can I live?" to unravel the catastrophic impact of the "catalogues of atrocities enacted on black people" (172). In this process, Sharpe mobilizes "care counter to what is offered and enforced by the state (many states, any state), which imagines and enacts care for the poor, the black, the trans, the queer, the migrant, the vulnerable as prison cell, grave, mental institution, prison-school, poisoned air and water, abandonment, extraction, 'tender-age shelters,' and 'baby jails'" (174). This form of counter care is a practice integral to ways of doing (Malatino 41), on which trans studies theorists also insist. A commitment to an active praxis of care is

FIGURE 10.2 *Activist Portrait Series: Portrait of Queen Tite Opaleke.*
(Graphite on paper, 6 × 12 ft, 2015. Photo courtesy of Syrus Marcus Ware.)

evident in Ware's installation *Activist Wallpaper Series: Vancouver,* inspired by his *Activist Portrait Series* and which was part of Vancouver Mural Festival in early 2021. Here Ware "began creating wallpaper with the portraits to imagine a different landscape wherein activists were honoured and cared for—centered in our day" (*Activist Wallpaper*). The Vancouver installation is accompanied by a poem that becomes an ordinary note of care occupying the street, to use Sharpe's phrasing. One of Ware's verses reads, "our movements are pulsating with life," situating aliveness—symbolized by the pulse—at the centre of the aesthetic and political praxis. In Ware's multimedia installations, the street becomes a site of storytelling that at least, momentarily, disrupts normative ways of seeing.[4]

Ware's portraits continue to enter other spaces beyond the street and the art gallery. For instance, Ware took this archive into his PHD in environmental studies, which he titled *Irresistible Revolutions*, borrowing a quote from the late African American filmmaker and activist Toni Cade Bambara. Challenging the conventions of the genre, his doctoral work contained scholarly articles, together with twenty twelve-foot by five-foot graphite portraits of disabled arts activists in Canada (Smith 2021). Coyote's and Ware's ungovernable archives practice care by inviting readers and viewers to act as collectors of the ordinary in ways that counter individualistic and cis-centric impulses. They are both archivists of the ordinary invested in "documenting" their realities, borrowing Ware's words, to forge more capacious sites of trans life. In this ungovernable archive, "aliveness sets the parameters" and becomes world making (Quashie 10). Their written and visual works, as I have shown, challenge generic traditions to imagine trans aliveness as antiracist feminist world making.

For writers, artists, and activists such as Coyote and Ware, making feminist worlds requires labour, experimentation, creativity, and resources. Similar to care itself, acts of feminist worlding are not abstractions but entail a series of practices and doings. The etymology of the word *praxis* as habitual modes of action is particularly pertinent for my argument here, as it allows thinking about how the ordinary can be transformative and lead to change. Writing a note of care or drafting an activist love letter, as Coyote's and Ware's collective worlds illustrate, can be charged with political and ethical meaning. Their respective bodies of work resonate with other feminist, trans, and Black modes of collective autotheory, where memoir and autobiographical storytelling fuses with theory and philosophical commentary and with which I learn with: Erin Wunker's *Notes from a Feminist Killjoy: Essays on Everyday Life* (2016), Kai Cheng Thom's *I Hope We Choose Love: A Trans Girl's Notes from the End of the World* (2019), and Katherine McKittrick's *Dear Science and Other Stories* (2021). And as I always tell my students, the etymology of the term *theory* invites us to look at, to contemplate, to speculate about the world differently; to experiment with ways of seeing for "thinking and living otherwise" (Ieven et al. 1). Theory, as McKittrick reminds us, is also "a form of storytelling" (7), and, in that sense, Coyote is an exceptional theorist. For most of my adult life, feminist theory has sustained me, offering words and worlds that seemed impossible to me. As such, inspired by Ware's vital project, I want to close this essay by sharing my activist love letter to Coyote.

| Dear Ivan,
I hope this note finds you on the road again, breathing an air of possibility outside! I am writing this letter from Trondheim, a place in Norway that is not quite home. I am so grateful for your stories in *Care Of*...what a tremendous collection, omgoddess. I have carried your words from the introduction since I first read them: how to understand oneself without being in transit. To take in moments of impasse, of stillness, of quietness and not drown... (no, the watery imagery will not do)...I imagine the ocean when I try to escape but these months of partial isolation have felt more like inhabiting a volcano, susceptible of erupting at every turn, at every phone call from Spain, where I was born and where my parents live; yet another place I call not quite home; fear nesting in the body and the shame of living and surviving. And then your words, your stories, your act of responding to others...what a feminist archive of trans aliveness you have built! I would love to share a coffee with you and listen attentively to your views on the alarming spread of anti-feminist discourses that seek to co-opt the term feminist in dangerous ways.

    I am a forty-four cis feminist parent, researcher, and educator, of queer and transnational dis/orientations, who thinks with trans knowledges and artistic practices as instances of feminist world making. For years now, I urge students to read bell hooks's essay from 1984 where she reminds us that feminism is the movement to end sexist oppression and that interlocking systems of oppression of race and class do matter. How crucial it is to for cis and trans feminists to work together through rupture and paradox, and forge alliances grounded on difference. The stories you revived in *Care Of* are, in my view, a testimony to this need to unlearn and unhear sexist, racist, and transphobic discourses that are wired in our brains, bodies, and actions. I love how you think with Judith Butler and insist, in one of your response letters, on the "need to cherish the longer forms" (78). To me this means slowing down in our writing, theorizing, and artistic practices; stretching time and space, in their potential malleability, to forge futures otherwise.

This is what Syrus Marcus Ware does: to desire the longer forms. Have you seen any of his installations? I wish I can go back to Canada one day, where I spent some of the best and worst days of my adult life (in Edmonton and Winnipeg!); an idealized space in my imagination (a place that felt like home for the first time in my life) and read his love letters to activists and portraits. His work inspired me to write this letter, an activist love letter, to you, Ivan! Ware loudly exclaims, "we are in a time of profound love" ("Love" 00:05:49). What an extraordinary provocation. The stories in *Care Of* make me want to touch this love, feel this love, breathe this love for a feminist life, with its paradoxes and its impossibilities. I will carry your stories with me, as I try to raise my child, and as I learn and unlearn how to build more generous worlds with my students. Warm thanks, Ivan, for your capacious archive of life, your radiant moments of ordinariness, your inimitable craft, and your tender fierceness.

With feminist love,
Libe

Notes

1. As Malatino contends, in relation to a course he taught with Aren Aizura in 2019, the classroom is also a space where trans and queer labour occurs (42). As a university professor in teacher training, I am grateful for Coyote's monumental written archive, which can help educators and students begin to unlearn normative pedagogies.
2. Coyote thanks both grandmothers in the book, describing them as "leaders" and "moral compasses" (71), together with their agent, Rachel Letofsky, for guidance and their shared love for "smashing the patriarchy" (241).
3. In this chapter, I have used the terms *ordinary* and *quotidian* interchangeably. I recognize, nonetheless, that these are concepts with extensive critical genealogies. In the context of Canadian studies, for example, Paul Barrett has written about the poetics of the quotidian in relation to Black diasporic writing. Dionne Brand's oeuvre, in Barrett's words, "not only contextualizes the quotidian within the black diaspora, but also constitutes a language for these unspoken traumas, longings, and absented histories" (26). See Barrett, *Blackening Canada*, for further reference.
4. Ware's multimedia installation *Radical Love* (2020), which centres Black and Afro-Indigenous trans women and non-binary people, stands as another example of how urban spaces can be reclaimed as locations of aliveness.

Works Cited

Ahmed, Sara. "A Mess as a Queer Map." *Feministkilljoys* blog. 23 Dec. 2020. https://feministkilljoys.com/2020/12/23/a-mess-as-a-queer-map/comment-page-1/.

Barrett, Paul. *Blackening Canada: Diaspora, Race, Multiculturalism*. U of Toronto P, 2015.

Brand, Dionne. *A Map to the Door of No Return: Notes to Belonging*. Doubleday, 2001.

Coyote, Ivan. *Care Of: Letters, Connections, Cures*. Penguin Random House, 2021.

Coyote, Ivan. *Rebent Sinner*. Arsenal Pulp Press, 2019.

Freeman, Elizabeth. *Time Binds: Queer Temporalities, Queer Histories*. Duke UP, 2010.

González-Díaz, Isabel. "Reassembling Components: Ivan Coyote Writes Down Difficult Things." *Journal of Commonwealth Literature*, vol. 56, no. 3, 2021, pp. 416–430.

Gossett, Reina, et al., editors. *Trap Door: Trans Cultural Representation and the Politics of Visibility*. MIT Press, 2017.

Ieven, Bram, et al. "Introduction: Taking Aesthetics from Resistance to Resilience." *Art and Activism in the Age of Systemic Crisis: Aesthetic Resilience*, edited by Eliza Steinbock, et al., Routledge, 2021, pp. 1–5.

Malatino, Hil. *Trans Care*. U of Minnesota P, 2020.

McKittrick, Katherine. *Dear Science and Other Stories*. Duke UP, 2021.

Peers, Danielle. "Inclinations." *Pierre Elliott Trudeau Foundation Alumni Newsletter*, 5 May 2020, https://www.trudeaufoundation.ca/updates/publication/danielle-peers-inclinations.

Quashie, Kevin. *Black Aliveness, or A Poetics of Being*. Duke UP, 2021.

Sharpe, Christina. "And to Survive." *Small Axe*, vol. 22, no. 3, November 2018, pp. 171–180.

Sharpe, Christina. *Monstrous Intimacies: Making Post-Slavery Subjects*. Duke UP, 2010.

Smith, Elaine. "Non-traditional Theses Becoming New Tradition for Faculty of Graduate Studies." *YFile*, 20 May 2021, https://yfile.news.yorku.ca/2021/05/20/non-traditional-theses-becoming-new-tradition-for-faculty-of-graduate-studies/.

Stanley, Eric. "Near Life, Queer Death: Overkill and Ontological Capture." *Social Text*, vol. 29, no. 2 (107), 2011, pp. 1–19.

Ware, Syrus Marcus. *Activist Love Letters*. 2012, https://www.syrusmarcusware.com/art/activist-love-letters. Accessed 11 Mar. 2024.

Ware, Syrus Marcus. *Activist Portrait Series*. 2016, https://www.syrusmarcusware.com/art/activist-portrait-series. Accessed 7 Apr. 2022.

Ware, Syrus Marcus. *Activist Wallpaper Series: Vancouver*. 2021, https://vanmuralfest.ca/blog/syrusmarcusware. Accessed 19 Sep. 2023.

Ware, Syrus Marcus. "Art, Activism, and Futurity." Tanenbaum Lecture. Ryerson University, 27 Nov. 2020, https://www.youtube.com/watch?v=wjvxavPg4J0.

Ware, Syrus Marcus. "The Black Radical: Fungibility, Activism, and Portraiture in These Times." *Art and Activism in the Age of Systemic Crisis: Aesthetic Resilience*, edited by Eliza Steinbock, et al., Routledge, 2021, pp. 158–168.

Ware, Syrus Marcus. "Love and Living." *Creative Time Summit: Of Homelands and Revolution.* Toronto, 20 Nov. 2017. https://www.youtube.com/watch?v=F1UtY6wQ1A8. Accessed 3 Nov. 2021.

11
(Dis)(Re)Learning with Liz Howard's *Infinite Citizen of the Shaking Tent*

ANNE QUÉMA

A FIRST READING of Liz Howard's 2015 *Infinite Citizen of the Shaking Tent* might prompt a predictable categorization of her book as experimental poetry. Howard's approach—which led to the creation of the AvantGarden group (2010–2014) and includes references to writers such as Gail Scott, Margaret Christakos, M. NourbeSe Philip, Lisa Robertson, and Erín Moure— revolves around experimental practices of poetic constraint and citational *détournement*.[1] Her book is thus inscribed in a genealogy of experiments that upset normative systems preceding the act of writing. However, in an interview with rob mclennan, Howard describes her book in terms that qualify her approach to experimentation: "Here, this here where all are invited, contains the urban, the boreal forest, Descartes, Wittgenstein, Plath, Stein, Keats, Anishnaabe cosmology, lumberjacks, punk rock, autobiography, the tension between unintelligiblity and TMI, poverty and science. It's a party, a séance, a powwow, a wake" (mclennan). This gathering of percussive practices and origins speaks to what Howard calls a "First Nation's approach to poetics" ("Against Assimilation" 32) that reconfigures expectations about experimental writing.

Nestled within her writing is the historical and political fact that the whole question of experimental citation is charged with the genocidal effects of the colonization of Indigenous knowledge, land, and cultures. If language is at the heart of Howard's experiment, it is in the grip of a violent dynamic of citation. On the one hand, citing Western language is necessary to dismantle it; on the other, Indigenous languages have been muted as pre-existing grounds of reference. Resisting what Yellowknives Dene writer Glen Coulthard calls the colonial politics of recognition, Howard's poetry mobilizes levels of citation: the language that oppresses, the language that shadows the poems, and the language of experimental poetry that Howard, a mixed settler-Anishinaabe from Treaty 9, re-sites. In re-citing and disturbing Western discourses of knowledge and appropriation, her poems undo epistemic hegemony through a process of dis/re/learning to invoke poetry as ceremonial cognition and land as the "lectern of origin" (*Infinite* 73).

In 2016 Cree-Métis scholar Deanna Reder and Linda M. Morra published *Learn, Teach, Challenge*, a major collection gathering a multiplicity of Indigenous and non-Indigenous writers to reflect on the ethical and political challenges that attend critical approaches to Indigenous literatures. A recurrent theme of discussion concerns methods of reading and responding to storytelling that do not reproduce acts of colonization. Among contributors, poet and photographer Kimberly M. Blaeser, of the Minnesota Chippewa Tribe, describes the search for "a critical voice and method which moves away from the culturally centered text outward toward the frontier of 'border' studies, rather than an external critical voice and method which seeks to penetrate, appropriate, colonize, or conquer the cultural centre, and thereby change the stories or remake the literary meaning" (232). This approach calls into question the practice of interpreting texts according to a masterful deployment of knowledge premised on the subject-object of Cartesian tradition. This critical regime is haunted by the extractive and assimilative drive of interpretation which Tuscarora writer Alicia Elliott calls "literary colonialism," and which reinforces "troubling attitudes of colonial ownership over Indigenous people within the literary community…[and] what Native writers can write about, and even whether they count as Native at all" (153–154). The task of reimagining criticism ought to concern settler critics in their encounter with Indigenous artistic expressions. If criticism is an act of creating knowledge through an address, how does one address Howard's poetry without reproducing patterns of colonization through the application of critical concepts that stem from Western epistemology?

As a settler critic, my intent is to contribute to the unsettling of this assimilative drive of interpretation through a process of writing that invokes other Indigenous writers and artists in the act of reading Howard's book of poetry. In this respect, I heed Métis writer Jo-Ann Episkenew's insistence that studying Indigenous texts hinges on conversing with Indigenous people. This conversation also takes place among Indigenous artists. Indeed, referring to Indigenous writing in the United States, Blaeser suggests that "contemporary texts contain the critical contexts needed for their own interpretation, and, because of the intertextuality of Native American literature, the critical commentary and contexts necessary for the interpretation of works by other Native writers" (237). So, rather than establish a context or theoretical framework and then focus on Howard's book in isolation, my purpose is to acknowledge that her book is part of the resurgence that Michi Saagiig Nishnaabeg writer Leanne Betasamosake Simpson invokes in *As We Have Always Done*. Such a resurgence speaks to a collective movement of creative resistance to a legacy of genocidal erasure and revolves around a foundational conception of relationality as governance:

> All of our political structures are plugged into the essence and real power of life that exists across time and space as worlds of nonhuman beings, some of which are spiritual beings and some of which are our Ancestors. Decision making and leadership in a highly networked, diffuse political system that is grounded in relationship to spiritual power have to be actively generated, sustained, and maintained within Indigenous bodies and the relationships that forms these hubs. (Betasamosake Simpson, "Land Pedagogy" 117)

In citing and referring to other Indigenous writers and visual artists, my own approach foregrounds an intertextual and intermedial web of practices that I intend as a respectful acknowledgement of the centrality of Indigenous relationality not only in the political but also in the creative and cognitive sense of the term. The purpose is one of *reading with* Indigenous texts and images to materialize a critical practice that remains contextualized by and attentive to the modes of learning nestled in the visual and textual citations.

The history of colonial disaster casts a long shadow on *Infinite Citizen of the Shaking Tent*. In Canada, colonization expanded by drawing on the conjunction of land appropriation, linguistic erasure, genocidal destruction, and social assimilation that each demanded the submission of bodies and spirits undergoing regimes of incarceration in reserves and residential schools. Today, Indigenous struggles to reconnect with severed links are all the more traumatic as they coincide with an entry into history—individual and collective—that is violent and reiterative:

> for all history
> awaited you
> was open to you
> bade you
> entrance (*Infinite* 45)

Two names stand out in Howard's book: Jacques Cartier (1491–1557) and René Descartes (1596–1650). Both figures represent the convergence of two types of mastery, one over land for the purpose of extraction, the other over doubt through the assertion of the rational subject. In this colonial scenario, the conquest of land engenders a discursive space for the exercise of a subject endowed with superior knowledge and deliberative, linguistic, and economic know-how. Both types of mastery contributed to a governance dependent on the suppression of Indigenous modes of being revolving around relationships to land and non-humans that are nurtured through ceremonial protocols and learning practices.

In *Infinite Citizen of the Shaking Tent*, motifs of dismemberment and blood point to a transgenerational plight that has led to the disruption of kinship. In the third part of the book, "Skullambient," the spiritual link to land and non-humans recedes and is replaced by a "psychogeography" that spreads out over several pages where the "I" moves eerily through a series of disparate memories of places and events. Howard's speaker is often located between the spiritual and the profane, as in "to be small and dreaming parallel / to ceremony and decay" (*Infinite* 65). Receiving a blessing from an Elder— "*diabetic amputee / from the farthest reserve*" (54), she bears witness to the abjection of the body of her people and culture.[2] The time of colonial ravage is "STANDARD TIME," the recurring title of four sections that record the "caustic history / of moisture" (53), as genocidal domination holds the lines and stanzas in its grip:

> Our throats flecked with pyrite and broken glass
> swift foxes, insulin pumps, pink cyclical rivers
> know the jet stream to be a Sanguine (5)

While historically contact is associated with 1492, Howard's poems speak to the continuation of contact in the form of what Achille Mbembe identified as a mode of necropolitical governance that creates "*death-worlds*, new and unique forms of social existence in which vast populations are subjected to conditions of life conferring upon them the status of *living dead*" (39–40).

Historically, necropolitical governance has combined with the attempt to mute what Sandra Styres has called Land Literacies, which generate "stories [that] are etched into the essence of every rock, tree, animal, pathway, and waterway…in relation to the Indigenous people who have existed on the land since time immemorial" (29). Land Literacies thus speak to interacting practices of cognition, language, and kinship that sustain relational modes of governance. Contact disrupted Land Literacies. In *Moon of the Crusted Snow* (2018), Waubgeshig Rice of the Wasauksing First Nation re-enacts the first contact with necropolitical governance in a scene between Evan, a member of a northern Anishinaabe community, and a white survivalist who is later revealed as a Wendigo-like figure surviving on the flesh of Indigenous bodies: "Trees cracked under the weight of snow in the still, crisp air. As he stood up, the stranger's stature stunned Evan. He was a beast of a man who was invading his people's space. 'I come in peace.' The man's voice echoed across the barren landscape. Then he started to laugh, a mild chuckle, that quickly escalated into sharp guffaws" (100). In Howard's book, contact eats away at poetic lines trapped in abjection. The lines bear the traumatic signs of a historical severance from reciprocal relationships to the land that act as a way of grounding being and learning.

Colonial extraction prepared the ground for the technical scientific discourse that currently organizes institutional knowledge and that demands the sacrifice of what Coulthard calls "grounded normativity," which he defines as an ethical framework generated by the notion that "land as a mode of reciprocal relationship (which is itself informed by place-based practices and associated form of knowledge) ought to teach us about living our lives in relation to one another and our surroundings in a respectful, nondominating and nonexploitative way" (60). The colonial violation of land, kinship, and languages is predicated on a persistent process of assimilation that relies on the domination of Western knowledge. In resisting this legacy, Howard's book asks, how does one learn to be, speak, and live through practices that reaffirm a broad sense of kinship that has been under erasure? Knowledge is therefore a relational question of survivance whereby learning is *learning with*.[3] What makes Howard's practice of experimental poetry singular is its affect, as it oscillates between resistance to colonial power and the loss of *being with*. For the challenge is to find the ground from which to exit colonialism while at the same time knowing that the link to the ground has been damaged and that learning always hinges on an affective relationship to knowledge, including the modes of learning that are also at the origin of assimilation and economic spoliation.

In revolving around assemblages of Western science and Indigenous culture, Howard's book recalls the Two-Eyed Seeing methodology that in 2004 Albert Marshall, Elder of the Mi'kmaw Nation in Unama'ki-Cape Breton, created: "Two-Eyed Seeing is the gift of multiple perspective treasured by many aboriginal peoples…It refers to learning to see from one eye with the strengths of Indigenous knowledges and ways of knowing, and from the other eye with the strengths of Western knowledges" (Bartlett et al. 335). At the same time, the labour of writing from within epistemological frameworks established during colonization cannot but bear the signs of disconnect: "poet   scientist   Anishinaabe" (Howard, *Infinite* 74). The gaps between these three modes of being speak to a division among unreconciled modes of creating, knowing, and being. In its configuration of the page, "Watershed and Shield Reminiscence" concretizes in a few strokes the devastating aftermath of Western mastery over land and knowledge. The left column constitutes a timespace of desolation and petrochemical pollution; the right column offers a fragmented lineage of memories associated with the great-grandfather's traplines, the killing of a horse suffering from a broken bone, and the protective gesture of an amputated Elder who

> *called upon*
> *Gitchi Manitou*
>
> *to secure my exit*
> *from poverty* (54)

In between the columns lies a chasm to which the poet bears witness. The deprivation of cultural origins haunts the poems, as in

> Sweet citizen, I know you
> as I know myself: a fictive province
> of selves within
> doppler range (70)

In Howard's book, the poetic page is the site for a poetics of resistance to the dislocating effects of epistemic hegemony. The metamorphic processes by which Howard's lines rip scientific terms from their habitual and normative contexts—turning them into *objets trouvés*—could be read as the twists and turns of a knowledgeable, wry trickster adept at both the simulation and *détournement* of Western scientific language. The book can thus be read as a prodigiously complex process of (un)(dis)learning through the creation of poetic constraints that speak to the strictures of a persisting colonial will to power. What settler readers see first and foremost is the citation of a scientific lexicon that has been torqued beyond recognition, and this for three reasons: readers not familiar with the words are at sea; bewildered readers seek in vain a mirror image of their reading self; and, to make matters worse, the presumable objectivity of the scientific lexicon and its association with progress clash with the dereliction that it names. A vast citational procedure unfolds inexorably as the poems are impaired by "a contagion of words" (*Infinite* 12):

> In our woods: hemodynamic snow
> a terrarium of lung-fed prosody
> tucked inside a small body of rusted air (5)

The taxonomy of Western knowledge contaminates lines as if the page were a site to be conquered and mastered. Instead of an outright rejection, the lines proceed to refurbish the cognitive lexicon by detaching it from a discourse that seeks coherence.

This reconfiguring indicates that Howard's poetry is not an *object* of criticism but a fusion of cognition and creation. Therein lies the energy of her resistance. Unravelling and splicing heteronomies, some of the poems unfold like the double-stranded structure of molecular DNA. Dividing and replicating strands of scientific knowledge, Howard's lines generate outlandish possibilities of meaning. For instance, "Neural Cascade: A Chandelier of Forest Bones" combines Cartesian doubt with a vision of dendrites storing ancestral memory while it alludes to Nanabozho as in "a hare gone / to rut in the reverb of / precognition" (4). The lines that create this phantasmatic collage are organized according to a pattern of indentation that replicates a neural cascade, that is, a visualization of neurological and biochemical events in the brain.

In the context of this *détournement* of Western epistemology, the poems reveal the loss of *being with and knowing with* through the silencing of Indigenous languages. The poem "Steinian Aphasia" not only refers to Gertrude Stein's avant-gardist prodding of American linguistic practices, but it also signals an approach to writing spurred by the experience of colonizing assaults on speech. Repeatedly, Howard's speaker underlines a state of mutism:

> south of the fortune
> cookie factory on the
> street where I lived I
> lost the nerve to speak (61)

Similarly, the tale of the poems evaporating from camels' humps after the ants have eaten the flesh away concludes with aphasia and anonymity: "we had no words / our faces became / indistinguishable" (72). This traumatic deprivation of antecedence and tongue recurs through the work of Nisga'a poet Jordan Abel and its dismantling of the invasion of Western narratives of anthropology and literature in *The Place of Scraps* (2013) and *Injun* (2016). In *NISHGA* (2020), which also tells of the sacrifice of kinship and place of origin, Abel includes a transcript of an interview that took place in 2017, in which he comments on *The Place of Scraps*: "the moments that precede these excerpts are the moments when I am forced to search for Indigenous knowledge through Marius Barbeau" (78). Howard's *détournement* of English scientific terminology exposes this forced detour of Indigenous knowledge through colonial ventriloquism. Common to Abel's and Howard's writing is the elusiveness of a language of origin whose presence is paradoxically signified by the silencing effects of a hegemonic language. Mourning a history of decimation coinciding with the loss of her father, who named himself December, the speaker says,

> when presented with history in the form of an ellipsis
> I must continue
>
> feral, I enter
> the court of words, December, December
> of my mind (*Infinite* 77)

This court of words is the site of potential injury which in turn engenders acts of creativity in search of ancestral sounds and voices. Thus, in *The Pemmican Eaters* (2015), Cree-Métis poet Marilyn Dumont contests the demeaning of Michif and gathers the sounds of "wintering words":

> Métis traders, speak la lawng of double genetic origin
>   pleasure doubled   twice the language   twice the culture (16)

Each and every unarchiving endeavour bears witness to the enduring will to regraft cultural antecedents onto contemporary creation.

If poets have only words at their disposal, then Howard's words are aleatory from the start, as they can be both bearers of dispossession and pods of regeneration. This intractable relation to one's tools of creation is the colonial legacy of the deprivation of Indigenous languages. It is illustrated by Howard's complex approach to the history of experimental poetry. In a citational gesture to Arthur Rimbaud, whose Symbolic poetry is often regarded as a forebear of experimental poetry in European literature, the last section of "North by South" Indigenizes the synesthetic poem of *Voyelles* (1871):

> *A* is red in my mind and the number I is white
> inimical as the perjured self
> …
> 2 is red in my mind and the letter *I* is white (78)

This writing-over is all the more complex as one recalls the historical contexts of experimental art and its bouts of colonial fever, including Rimbaud's firearms trafficking in Ethiopia. In a section of "Standard Time," the iterative time of colonization, Howard concludes with lines that speak to the injurious affect of words: "the word is a purple gash I could write / a

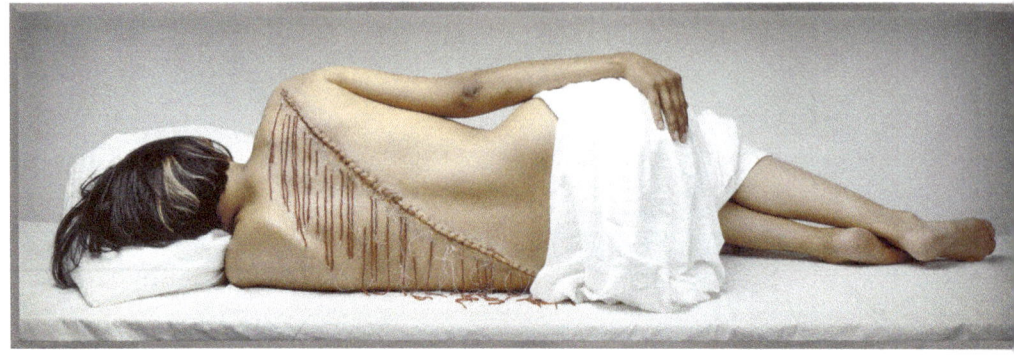

FIGURE 11.1 Rebecca Belmore, *Fringe*, 2008. (Inkjet print transparency in LED lightbox, 81.5 × 244.8 × 16.7 cm, National Gallery of Canada, Ottawa. Artwork © Rebecca Belmore. Photo by NGC, used with permission.)

surgical line through this day" (78). Howard's lines can be read in the context of *Fringe* (2008), a photograph by Anishinaabe artist Rebecca Belmore from Lac Seul First Nation that captures a mise en scène: a woman lies on her side presenting her back to the viewer. Her head lies on a white pillow and her buttocks are covered with a white cloth. She could be sleeping, her right arm resting on her hip. From the top of her right shoulder to the base of her back runs a diagonal line scarified into her skin, as if a seam had been created to suture the two sides of her back. Streaks of blood drip down from the line, creating the pattern of a fringe (Figure 11.1).

Fringe exposes an embodied history of genocidal assaults on Missing and Murdered Indigenous Women and Girls. Like Howard, Belmore works through the political history of signs and the constraints they impose on acts of representation. On the one hand, the word *fringe* recalls the sartorial feature of Indigenous deerskin clothing, but also the stereotypical representation of Indigenous characters in novels and movies, and its appropriation by settler heroes. The photograph exposes genocidal violence by turning the sartorial motif into the fringes of a surgical line. On the other hand, if we look again at *Fringe* in the context of Howard's writing, it is also possible to perceive the lying figure as the potential for a regenerative experience of the real. Howard writes, "without cameras / everything becomes the fringe / of our interior" (*Infinite* 21). The words speak to an understanding of the cosmos according to which there is no duality between subject and object. Instead, the outside is but the fringe of the inside, or the being of the self is but the lining of the cosmological fabric. What is the resting figure dreaming of and on what terms?

It is this cosmological vision and its implications for modes of being that colonial writers such as Henry Wadsworth Longfellow trampled in their eagerness to appropriate the dreams of others. In the second part of the book, "Of Hereafter Song," Howard satirizes Longfellow's *The Song of Hiawatha* (1855), a trochaic tetrameter faux epic addressing what Lenore Keeshig, Chippewas of Nawash Unceded First Nation, has called the theft of voice, and what Gerald Vizenor of the White Earth Nation of the Anishinaabe has described as "simulations of manifest manners": "how ironic that the most secure simulations are unreal sensations, and become the real without a referent to an actual tribal remembrance" (160). Through fakery, Longfellow pretends to tell an epic story on behalf of Indigenous people. At stake is the fact that, through centuries, the poem has paraded as a staple of poetry taught in North America and a source of knowledge. It comes across as a subterfuge combining assimilation and simulation—begetting assimilation—to coin a term. *Hiawatha* first recounts the moment of contact between Hiawatha and a Jesuit priest, then it proceeds to recast an Indigenous myth of origin into a Christian and patriarchal narrative:

> "As unto the bow the cord is,
> So unto the man is woman,
> Though she bends him, she obeys him,
> Though she draws him, yet she follows,
> Useless each without the other!" (Longfellow X, 1–5)

The faux story epic culminates in the triumphal killing of a deer without any sign of the Indigenous protocol of thanking life for providing sustenance. The twenty-two sections constituting *Hiawatha* read like a prototype for American narratives of masculinist superheroes with a relentless focus on the self-centred protagonist cut off from any sense of community. Longfellow's epic is a pastiche to start with, yet it claims precedence through naming and knowing. The pastiche is the reverse of *reading with*, as it enacts cultural and political extraction and leaves Indigenous culture fallow, as in "fictive tree fictive finch fictive treaty / rails and rails beyond" (*Infinite* 25). Howard's parody talks back to Longfellow by scratching the surface of his vinyl. Upping the ante on the meaning of Minnehaha—laughing waters—Howard writes,

> in some marsh
> of insufficient housing
> laughing
> all the time Christ thought me
> a fossil (47)

The continuous effects of extraction are captured by the *détournement* of the faux epic through the use of words that forces the sham narrative into material, social, economic, and political reality:

> I, Minnehaha, a small LOL
> fiction antecedent
> to quarry a nation
>
> I gave you this name then said
> *Erase it* (48)

Howard's mock-heroic is part of a larger web of references that includes Kent Monkman of the Fisher River Cree Nation. In encyclopedic revisions of Eurocentric painting, Monkman mixes satire with pastiches of Western iconology—from the colonial picturesque to Picasso's appropriative abstract art—to carry out a critique of Canadian colonization that includes the pricking of national consciousness, as in *The Daddies* (2016). Similarly, Howard's satire takes stock of an eternity of cultural extraction and land pollution, turning Longfellow's vision of the hereafter into a governance of genocidal hatred: "no plenitude abound no abhorrence / no abhor / original" (*Infinite* 33). The parody of the faux epic reveals the disfiguration of the land that Longfellow's text was commissioned to exalt.

Poems such as "Contact," "A Rude Inscription at the Top of Heaven," "Henceforth through the Forest," "Tender Pathos: A Denser, Blue Vapour" are marred by the clouds, tail ponds, landfills, dead rivers, and poisoned salmon streams that capitalistic extraction would like to wipe out through acts of duplicitous, collective amnesia. Howard's critique recalls *Tower* and *tarpaulin* (2018), an installation consisting of two clay sculptures in which Belmore exposes how a pervasive culture of extraction-based consumerism depends on the pauperism of Indigenous people and the erasure of their knowledge (Figure 11.2). On the left, a phallic tower of red earth thrusts its way through

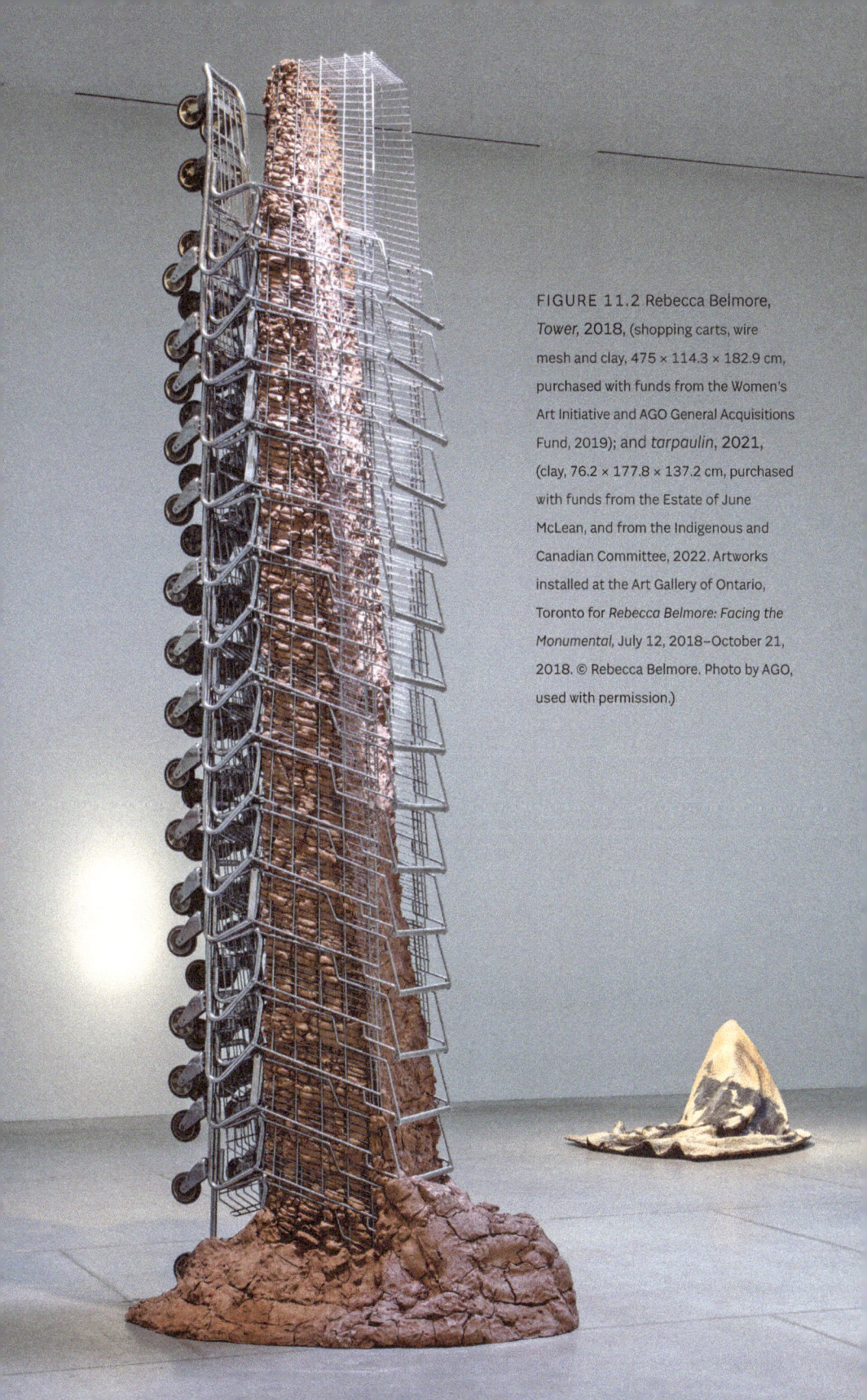

FIGURE 11.2 Rebecca Belmore, *Tower*, 2018, (shopping carts, wire mesh and clay, 475 × 114.3 × 182.9 cm, purchased with funds from the Women's Art Initiative and AGO General Acquisitions Fund, 2019); and *tarpaulin*, 2021, (clay, 76.2 × 177.8 × 137.2 cm, purchased with funds from the Estate of June McLean, and from the Indigenous and Canadian Committee, 2022. Artworks installed at the Art Gallery of Ontario, Toronto for *Rebecca Belmore: Facing the Monumental*, July 12, 2018–October 21, 2018. © Rebecca Belmore. Photo by AGO, used with permission.)

staggered shopping carts. The temporality of this sculpture revolves around colonial history—which Howard identifies as STANDARD TIME and its "missionary position" (*Infinite* 21)—and colonial extraction with "dark stars for lease in the divisible world / at all hours culling a distemper of infinity" (5). Below and on the right, a soiled tarpaulin rests on the ground in a conic shape, "its loamy brown folds rising up from the ground like rugged topography" (Adler), as if sheltering an invisible presence. The juxtaposing between the tower and the tarp reveals the abysmal gap between a consumerist-based economic system and the land-based hubs of governance that Betasamosake Simpson consistently invokes in all of her works. It also underscores the immense task of reconnecting to what Cree-Métis writer Emma LaRocque calls "an aboriginal ground to Aboriginal literature" (63).

Howard's poetics of resurgence revolves around a regenerative experience of time. Calling upon Anishinaabe spirituality and cosmology, Howard invokes the ancestral and ceremonial ritual of the Shaking Tent, striving to loosen the transgenerational grip of colonial power. In communication with the ancestral past, learning can be reconfigured through dream as a mode of knowing based on spiritual relations between land and bodies. In 1958 Ojibway painter Norval Morrisseau began to use acrylic on birch bark to paint *Ancestors Performing the Ritual of the Shaking Tent*.[4] The conic shape of Belmore's *tarpaulin* reappears in his painting, but this time it delineates the red hoods of Elders performing a sacred Midewewin ceremony, their drum sending off vibrations into the communal space that their three bodies create. Sheltering invisible presences, the Shaking Tent is delicately sketched in a round outline with an opening in the middle. In *The Thunderbird Poems* (2015), Anishinaabe-Ojibwe poet Armand Garnet Ruffo of Chapleau Cree First Nation presents an ekphrastic poem describing Morrisseau's painting, including the following lines:

> Bound hand and foot,
> [the Shaman] first calls Mikkinnuk, Turtle,
> to interpret for all the other spirits.
> ...
> if the ceremony is strong enough,
> Mikkinnuk will enter the tent
> And blow away the Shaman's bindings.

> Then whoever or whatever may be…follows,
> the spirits exuding such power
> that each response they give
> lifts the tent off the ground,
> wants to tear it from its mooring.
> A cacophony of voices slamming into it,
> all the force of a storm (17–18)

Invoking the ancestral ceremony of Ruffo's description, Howard's speaker creates the THINKTENT as a mobilizer of transformation from within the first and fourth parts of the book, both titled "Hyperboreal." Spurred by the energy of the ceremony, lines enact a shift from selves within doppler range to an experience of the present grounded in the spiritual and the sensorial. In an upsurge of energy, the speaker leaves behind standard time, as if floating in liquidity, as the recurrence of liquid consonants conveys: "I'm all in and over the limit / the limit, the eliminative, the lumens, the mens rea, the loom" (17). Howard uses experimental poetry as a vehicle for excess, "a desire for more than" (1), something bigger than normative frameworks of colonial control and domination.

At the outset of the book, the desire to shake off constraints to enter a different world arises. Lulled into a hypnagogic state, the speaker invokes an experience of the hyperbo-real, a means of engendering a hyperbolic arc of being that exceeds the real towards infinity:

> Spent shale, thigh haptic fisher, roe, river
> delta of sleep-inducing peptides abet our tent
> in a deep time course, in Venus retrograde
>
> we coalesce into the Cartesian floral pattern
> of heritage where I hunt along a creek as
> you pack bits of bone away within a system
>
> of conservation the site was discovered
> during construction of a new venous
> highway for stars birthing themselves

out of pyroclastic dust and telepathy
in the time zone of some desperate hour
when all our exits are terraformed

...

O creek, bleeding hills, census inveterate
let me sleep five more minutes just five
minutes more before we default on

eternity (1–2)

The oneiric experience inaugurates a place of *being with*: "all of us a congress / of selves a vibrational chorus...this potlatch we call the present moment" (16). The shift from census to the senses is crucial, as it is through a sensorial-spiritual cognition of the land that kin can be rekindled: "*in extremis* // hyperborean / all of us*" (24). The THINKTENT and its hyperboreal timespace are key to the transformation taking place side by side the description of the colonial disaster because it exceeds the normative and the extractive, and in reconnecting the self to land, asters, and kin, it ushers in processes of re-learning. The invocation to dream is an invocation to an expanded cognition of the world whereby the experience of time and space is not predicated on the Western subject-object split. Instead, "everything becomes the fringe / of our interior": "tender stairwell of mares / limbic foals all *miskwaa nibowin*" (*Infinite* 51). Dreamtime counters STANDARD TIME. As Anishinaabe poet Annharte of the Little Saskatchewan First Nation writes,

Takes five centuries for resurgence to take back
ancestral dreamtime before us forgotten women
use imperialist nostalgia to reconnect the power:

resistance revitalization regeneration revolt (94)

What Howard calls "a fur-lined oneirophrenia" (*Infinite* 51) taps into precognition, as in cognition *before* the Cartesian *ergo sum* and cognition *before* European contact. Dreaming of walking on the rivers flowing north from the Arctic Watershed and of experiencing the "ministry of the shaking dress" (47), the speaker sees into the human hearts of the Missing and Murdered Indigenous Women and Girls—*The Named and the Unnamed* (2002) of

Vancouver's Downtown Eastside to whom Belmore's video installation pays homage.

Dream and land thus work in concert and open up the way to ancestral knowledge and being. In a conversation with Shannon Webb-Campbell, Howard explains how poetry has "tied humanity in rhythm with the seasons of the land, a mnemonic, a way to be, an archive" ("In Conversation"). This vision of archiving land re-emerges in the book: "a river of somnolent fauns / heady, white-tailed apnea / our sleep a fossilized memory sequence" (*Infinite* 55). These lines occur in the poem "Foramen Magnum"—fantastic, polysonic terms that refer to the hole at the base of the skull where spinal cord and brain stem meet, and from which the spine stretches all the way down to the sacrum, the bone structure that links the two symmetrical parts of our hip bones to the coccyx and the sacral canal.

Through time, humans have shared a capacity to dream that their anatomical bone structure supports and that has translated into the visionary petroglyphs of the land. In regenerative lines that seek to honour those whose lives were sacrificed and whose bodies were surreptitiously buried, Cree poet Louise Bernice Halfe writes, "The prairie is full of bones. The bones stand and sing and I feel the weight of them as they guide my fingers on this page" (20). It is this kinship between land and body that generates the vision of Howard's "Some Americas" in which the Cordillera links the spine and vertebra of the speaker's body:

> The vertical interior of the Americas
> dreamt my spine, pulling through the eye
> of each vertebra a tactile thread
>
> connecting the nape of my neck
> to the foot of Tierra del Fuego (25)

These lines offer a counterpoint to the necrotic pall of the third part of the book, "Skullambient," by imagining an immemorial symbiosis between land and body. What should also catch the eye in these lines is the action attributed to land. Howard's poetry performs a reversal that calls into question a Western belief in the precedence of language over land and body—so that land is not the signified but the "lectern of origin" (*Infinite* 73). In the Shaking Tent ritual, the role of the translation of knowledge from the animal spirits to the community is assigned to the Mikkinnuk, and in "Thinktent" Howard reassigns the task of translating to her speaker:

> method amphibious
> of two minds
> that's the translator
> her task to receive
> the call that comes
> down the barrel
> of the future (16)

The THINKTENT is a time-site where utterances occur not from a grammar-based seat of knowledge but from ground-based cognition whereby animals and spirits speak. Thus, Howard's book engages with a process that effects a fundamental reversal of Western ontological and epistemological conceptions of being and knowing.[5]

This reversal signals the passage from a history of assimilation to an "anarchaeology of lichen," the title of a poem in the book (*Infinite* 51). The portmanteau word combines anarchy with an archaeology of the past that reconnects to land as antecedence. This reversal is equally illustrated by Belmore's two separate works that materialize a crucial understanding of the relationship between land and language. *Speaking to Their Mother* (1991) consists of a gigantic megaphone that Belmore transported to various locations to speak to Mother Earth. Twenty-six years later, Belmore created a series of sculptures that reversed the sense of communication: *Wave Sound* and its multilocational earpiece-like sculptures (*LandMarks* 2017) invite those who happen to be there to listen (Figure 11.3). Speech is common to both works, but while in the first instance humans address Earth, in the second instance land speaks to them as they listen.

Howard's poetics of antecedence can be reread in light of Belmore's installations. In both cases, resurgence coincides with land as the ground for meaning through exchange. In this context, the lines "what else is a river but the promise of a text / this is my delta some neural asymptote / where else could you cull such a clanging nerve?" (*Infinite* 56) upset a century of linguistics and philosophy that have sought to assert that language precedes our relation to the world. While some poems bear the trace of doubt and

FIGURE 11.3 Rebecca Belmore, *Wave Sound*, 2017. (Sculpture, *LandMarks2017Repères2017*, Partners in Art. Artwork © Rebecca Belmore. Photo by Kyra Kordoski, used with permission.)

Wittgensteinian questioning, others pivot towards a different conception of sense-making and agency that generates lines such as

> this account of light
> as an acquired characteristic
> became propositional
>
> just as every forest
> would come to speak to us
> as a verb (69)

Ruffo echoes this vision by saying "Loon shapes the canoe / in an elegant song / of loyalty / and beauty" (*Thunderbird Poems* 101), and Webb-Campbell

Anne Quéma   185

rejoins, "I am a body of land unlearning / what cannot be expressed. / Dig to find a physical knowing, ceremony" (*I Am* 32). This conception of knowledge destabilizes the subject of Western cognition by making the land the basis for measure as opposed to being an object of analysis:

> All night the blood moon measures the dilation
> of your pupil, pinprick or dinner plate
> in this plenum where our attention fails to die (*Infinite* 9)

The lines reverse the Cartesian theory of dioptrics and light refraction, illustrated by a diagram that Howard's book cover reproduces in a phantasmagoric mise en scène of a female écorché (with a bun)—her eyes pulled out her sockets and aligned with geometric lines of two triangles to establish coordinates.

To pause on the Cartesian diagram is to grasp the gap between a dualistic conception of cognition and a land-based cognition, as illustrated by Denesuline painter Alex Janvier of Cold Lake First Nations and his use of lines, planes, and colour to translate the rhythms of the mind in relation to the land—its curves and nodes of energy, as in his painting *Untitled* (1986) (Figure 11.4).[6] What brings together Belmore's *Fringe*, Morrisseau's *Thunderbird,* and Janvier's *Untitled* is the oneiric passage towards a symbiosis of being and cosmos which the first poem of Howard's book invokes in its desire for sleep. While Janvier's painting alludes to the horizontal and vertical lines of visual planes, his lines unfold as if in perpetual motion with brushstrokes veering and expanding on the canvas. These lines follow their own principle of relationality by acting as common seams between colour planes within which shapes are nestled: the outside is but the fringe of the inside. The tendril-like shapes recall the slow swirls of water and the crevices of a land that mirror the arborescent dendrites of precognition that Howard evokes in "Neural Cascade" (*Infinite* 3). To echo Howard, what else is the land but the promise of a painting? Outlined with delicate precision, Janvier's curvaceous lines share with Howard's practices of *détournement* the potential for generating new forms begetting renewed acts of interpretation that cannot exhaust the land as the lectern of origin.

The land has agency and is not lying passive waiting to be assessed, fenced, and drilled. In this context, the rhythm and motion of Howard's writing seek to escape the clutch of Western temporality and enact an

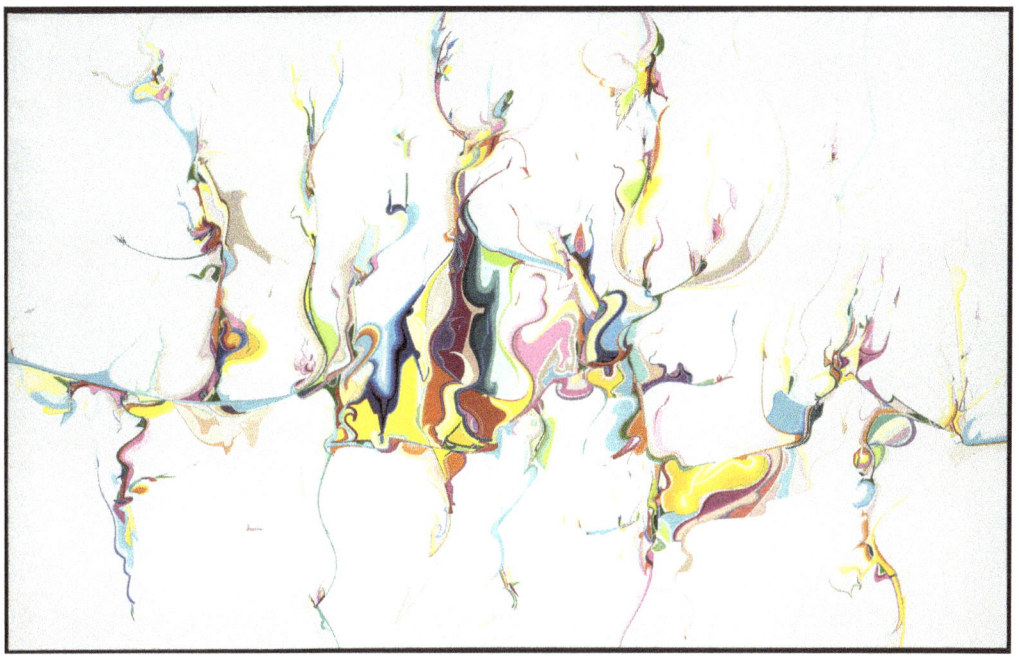

FIGURE 11.4 Alex Janvier, *Untitled*, 1986. (Acrylic on canvas, 165.1 × 266.7 × 6 cm, National Gallery of Canada, Ottawa. Artwork © Alex Janvier. Photo by NGC, used with permission.)

anarchaeology of lichen by drawing on dendrochronology, or the study of tree growth by dating the formation of tree rings. Ancestral memory is lodged in the kernel of trees, as it informs the experience and preservation of time around and in us. This attentiveness to time leads Howard to graft a narrative approach onto experimental poetry, which has tended to suspect narrative forms of trafficking in normative conceptions of the world, including neoliberal, patriarchal, racist, ableist, and classist storylines. However, the book does not give up on storylines, as it is inflected by a narrative rhythm that runs through stanzas.

Thus, in the first and fourth parts of the book, six prose poems recount memories from childhood and adolescence before the speaker's move from the boreal forest to the city. The poems are retrospective, as they deal with a bildungsroman of bruises and slights. Alternating with the elaborate and experimental aspects of other poems, they strike by their fluidity and compositional regularity. At the same time, a poem like "Boreal Swing" brings together storytelling and the visual patterns that concrete poetry practitioners cherish: anarchaeology, land, and dream coalesce as the lines on the page delineate the cavity of a moose belly hauled to tree trunks and within which the mother as child anchors herself as her father sends her swinging.

The narrative scope of the book is also at the source of Howard's extraordinary use of enjambment, which manages to combine a narrative drive with an experimental disruption of prosody. The narrative signs are subtle and almost imperceptible. For instance, starting with a capital letter, poems often display a sentence that runs its course from one stanza to the next. "Psychogeography" thus unfolds over five pages beginning with "From" (*Infinite* 61). In following the meandering of the sentences, readers *read with* the immediacy of sounds and the pivoting of meaning through enjambment. The lines thus materialize the uncertainty underlying reading while they also generate time—the time to read the lines. Drawn on by the impetus of enjambment, readers experience time somehow between suspension and duration as meaning is adumbrated through the pivoting onto the next line or the next stanza. This potentializing of meaning occurs from the get-go in the very first poem, "Terra Nova, Terraformed," which can be read as the exfoliation of three sentences signalled by the occurrence of three capital letters.

Finally, the desire to reconnect with kin also follows the rhythms of dendrochronological poetics. In "A Wake," the book suddenly switches from the citational cut-ups of scientific proliferation to a variation on a villanelle that both laments the loss of kin and longs for the awakening of a lost speech: "If I moan from an animal throat it is in hope you / will return to me what I lost learning to speak" (*Infinite* 12). This recombinant approach characterizes not only the "Revenant" suite (82–84), but also the relationship between the first and fourth parts of the poems, which bear the same title, "Hyperboreal." The iterative composition of Howard's book recalls Métis artist Christi Belcourt's extraordinary floral painting. In works such as *The Wisdom of the Universe* (2014), *The Conversation* (2002), or *This Painting Is a Mirror* (2012) (Figure 11.5),[7] exfoliation expands according to a delicate pattern of precise symmetry whereby the left side of the painting is the mirror image of the right side.

In her book, Howard refers to the "iterative gasket" (22), which sounds like a Dadaist fantasy. In fact, the term refers to Sierpinski's theory of fractal

FIGURE 11.5 Christi Belcourt, *This Painting Is a Mirror*, 2012. (Acrylic on canvas, 185.4 × 272 cm, Indigenous Art Collection, Crown-Indigenous Relations and Northern Affairs Canada. Artwork © Christi Belcourt. Photo by Lawrence Cook, used with permission.)

patterns through an infinite iterative serial pattern. This geometric pattern re-emerges in practices such as tessellation, weaving, and the Indigenous and Métis beadwork on which Belcourt's floral work draws. In describing beadwork, Dumont reveals how this ancestral knowledge of iterative patterns sustains a spiritual and relational process linking art and land: "the bead's colour makes no sound / but it is cranberry, moss, and fireweed / it is also wolf willow, sap, and sawdust / as well as Chickadee, Magpies, and Jackrabbit" (35). At the heart of Belcourt's floral compositions, whose roots to the land are always made apparent, are centuries of transmission of knowledge that has evolved into the complexity of reiterative beadwork. It is this specular pattern that holds Howard's book together, with in between Longfellow's faux epic and skullambient—the thievery and decay—threatening the beating pulse that symmetry harbours in its centre.

Notes

1. For an account of the creation of AvantGarden, see Taylor.
2. In "Against Assimilation I Rose into Poetry," Howard names and honours the Elder as James Douglas Wesley from Brunswick House First Nation, in Chapleau, Ontario.
3. Referring to Gerald Vizenor's concept of survivance, Howard writes, "The estate of my survivancy is poetry. In poetry I am never a victim. I am most alive" ("Against Assimilation" 32).
4. This painting can be seen on Carmen Robertson's website, https://www.aci-iac.ca/art-books/norval-morrisseau/style-and-technique.
5. In "North of Invention: The Shaking Tent with Liz Howard" and in a conversation with Klara Du Plessis, Liz Howard discusses the significance of the ritual for her poetics of writing.
6. All of which are reproduced in Greg Hill, pp. 147, 183, 189, 221, and 227.
7. See Nadia Kurd, pp. 56, 57, and 60.

Works Cited

Abel, Jordan. *Injun*. Talonbooks, 2016.

Abel, Jordan. *NISHGA*. McLelland and Stewart, 2020.

Abel, Jordan. *The Place of Scraps*. Talonbooks, 2013.

Adler, Solomon. "Rebecca Belmore: *Tarpaulin No. 1*, 2018." San Francisco Museum of Modern Art, June 2021. https://www.sfmoma.org/essay/rebecca-belmore-tarpaulin-no-1/. Accessed 19 Mar. 2022.

Annharte. *Indigena Awry*. New Star Books, 2015.

Bartlett, Cheryl, Murdena Marshall, and Albert Marshall. "Two-Eyed Seeing and Other Lessons Learned within a Co-learning Journey of Bringing Together Indigenous and Mainstream Knowledges and Ways of Knowing." *Journal of Environmental Studies*, vol. 2, 2012, pp. 331–340.

Belcourt, Christi. *The Conversation*. 2002, Thunder Bay Art Gallery, https://theag.ca/the-conversation/. Accessed 3 Mar. 2022.

Belcourt, Christi. *The Wisdom of the Universe*. 2014, The Art Gallery of Ontario, https://ago.ca/agoinsider/artists-statement-christi-belcourt-wisdom-universe. Accessed 3 Mar. 2022.

Belmore, Rebecca. *The Named and the Unnamed*. 2002, https://www.rebeccabelmore.com/the-named-and-the-unnamed/. Accessed 19 Mar. 2022.

Belmore, Rebecca. *Speaking to Their Mother*. 1991, https://www.rebeccabelmore.com/ayum-ee-aawach-oomama-mowan-speaking-to-their-mother-2/. Accessed 19 Mar. 2022.

Betasamosake Simpson, Leanne. *As We Have Always Done: Indigenous Freedom through Radical Resistance*. U of Minnesota P, 2017.

Betasamosake Simpson, Leanne. "Land Pedagogy: Nishnaabeg Intelligence and Rebellious Transformation." *Decolonization: Indigeneity, Education & Society*, vol. 3, no. 3, 2014, pp. 1–25.

Blaeser, Kimberly M. "Native Literature: Seeking a Critical Centre." *Learn, Teach, Challenge: Approaching Indigenous Literatures*, edited by Deanna Reder and Linda M. Morra, Wilfrid Laurier UP, 2016, pp. 231–238.

"Cascade." Illustration. https://www.researchgate.net/figure/Illustration-of-the-cascade-neural-network-architecture-used-in-this-work_fig3_261513051. Accessed 19 Mar. 2022.

Coulthard, Glen Sean. *Red Skin, White Masks: Rejecting the Colonial Politics of Recognition*. U of Minnesota P, 2014.

Dumont, Marilyn. *The Pemmican Eaters*. ECW Press, 2015.

Du Plessis, Klara. "In Conversation with Liz Howard." *carte blanche*, vol. 31, Fall 2017, https://carte-blanche.org/articles/conversation-liz-howard/. Accessed 19 Mar. 2022.

Elliott, Alicia. *A Mind Spread Out on the Ground*. Doubleday, 2019.

Episkenew, Jo-Ann. "Socially Responsible Criticism: Aboriginal Literature and the Literary Cannon." *Introduction to Indigenous Literary Criticism in Canada*, edited by Heather MacFarlane and Armand G. Ruffo, Broadview Press, 2015, pp. 188–200.

Halfe, Louise Bernice. *The Poetry of Sky Dancer Louise Bernice Halfe,* selected and introduced by David Gaertner, Wilfrid Laurier UP, 2018.

Howard, Liz. "Against Assimilation I Rose into Poetry." *Avant Canada: Poets, Prophets, Revolutionaries*, edited by Gregory Betts and Christian Bök, Wilfrid Laurier UP, 2018, pp. 29–35.

Howard, Liz. *Infinite Citizen of the Shaking Tent*. Penguin, 2015.

Howard, Liz. "North of Invention: The Shaking Tent with Liz Howard." *Poets House*, 17 Oct. 2019. Reading. https://poetshouse.org/event/north-of-invention-the-shaking-tent-with-liz-howard/. Accessed 19 Mar. 2022.

Hill, Greg A., ed. *Alex Janvier*. Musée des beaux-arts du Canada, Ottawa, 2016.

Janvier, Alex. https://www.alexjanvier.com/. Accessed 19 Mar. 2022.

Keeshig, Lenore. "Stop Stealing Native Stories." *Introduction to Indigenous Literary Criticism in Canada*, edited by Heather MacFarlane and Armand G. Ruffo, Broadview Press, 2015, pp. 34–36.

Kurd, Nadia. *Christi Belcourt*. Goose Lane Editions, 2020.

LaRocque, Emma. "Teaching Aboriginal Literature: The Discourse of Margins and Mainstreams." *Learn, Teach, Challenge: Approaching Indigenous Literatures*, edited by Deanna Reder and Linda M. Morra, Wilfrid Laurier UP, 2016, pp. 55–72.

Longfellow, Henry Wadsworth. *The Song of Hiawatha*. 1855. *Maine Historical Society Website*, 2000–2022, https://www.hwlongfellow.org/poems_poem.php?pid=296. Accessed 19 Mar. 2022.

Mbembe, Achille. "Necropolitics." Trans. Libby Meintjes. *Public Culture* vol. 15, no. 1, 2003, pp. 11–40.

mclennan, rob. "A Short Interview with Liz Howard." *jacket2*, 2015. https://jacket2.org/commentary/short-interview-liz-howard. Accessed 19 Mar. 2022.

Monkman, Kent. *The Daddies*. 2016, https://www.kentmonkman.com/painting/2017/1/9/the-daddies. Accessed 19 Mar. 2022.

Morrisseau, Norval. Ancestors Performing the Ritual of the Shaking Tent, c. 1958–61. *Norval Morrisseau, Life & Work, Carmen Robertson, Art Canada Institute*, https://www.aci-iac.ca/art-books/norval-morrisseau/style-and-technique/. Accessed 19 Mar. 2022.

Rice, Waubgeshig. *Moon of the Crusted Snow*. ECW Press, 2018.

Rimbaud, Arthur. "Voyelles." *Poésies: Une Saison en Enfer, Illuminations*, prefaced by René Char, edited by Louis Forestier, Gallimard, 1999, p. 114.

Robertson, Carmen. *Norval Morrisseau: Life & Work*. Art Canada Institute, https://www.aci-iac.ca/art-books/norval-morrisseau/. Accessed 19 Mar. 2022.

Ruffo, Armand Garnet. "Poetry, Place, and Indigeneity: Dialogue between Liz Howard and Armand Garnet Ruffo." *The Walrus*, 2 Jan. 2019, https://thewalrus.ca/poetry-place-and-indigenous-identity/. Accessed 19 Mar. 2022.

Ruffo, Armand Garnet. *The Thunderbird Poems*. Harbour Publishing, 2015.

Styres, Sandra. "Literacies of Land: Decolonizing Narratives, Storying, and Literature." *Indigenous and Decolonizing Studies in Education*, edited by Linda Tuhiwai Smith, Eve Tuck, and K. Wayne Yang, Routledge, 2019, pp. 24–37.

Taylor, Jess. "'Make it a Collaborative Enterprise': Liz Howard on AvantGarden." *The Town Crier*, 5 Oct. 2013. https://ex-puritan.ca/blog/make-it-a-collaborative-enterprise-liz-howard-on-avantgarden. Accessed 30 Mar. 2024.

Vizenor, Gerald. "Postindian Warriors." 1994. *Learn, Teach, Challenge: Approaching Indigenous Literatures*, edited by Deanna Reder and Linda M. Morra, Wilfrid Laurier UP, 2016, pp. 155–167.

Webb-Campbell, Shannon. *I Am a Body of Land*. Book*hug, 2019.

Webb-Campbell, Shannon. "In Conversation with Liz Howard." CWILA, 2016. https://cwila.com/in-conversation-with-liz-howard/.

12
Breathing in the "Pulmonary Commons"

Conspiring against Canada's "Settler Atmospherics" in Rita Wong's undercurrent

STEPHANIE OLIVER

PUBLISHED IN 2015, *undercurrent* is a poetic exploration of Rita Wong's commitment to water. A work of ecopoetry, *undercurrent* takes up concepts from feminist new materialisms while centring Indigenous worldviews that originally gave them voice. Indebted to the Indigenous water keepers with whom she does activist work on the unceded territory of the Tsleil-Waututh, Musqueam, Squamish, and Stó:lō Nations (Wong, *undercurrent* 89), *undercurrent* critiques the intersecting micro and macro impacts of settler colonialism, resource extraction, petrocapitalism, and environmental injustice—with their disproportionate effects on Indigenous Peoples, racialized communities, the poor, and women—by developing a poetics and ethics of water. Emphasizing the detrimental effects of treating water as a commodity resource, Wong calls upon "(un)settlers" like herself to combat colonial capitalist resource logics and engage in a "participatory water ethics" that honours water as a life-giving ancestor. Inspired by Stó:lō writer Lee Maracle's words, "We do not own the water. The water owns itself" (qtd. in Wong, *undercurrent* 5), Wong's decolonial feminist ethics honours water as a facilitator of interdependencies between human and non-human beings that offers valuable lessons about reciprocity and respect (Wong, "Waters as" 210).

Unsurprisingly, most scholarship on *undercurrent* focuses on Wong's water ethics.[1] Much of this work takes up the concept of the "hydrocommons," "that which we share through a water-based ecology, including plants, plankton, rivers, even the moist breath that we exhale or transpire into the environment" (Wong, "Waters as" 216). Developing what Heather Milne calls a "poetics of interconnectivity," Wong's hydrocommons underlines humans' role in environmental crises while decentring "the human," de-anthropomorphizing nature, and emphasizing the raw materiality of bodies embedded in networks that are at once locally situated and globally connected, multiple and dispersed (125, 129). This essay builds on this work by situating Wong's water ethics in relation to her poetic investigation of breath and atmosphere, realms of exchange inextricably linked to water. While water is Wong's focus, air constitutes an undercurrent in her work that deserves closer attention. As a white settler living on Treaty 6 territory in Alberta—a cornerstone of the Canadian petrostate examined in Wong's poems—I argue for a more fulsome understanding of Wong's ethics and poetics by considering her investigation of the "pulmonary commons," a set of striated atmospheric relations shaped by airborne toxins that, like the neocolonial structures that produce them, often evade perception. If, as Rob Nixon argues, slow forms of chemical and radiological violence are particularly invisible (6), then attending to how these and other forms of atmospheric violence impact the hydrocommons, and vice versa, is necessary for understanding Wong's poetry and how settler colonial violence works atmospherically.

To theorize the pulmonary commons, this essay puts *undercurrent* in conversation with Paiute scholar Kristen Simmons's concept of "settler atmospherics." Reflecting on how law enforcement deployed atmospheric weapons to debilitate Indigenous water protectors at Standing Rock, Simmons suggests that air is a site of colonial violence. Building on Kahnawake Mohawk scholar Audra Simpson's discussion of the "strangulated political order" of Indigenous nations (qtd. in Simmons) and Christina Sharpe's claim that anti-Black racism is as "pervasive *as* climate" (106), Simmons contends that "settler atmospherics are the normative and necessary violences found in settlement—accruing, adapting, and constricting indigenous and black life in the US settler state" (Simmons). These violences enact a "relational severing" that not only asphyxiates political resistance to state power, but also enacts "toxic strangulations—social and chemical"—that disproportionately affect Indigenous nations and marginalized communities in ways that are difficult to trace and often remain visible, as "we are trained not to see them" (Simmons).

Given atmospheric phenomena like toxic drift, a process by which pollutants are carried "away" by winds beyond the realm of corporate or state responsibility, Wong's poems explore how the toxic dynamics of settler atmospherics emerge in relation to bodies, geographies, and settler colonial contexts embedded within global and planetary networks. Her poetry maps the multi-scalar dynamics of settler atmospherics in Canada by linking large-scale forms of toxic strangulation—such as the burning of fossil fuels, accumulation of airborne chemicals, and toxic drift of radioactive waste—to small-scale inhalations and exhalations, including the basis of carbon-based life: breath. A relational process that is often idealized—and taken for granted—when unconscious, breathing connects porous bodies to the hydrocommons and pulmonary commons. As Simmons argues, breath's "porous relationality" attunes us to how others can and cannot breathe, thereby opening us up to new ways of relating. Breathing thus embodies a "relational ethics based on reciprocity and obligations with the land and other-than-humans" (Simmons). Noting that the Latin root of *conspire* means breathing together, Simmons asserts, "We need to conspire to strategize logics of agitation, which displace and unsettle." Breathing together enacts a conspiratorial ethics based on reciprocity that "stage[s] the grounds for a collective reimagining" of an "atmospheric otherwise" (Simmons).

Breath links breathing beings to the water cycle, embodying reciprocal ethics at a cellular level. Yet the vital connection between water and breath often goes unacknowledged, not only because of the separation of "cycles" in Western science, but also because of the tendency to idealize unconscious breath, a privilege available to few in settler atmospheres. Wong's poetry suggests that modern air, like Jamie Linton's concept of "modern water," is structured by power. When confined to the privileged realm of the unconscious and imperceptible, breathing's reciprocal ethics serve capitalism and state power. These issues gained global attention in 2020 with the murder of George Floyd, a Black man murdered by Minneapolis police officers pinning him down and kneeling on his throat. Floyd's last words—"I can't breathe"—became a rallying cry for the Black Lives Matter movement amidst a COVID-19 pandemic that has disproportionately impacted Black, Indigenous, and marginalized communities. Floyd's words echo those of other Black people killed by police such as Eric Garner, a man who suffered from chronic asthma; his 2014 death informs Sharpe's framing of anti-Black racism as a pervasive climate.

Arguing that poetry, with its connection to orality, is an ideal site for investigating the often unconscious act of breathing, I contend that *undercurrent* makes visible the toxic relations that structure Canada's settler atmospheres and gives voice to a pulmonary commons. Yet Wong also underscores how different modes of perception are needed to detect that which eludes vision and hearing, senses privileged within Western hierarchies of knowledge. Attending to diverse forms of perception from smell to atmospheric weight, Wong's poetry deploys breath strategically, thematically and formally defamiliarizing breath's "porous relationality" to attune readers to their own breathing patterns and open up new ways of relating in the pulmonary commons.

Linking the Hydrocommons and the Pulmonary Commons

For Wong, the notion of the commons is inextricably tied to breath. In a 2012 essay, she writes, "In the face of widely dispersed contamination that we share through winds, watersheds, and food networks, I find it increasingly urgent to respect and attend to the commons, by which I mean shared stewardship, management, and use by a community" formed through interdependence and cooperation ("Cultivating" 533). Wong continues, "As we inhale and exhale, we are arguably sharing a commons right now, one atmosphere, one planet, on which we all rely as we breathe" (533). Wong began giving voice to the pulmonary commons in "parent(h)et(h)ical breath," a poem in her 2007 collection *forage*. Extending Roy Miki's notion of the "poetics of apprehension," a phrase that describes Wong's critique of capitalism's plastic and GMO experiments on unconsenting bodies (185), I read this poem as an attempt to "apprehend" the pulmonary commons, or know it in a felt sense ("Apprehension"), through breath. The speaker, a "perambulatory witness to neo-colonial streets in saltwater city, / Aboriginal Columbia," situates herself in relation to "a pulmonary commons called planet" and

> a breath that met another in the commotion of nouns, gerunds, subordinate clauses cluttering the historical air: *whoo-oosh! ping!* (55)

The speaker bears witness to neocolonialism through walking, an act that increases her pace of breathing and attunes her to her surroundings. As Andrew Kay argues, "to foreground breathing as a major event in acts of perception is to involve the body in the task of apprehending the world" through "felt interpretation" (568). Perambulation encourages a felt sense of the link between the macro (the planetary) and the micro (breath). The pulmonary commons foregrounds a set of relations premised on breathing together amidst a clamor of speech and syntax that visually mimics and orally requires exhalations of breath ("*whoo-oosh!*"). The poem enacts a "conspirational understanding of poetry" by formally signalling physiological cues for readers to instantiate and complete (Kay 578). While *forage* offers a preliminary exploration of the pulmonary commons, *undercurrent* delves deeper into the ethics of breath in a pulmonary commons under threat.

Wong opens *undercurrent* with "Pacific Flow," a poem that outlines the speaker's humble approach to learning the so-called syntax of water. The poem establishes the speaker's commitment to the hydrocommons, suggesting that "water has a syntax" that she is "still learning" (9), and underscores the fundamental role that marine organisms play in supporting the pulmonary commons:

> saltiness grows over eons   plankton provides half our oxygen
>   what we cannot see   matters as kin (9)

Using a lowercase "i" that destabilizes the Eurocentric, humanist "I" associated with Romantic lyric poetry (L'Abbé), the speaker acknowledges her reliance on watery kin, giving voice to water and making visible the microscopic organisms that breathers rely on for oxygen; the collective pronoun includes readers in this shared breath. Abandoning punctuation that would conventionally signal when to breathe, the space in the middle of each line formally creates "breathing room" for readers while thematically drawing attention to how breath is made possible by unseen kin.

Breath, like water, constitutes a sacred bond between humans and nonhumans in *undercurrent*. Invoking the formal language used by governments and corporations to sever relationships, enshrine colonial laws, and uphold legal contracts framing Indigenous land as property rich in resources to be extracted, "Declaration of Intent" declares the speaker's allegiance to water rather than the settler colonial state: "let the colonial borders be seen for the pretensions that they are / i hereby honour what the flow of water teaches us" (14). The speaker describes water as

> a sacred bond, embedded in our plump, moist cells
> in our breaths that transpire to return to the clouds that gave us
> life through rain (14)

Just as the fluidity of water defies containment by borders that have been imposed on Indigenous Peoples and their lands (Milne 131), the diffuseness of air challenges artificial barriers that attempt to contain it. The poem honours the flow of both water and air by suggesting that water's sacred bond—an "ethical promise or imperative...premised on radical interconnectivity across life forms" (125)—is embedded in "our breaths," a phrase that implicates readers in a shared pulmonary commons. The long, word-laden lines describing this bond build on themselves by repeating "that," "in," "to"—a conjunction and two prepositions, parts of speech that link and show relationships, respectively. Offering little room to breathe, the enjambed lines develop a syntax and breathing pattern that emphasize reciprocal relationships between cells, breath, and water, enacting how water feeds back into the atmosphere as clouds and rain. Notably, transpire—meaning "to breathe through or across"—refers to an event that has occurred and a process of becoming known, particularly "by obscure channels, or in spite of secrecy being intended" ("Transpire"). With no end-stopped lines and few caesuras, readers transpire to breathe through or across the lines with little opportunity to catch their breaths. Like water's fluid syntax, the diffuse syntax of air creates a felt sense of readers' implication in this bond, drawing attention to the often-obscured channels that link porous bodies in the pulmonary commons.

The speaker's declaration models how readers can reflect on their responsibilities as part of this bond. Emphasizing how there is no way to separate ourselves from the problem in an interconnected world, the poem states variations of the phrase: "because i am part of the problem i can also become part of the solution" (15). As Alec Follett argues, the lowercase "i" creates a bond between speaker and reader, implicating the latter in "the problem," while the abstract diction allows people in different subject positions "to locate themselves within these broad categories so that they can work toward a solution" (55). Wong models this process in the acknowledgements by locating herself, like the Chinese Canadian poet-speaker, as "an (un)settler whose ancestors hail from the Pearl River delta" (*undercurrent* 89). According to Gillian Roberts, Wong's use of the term "(un)settler" "invoke[s] the position of settler while acknowledging the ambivalent position of racialized Canadians with respect to colonization in Canada and alluding to her efforts to work as an ally to Indigenous peoples" (79). As the poem's speaker states, "i will learn through immersion" (14). *undercurrent* creates a felt sense of this learning by thematically and formally immersing readers in the pulmonary commons.

"Flush" explores how people break these sacred bonds through daily activities large and small. In a lengthy opening sentence that flows from one line to the next like the "unstoppable rush" of rain, the speaker praises raindrops as "gifts from the clouds, pooled over centuries and channeled to power us" (42). This take on the ode paints an image of how age-old rainwater is piped into homes through hidden infrastructure that consumers rely on for survival. The speaker honours rain as the "anonymous agent of all that we, unwitting beneficiaries, do" (42). The image of water's journey defamiliarizes how it is transformed from a life force into H_2O or "modern water," an abstract resource often taken for granted with no regard for its source or destination (Linton qtd. in Wong, "Waters as" 209). This relational severing obscures people's obligations to water. Challenging convenient forms of settler forgetting that characterize the extraction and consumption of water-as-resource, the speaker reminds unconscious consumers that water does not simply appear in all homes at all times.[2] Water bears the burden of atmospheric waste carried by rain on our behalf. Modelling a different relationship that acknowledges water's connection to the pulmonary commons, the speaker "refus[es] the inertia of amnesia" and "welcome[s] the memory of rain / sliding into sink and teacup, throat and bladder, tub and toilet" (42), embracing the material traces of the commons that accumulate in teacups, throats, tubs, and toilets. The alliterated objects represent everyday interactions with water,

> bountiful abundant carrier of what everyone emits into the
> clouds, be that exhale or smoke, belch or chemical combustion,
> flame or fragrance (42)

Water bears the weight of atmospheric emissions, from the seemingly minor effects signalled by single syllable words such as "belch" to large-scale forms of violence encompassed by multisyllabic terms such as "chemical combustion." Though everyone emits, not everyone emits equally, nor are the effects of these emissions equally distributed. Punctuated by caesuras, the list of emissions offers numerous places to pause and breathe, inviting readers to situate themselves in relation to their own exhalations large and small. As Wong reminds readers, rain "gives it all back to us in spates" (42); the reciprocal relationship between water and air will inevitably confront breathers with the impacts of these emissions.

Wong examines fantasies of containment and regulation more closely in "for Gregoire Lake *which way does the wind blow?*" Another take on the ode, the speaker expresses gratitude for Gregoire Lake, a body of water downstream from the tar sands, on a healing walk. The poem juxtaposes the speaker's encounter with the lake on the left side of the page with an italicized list of chemicals on the right. The titular question *"which way does the wind blow?"* gestures toward the wind's powerful yet unpredictable role in spreading airborne toxins that governing bodies purportedly contain:

in the fresh morning	*hexavalent chromium*
i dip my hands into you tentatively	*arsenic*
thankful to camp on your shores	*aluminum*
amidst mosquitoes, mud & grass	*zinc*
knowing you hold airborne toxins	*thallium*
from the tar sands	*nickel*
though you look placid, peaceful	*dibenzothiophenes*
you hold bitter, bitumized depths	*phenanthrenes*
protracted violence has been done to you	*fluoranthenes*
to your fish, your birds, your dwellers	*benzanthracenes* (68)

The space between the columns formally signals the gap between the lake's "placid, peaceful" surface and its "bitter, bitumized depths" while linking the columns through enjambment. When the poem is read left to right, the chemicals disrupt the speaker's story (Follett 54). The toxins also appear when readers might otherwise breathe, inviting them to consider the chemical makeup of the air around them.

Though the lake is polluted, the speaker holds it in her hands, just as the poem holds space to make these toxins visible. The lines "a lake is surrounded / though not usually in this way" (Wong, *undercurrent* 68) use military language to suggest that oil companies hold the lake hostage, exploiting it for water-intensive bitumen extraction and polluting it with toxins that threaten its ability to support life. The poem refutes industrialism's "capital-intensive" fantasy of containment which, as Kim Fortun argues, relies on an "essentialist, functionalist logic that privileges what goes on inside...fencelines" and frames pollution as an "externality" with links to industrial production that can be confused or denied (qtd. in Ahmann and Kenner 420–421). Generated from a 2011 Government of Alberta report on "contamination of the Athabasca River System by Oil Sands operations" (Wong, *undercurrent* 68), the poem's list of chemicals underscores toxicology's limits as an industrial discipline that serves corporate technoscience by decontextualizing chemicals, studying them in isolation, and constructing risk assessments that fail to capture how toxins interact, spread, and accumulate.[3] Centring more nuanced forms of perception disavowed by risk assessment tools, the poem places the tar sands' airborne toxins in context, situating the chemicals in relation to their source and highlighting their impact on the lake and its human and non-human inhabitants. Dispelling fantasies of purity that support fictions of containment, the final lines—"even in our compromised states / we remember why we are here" (68)—emphasize Gregoire Lake's inherent value and expose the toxic relations of morally compromised nation-states while implicating both speaker and reader through the collective pronoun. By acknowledging her own complicity and opening up to new ways of relating to both the lake and the airborne toxins, the speaker demonstrates how to contribute to "the solution" while still being part of "the problem."

Immersed in Settler Atmospheres

For Wong, immersion becomes a key poetic strategy for capturing embodied relationships with air.[4] In "Immersed," Wong uses anaphora, the repetition of the same phrase at the beginning of each line, to immerse readers rhetorically and visually in a list of atmospheric phenomena:

> immersed in chlorinated water
> immersed in formaldehyde off-gas

> immersed in car exhaust
> immersed in the oxygen produced by oceanic plankton
> immersed in windy chinook
> immersed in barbecue aroma
> immersed in smog
> immersed in someone's sneeze
> immersed in the oxygen produced by cedar
> immersed in the oxygen produced by fir
> immersed in the oxygen produced by hemlock (32)

Here, life-giving oxygen mixes with life-threatening chemicals and other elements of everyday life. As Hannah Boast notes, Wong's poems are sometimes "strangely agentless" in that they often lack pronouns, which "emphasizes our lack of control" over our porous bodies (8). In this poem, the lack of a subject, combined with the past participle "immersed," contributes to a felt sense of being immersed in the material conditions of settler atmospheres. Notably, the poem represents marine organisms and trees as oxygen producers but places each noun at the end of the line, reinforcing how flora and fauna are not always respected as agential life forces. Wong invites readers to consider the unnamed sources of the other emissions and contemplate their own contributions to settler atmospheres. Jean-Thomas Tremblay argues that "as breathers, we take in particles that are nourishing *and* toxic—often beyond discernment. When being conscious of our breathing implies being conscious of our vulnerability or exposure to risk, we must perform breathing as a gesture that no longer feels natural" (223). The immersive effect of accumulating lines on the page denaturalizes breathing while defamiliarizing the nourishing and toxic blend of Canada's settler atmospheres. With no punctuation to suggest a breathing pattern, readers must decide where to breathe, thereby gaining a deeper awareness of their relationship to breath in this context. The poem concludes: "immersed in the irrepressible commons, come on! / immersed in q'élstexw" (33). The final call to the commons and reference to the Stó:lō word for return suggest that the toxic relations of settler atmospherics cannot repress the reciprocal ethics of the pulmonary commons (Stó:lō Research and Resource Management Centre / Stó:lō Nation). As Max Karpinski argues, Wong does not envision a romantic return to a pure pastoral past (220); in this instance, she concludes with an Indigenous word rooted in the land where she lives to suggest that returning is an ongoing process, an act ("come on!") and set of relations in which we are all immersed.

"Remembering the Future" represents burning fossil fuels as a form of environmental violence tied to the colonial occupation of settler atmospheres. The poem depicts car exhaust spreading through the air:

> as traffic empties into gasoline chambers into the atmosphere
>
> expanding into gas eight times its liquid weight (30)

Here fossil fuels enact "atmospheric imperialism," to use Martin Mahony's term (32), exceeding containment and continually expanding as the repetition of "into" suggests. The language of physics and expansive syntax accumulates, mimicking and producing what Nicole M. Merola calls "doom's affective quality: weight" (33). While the poem appears to offer readers "breathing room" in the ample visual space between lines, conceptually these spaces fill with invisible emissions. The next lines, "mutual promise unmet though embedded within our / compromised states" (30), implicate speaker and reader in a familiar pun, reinforcing the notion that there is an ongoing failure to fulfil the responsibilities required by breath's sacred bond. Drivers are implicated in the atmospheric imperialism of the morally compromised nation-state, which consistently breaks promises with Indigenous nations and devastates Indigenous land through resource extraction. For Wong, this scenario involves "hedging bets": "the bottom line, the one on which we all traverse, is as free / as the quiet air you breathe" (30). Referring to the weighted line of a fishing net, a "bottom line" describes a final balance on an account and a minimal acceptable standard; it also describes the crux of an argument or concluding point in a debate ("Bottom line"). Burning fossil fuels is a deadly gamble that exceeds corporate discourses of profit and political arguments about energy transitions. Survival—free breath— is at stake. A bottom line is also a boundary; governing bodies may claim to set boundaries by containing toxins, but atmospheric imperialism's tactic of occupying settler atmospheres is predicated on unfettered expansion.

Taking an even more expansive view, "Lupus, a Doubled Being" frames air, like water, as a system of global transportation that serves corporate capitalism in a way that "doubles back" on itself, creating a feedback loop that toxifies the pulmonary commons. Alluding to the wolf (*lupa*) that nursed the founder of Rome and his twin, the poem suggests that autoimmune disorders like lupus, in which the body's immune system attacks its tissues and organs, are the price of so-called progress, or the "dangerous fruit of empire" (52). As part of the global supply chain, this fruit is "born on wind & wave," confusing kidneys "filtering the truck of steamships, containers" (52). This

> precious cargo is double-edged, sore with steady emissions
> stolen from the source, from underground chambers
> taken in industrial mission & precision (52)

Alluding to the toxic accumulation of chemicals known as the "body burden," the speaker advocates for an energy transition to transform global capitalism's neocolonial relations:

>   transition
> to be shed like a stiff vinyl coat that no longer fits
> & doesn't breathe. (52)

A vinyl coat ostensibly offers protection against the elements, but like capitalist resource logics, this petroleum-based product smothers instead of protects, severing reciprocal relationships with the environment. This enjambed section is one of the only moments in *undercurrent* where the word "breathe" is followed by a period. After a lengthy sentence that spans fourteen lines, the period directs readers to catch their breaths, suggesting that only when we shed our addiction to fossil fueled capitalism will we be able to breathe and engage in life-giving reciprocal relationships. Contrasting the opening image of air as a global transportation system, the poem concludes with a powerful chorus that addresses readers directly: "*We are your very breath, the ancestral memory you inhale and the promises you exhale. We are the protocol of life, the Council of All Beings*" (53). This collective voice of the pulmonary commons reminds readers of the sacred bond between human and non-human beings, reiterating that each breath is a promise that deserves honour and respect.

Poetry and Perceptibility

For Wong, playing with language, syntax, and breathing patterns is a key strategy for making atmospheric violence perceptible. "Fresh Ancient

Ground" playfully exposes oil companies' toxic emissions, both chemical and rhetorical:

> "overburden removal" leaves poisonous polycyclic aromatic
>   hydrocarbons, pah
> the PAHs stink—swallow them and die a slow cancerous death (17)

Wong's evocation of the industry term "overburden removal" signals how, as Stephanie LeMenager argues, oil companies rhetorically transform "multiform, multipersoned life" that supports boreal forest to an abstract "burden" that "must be removed" to access bitumen (176). Writing against the logic of extraction, which, as Michi Saagiig Nishnaabeg scholar Leanne Betasamosake Simpson argues, "removes all of the relationships that give whatever is being extracted meaning" (qtd. in Boast 15), Wong deploys breath and sound to expose the multilayered effects of such violence. The poem's "noxious playfulness" puns on death with "*pah*—small case—the noise of exhalation, the poet's irritation, even disgust" and "PAH, a killing toxin" (LeMenager 176–177). The protracted plosive sound "pah" also requires an emphatic exhalation of breath—and therefore carbon dioxide—that draws attention to the speaker's and readers' implication in carbon emissions. By suggesting that the innocuous acronym PAHs "stink" and insisting on "poisonous polycyclic aromatic hydrocarbons" instead, Wong evokes sound and stench to expose how industry rhetoric mobilizes abstract language to obscure the deadly chemicals and lies that people "swallow." Though the speaker states, "*I have no words big enough for the horror I feel when I see and smell the tar sands*" (18), Wong attempts to capture this feeling and implicate readers through word play, breath, and multisensory language, demonstrating how poetry lends itself to perceiving extractivism's toxic relations in new ways.

Wong takes a different approach in "A Magical Dictionary from Bitumen to Sunlight," a poem that plays with the dictionary format to question singular, decontextualized notions of truth, objectivity, and knowledge. Juxtaposing words on the left side of the page with potential definitions on the right, the poem suggests that words do not exist in a logical vacuum but rather evoke multilayered meanings rooted in material contexts. The dictionary form authenticates these experiences and illuminates the "magic" of non-human ancestors, while Wong's refusal to organize definitions in alphabetical order suggests that the environment has its own cycles that resist imposed human structures. The poem redefines bitumen, a scientific term for distilled crude oil:

> bitumen   : buried ancestors, unearthed & burned to expand
>   the ocean
>   : pitched sacrifice zone wherever it bubbles up,
>   hellishly excavated (29)

Here bitumen is not inherently toxic; rather, the problem lies in toxic neocolonial capitalist relations that transform ancestors into resources to be violently extracted and burned.[5] Like Wong's magical dictionary, plants play a role in challenging these toxic relations, albeit in a different way. "Carries" is defined in two ways: "one act of the written word" and "a sapling song courtesy of xylem, transpires to / proliferate in the ether" (28). This definition resignifies xylem—the technical term for plant tissues that transport water and nutrients from roots to stems to leaves ("Xylem")—as a "sapling song." Like poetry, plants "carry" diverse forms of knowledge: they breathe through or across obscure channels, cleansing the air of carbon dioxide and producing oxygen for the pulmonary commons. By honouring the life-giving magic of non-human beings often viewed through an abstract scientific lens, Wong challenges conventional ways of knowing that define toxic neocolonial capitalist relations.

Decolonial Feminist Ethics and Its Alterlives

While many of Wong's immersive poems may appear to be agentless, other poems honour agents of change, creativity, and collective resistance—namely, Indigenous women, who have long cultivated a decolonial feminist ethics in the pulmonary commons and provide models for "(un)settlers" to follow. *undercurrent* thus responds to the need, articulated by Métis scholar Michelle Murphy, for "words, protocols, and methods that...honor the inseparability of bodies and land" while "grappl[ing] with the expansive chemical relations of settler colonialism that entangle life forms" (497). The poem "Dada-Thay"—Dene for "death rock"—considers how Dene women in northern Saskatchewan challenge one of the most notorious forms of toxic strangulation in settler atmospheres: radioactive waste leaking from uranium mines. As Nixon argues, the slowly unfolding, accumulating effects of radiological violence are "driven inward, somatized into cellular dramas of mutation" that remain "largely unobserved, undiagnosed, and untreated... particularly in the bodies of the poor" (6) as well as Indigenous Peoples and other racialized populations, as Simmons also suggests. While Wong "makes this 'slow violence' visible by drawing it into dialogue with the 'spectacular' violence of the nuclear war it enables" (Boast 12), she does not try to represent the spectacle of atomic warfare that links Dene and Japanese communities. Rather, the poem takes an expansive view, acknowledging the radiological damage of settler atmospheres while focusing on meaningful ways of relating to this slow violence. The poem centres the mourning Dene widows of husbands "lost to the brutal industry":

> they understand responsibility
> when western governments don't—
> they apologize to the survivors
> of Hiroshima
> & Nagaski for death
> rock taken from their homelands
> without knowledge
> of the consequences (Wong, *undercurrent* 70)

Wong's poetics of interconnectivity suspends damage, emphasizing instead how the women model a way of relating to this violence that differs from "western governments." In contrast, Saskatchewan, "the Saudi Arabia of uranium mining," continues to do damage,

> digging & burning up
> what rightfully belongs to the future
> leaking its deadly mess
> into our nervous, drenched bodies (71)

Though the women's nations and bodies have been compromised by the state, this does not preclude them from apologizing to victims located a world away in an expression of care and respect that recognizes the shared relations of the pulmonary commons. Since the short, pithy lines of this long stanza are enjambed and lack caesuras, readers must decide where to breathe and, by extension, how they relate to such acts of responsibility. The women's actions reflect what Murphy calls "alterlife": "life already altered" by "the molecular productions of capitalism" that "is also life open to alteration" (497). This "figuration of chemical exposures…attempts to be as much about figuring life and responsibilities beyond the individualized body as it is about acknowledging extensive chemical relations" that bridge past, present, and future (497). The women's actions may be understood within the context of alterlife, as their apology acknowledges how chemical relations necessitate a collective, interconnected understanding of life and responsibility that expands across space and time.

"Holders," Wong's penultimate poem, celebrates Indigenous women who breathe life into communities and conspire against attempts to asphyxiate political resistance. The poem opens:

> the women hold space like trees do, sweet fresh air between
> their tender branches. unseen roots draw deep down into dark
> moist substance, making homes for songbirds, windsong and
> children who puff with asthmatic exertion (80)

The simile aligns women with life-giving trees in the pulmonary commons. The women "hold space" for children, whose laboured breathing demonstrates how generations have been made vulnerable by toxic settler atmospheres. A multigenerational collective of women "stand in front of army trucks & policemen, uniforms & riot gear" and "crack open the ugly pavement of unjust laws & find old rivers / underneath" (80). This image of resistance and resurgence reflects the women's collective strength in challenging state attempts to strangulate political movements. Like the women in "Holders," these women may be at risk of being chemically and politically altered, but their lives are also open to alteration, as are toxic settler atmospheres. The women remake settler atmospheres through ceremony: "they pray & burn offerings for the / four directions to come together in sacred commitment to all of creation" (80). Recognizing the gendered and sexualized dimensions of Canada's atmosphere of colonial racism, Wong acknowledges how, in the face of the epidemic of Missing and Murdered Indigenous Women and Girls, "the women continue to stand together," working towards a thriving future as they "plant trees & gardens," "compost & compile recipes," "forage for mushrooms & cultivate stubborn corn" (80), and breathe life into a shared commons.

Echoing the earlier image of rewilding (Boast 14), the women "perch on the edge of teetering cities" (80), ready to reclaim colonized spaces. This reclamation would destroy zoning policies which, as Chloe Ahmann and Alison Kenner argue, ensure the majority white, wealthy occupants of residential centres enjoy clean air while those on the margins—typically poor racialized communities—suffer from asthma and other conditions linked to industrial air pollution (420). The poem's form attunes readers to how supporting Indigenous resistance and resurgence enables everyone to breathe better. Structured like a prose poem, "Holders" features a mix of long and short sentences in one paragraph-like stanza; unlike most other poems in *undercurrent*, punctuation appears when expected, creating a sense of flow and visually indicating that, in this context, readers have ample, predictable opportunities to breathe. The poem ends with the phrase "the women remain" (80). The lack of a closing punctuation mark signals that the women will persist, but for readers to persist as well—to continue the consistent and reliable breathing pattern established by the poem—they must hold space for Indigenous women's collective action against toxic settler atmospheres.

Something in the Air: Poetic Aspirations

"To aspire is to breathe," writes Sara Ahmed, and "with breath comes imagination" (qtd. in Ahmann and Kenner 426). Inspired by Indigenous women's decolonial feminist ethics, Wong aspires to futures forged through conspiratorial practices that displace and unsettle the toxic relations of settler atmospherics. Poetry and storytelling play a central role in building these futures. Like "Holders," "Night Gift" features full sentences in one long paragraph-like stanza, yet the syntax creates a different sense of flow that reflects the speaker's agitation. Punctuation clearly indicates where to breathe, guiding readers through the dark underbelly of "political / systems… stuffed full of suncorpse & tired old neocolonial / ego that refuses to stop growing until it reaches the limits of the planet's patience" (23). "Suncorpse," a play on energy company Suncor, underscores the deadly—and dead—set of relations that characterize the petrostate's vision of sunny energy futures. As LeMenager argues, "Suncor, as the name implies, aspires to be something other than an extractive industry, aspires to primal, solar force, to be a player—reciprocal, responsible—in the ecological longue durée" (177). Turning to the realm of night, the poem illuminates gifts that are often left in the dark: "the song of the night-cleaners, the lament of the wrongly /

imprisoned, the rage of the ragged, the dispossessed" (23). Critiquing "an arrogant elite that doesn't heed / the world's necessary stories," the speaker declares:

> jail the stories & the storytellers,
> but they will keep speaking the night, until empire expires, with
> or without the multitudes alive. (23)

In a line that anticipates Wong's arrest in August 2018 for protesting the Trans Mountain Pipeline, the poem asserts that incarceration cannot stop Indigenous water protectors and allies from conspiring against settler atmospherics.[6] Punning on the word "expires," the poem suggests that poets, storytellers, and activists will continue to use their breath—their voice—to speak truth to power until empire draws its last gasp of air. The final lines state, "the night replenishes us so that we may / continue to embody her songs" (23). By attending to the alternative "energy systems" of the unseen and unheard, Wong envisions her own model of conspiring against settler atmospherics through creative expression and collective action.

"Epilogue: Letter Sent Back in Time from 2115," the final poem, offers a hopeful vision of the future in which "empire expires." This poem is also organized as one long stanza in paragraph form, but the agitated syntax of "Night Gift" gives way to a slower pace and more relaxed breathing pattern, reflecting a different energy—and different energy future—where "everyone slows" (87). Wong locates this vision of "critical optimism" (Milne 132) firmly in the present through a deictic "here" (Karpinski 221): "here is wonder, despite armies of mistakes" (Wong, *undercurrent* 87). This imperfect future is both aspirational—future oriented—and already in the air. Though called "the great return," this world-building process where "rebalance / begins, practical & spiritual" (87) is ongoing. Built on a reciprocal ethics of care and respect rather than the neocolonial capitalist logic of resource extraction, this world embraces the shared responsibilities of the pulmonary commons: "We live in the world as if it were our only home, loving / dreamtime & full breath" (87). Access to full breath, unencumbered by the toxic strangulations of settler atmospherics, comes when "spontaneous compassion sprouts in / the cracks of collapsing systems," "the syntax of hope" percolates in waterways, "treaties mature, deepening respect," "we learn the language of roots & fungus medicines," and "balance quietly returns to the commons" as "indigenous resurgence slows climate instability / & deflates apocalyptic fervor" (87). Echoing "Holders," the poem demonstrates what might be possible when conspiring with Indigenous resurgence movements grounded in decolonial feminist ethics.

Reading and writing poetry may not be enough to "save the world" from the compounding crises that Wong tackles, but poetry does have the power to alter perspectives (Milne 150), making *undercurrent* important for inspiring—in the sense of breathing life into—action. In an essay written during the first year of the pandemic, Wong states, "I am weary. I don't have much energy to write poems these days…I feel a widely shared ecological grief at this desecration caused by short-sighted colonial occupation, and I cope…by directing my energy into supporting collective action" ("Afterword" 71–72). As we reflect on the multilayered meaning of energy and its relationship to poetry and activism in the wake of the COVID-19 pandemic, *undercurrent* attunes us to the pulmonary commons in new ways and invites us to conspire to create an atmospheric otherwise.

Notes

1. See Hannah Boast, Ryan Fitzpatrick, Alec Follett, Max Karpinski, and Heather Milne.
2. See Boast's discussion of Wong's poetry in relation to boil water advisories in Indigenous communities and increased rates of illness in communities downstream from resource extraction sites.
3. See Michelle Murphy and Chloe Ahmann and Alison Kenner for critiques of toxicology's decontextualized approach to the study of chemicals.
4. For a discussion of Wong's "ethics of immersion" in relation to the hydrocommons, see Boast.
5. See Warren Cariou and Jon Gordon for a discussion of how capitalism transforms bitumen into a harmful substance.
6. Wong was sentenced to twenty-eight days in prison after being arrested for breaching a Supreme Court injunction meant to prevent land protectors from accessing Trans Mountain facilities; she was released after eighteen days (Bradley x).

Works Cited

Ahmann, Chloe, and Alison Kenner. "Breathing Late Industrialism." *Engaging Science, Technology, and Society*, no. 6, 2020, pp. 416–438.

"Apprehension." *OED Online*, Oxford UP, June 2022.

Boast, Hannah. "Borrowed Waters: Water Crisis and Water Justice in Rita Wong's *undercurrent*." *Textual Practice*, vol. 35, no. 5, 2021, pp. 1–21.

"Bottom line." *Oxford English Dictionary*, Oxford UP, June 2022.

Bradley, Nicholas. "Biographical Note." *Current, Climate: The Poetry of Rita Wong*, edited by Nicholas Bradley, Wilfrid Laurier UP, 2021, pp. ix–xi.

Cariou, Warren, and Jon Gordon. "Petrography, The Tar Sands Paradise, and the Medium of Modernity." *The Goose*, vol. 14, no. 2, 2016, pp. 1–29.

Fitzpatrick, Ryan. "Material Frictions: Troubling the Ethics of Experiment in the Ecopoetic Work of Rita Wong and Christian Bök." *Studies in Canadian Literature*, vol. 45, no. 2, 2020, 181–204.

Follett, Alec. "'A life of dignity, joy and good relation': Water, Knowledge, and Environmental Justice in Rita Wong's *undercurrent*." *Canadian Literature*, no. 237, 2019, pp. 47–63.

Karpinski, Max. "Unsettled Solutions: Petropastoral Poetics in Rita Wong's *undercurrent*." *Studies in Canadian Literature*, vol. 45, no. 2, 2021, pp. 205–228.

Kay, Andrew. "Conspiring with Keats: Towards a Poetics of Breathing." *European Romantic Review*, vol. 27, no. 5, 2016, pp. 563–581.

L'Abbé, Sonnet. "'Infiltrate as Cells': The Biopolitically Ethical Subjects of *sybil unrest*." *Canadian Literature*, no. 210/211, Autumn/Winter, 2011, pp. 169–189.

LeMenager, Stephanie. "Sediment." *Veer Ecology: A Companion for Environmental Thinking*, edited by Jeffrey Jerome Cohen et al., U of Minnesota P, 2017, pp. 168–182.

Linton, Jamie. *What Is Water?: The History of a Modern Abstraction*. UBCP, 2010.

Mahony, Martin. "For an Empire of 'All Types of Climate': Meteorology as an Imperial Science." *Journal of Historical Geography*, vol. 51, 2016, pp. 29–39.

Merola, Nicole M. "what do we do but keep breathing as best we can this / minute atmosphere': Juliana Spahr and Anthropocene Anxiety." *Affective Ecocriticism: Emotion, Embodiment, Environment*, edited by Jennifer Ladino and Kyle Bladow, U of Nebraska P, 2018, pp. 25–49.

Miki, Roy. *In Flux: Transnational Shifts in Asian Canadian Writing*. NeWest, 2011.

Milne, Heather. "Water and Plastic: Trans-Corporeality in Rita Wong's *undercurrent* and Evelyn Reilly's *Styrofoam*." *Poetry Matters: Neoliberalism, Affect, and the Posthuman in Twenty-First Century North American Feminist Poetics*, U of Iowa P, 2018, pp. 129–160.

Murphy, Michelle. "Alterlife and Decolonial Chemical Relations." *Cultural Anthropology*, vol. 32, no. 4, 2017, pp. 494–503.

Nixon, Rob. *Slow Violence and the Environmentalism of the Poor*. Harvard UP, 2013.

Roberts, Gillian. "Writing Settlement after Idle No More: Non-Indigenous Responses in Anglo-Canadian Poetry." *Journal of Canadian Studies*, vol. 51, no. 1, 2017, pp. 64–89.

Sharpe, Christina. *In the Wake: On Blackness and Being*. Duke UP, 2016.

Simmons, Kristen. "Settler Atmospherics." Member Voices, *Fieldsights*, 20 Nov. 2017, https://culanth.org/fieldsights/settler-atmospherics.

Stó:lō Research and Resource Management Centre / Stó:lō Nation. "Language Resources." Digital *Sq'éwlets*, http://www.digitalsqewlets.ca/language_resources-ressources_linguistiques-eng.php. Accessed 6 May 2024.

"Transpire." *OED Online*. Oxford UP, March 2022.

Tremblay, Jean-Thomas. "Aesthetic Self-Medication: Bob Flanagan and Sheree Rose's Structures of Breathing." *Women & Performance: A Journal of Feminist Theory*, vol. 28, no. 3, 2018, pp. 221–238.

Wong, Rita. "Afterword: recommitting to peace, love, and justice." *Current, Climate: The Poetry of Rita Wong*, edited by Nicholas Bradley, Wilfrid Laurier UP, 2021, pp. 71–74.

Wong, Rita. "Cultivating Respectful Relations: A Response to Leroy Littlebear." *Journal of Chinese Philosophy*, vol. 39, no. 4, Dec. 2012, pp. 528–536.

Wong, Rita. *forage*. Nightwood Editions, 2007.

Wong, Rita. *undercurrent*. Blewointment, 2015.

Wong, Rita. "Waters as Potential Paths to Peace." *Material Cultures in Canada*, edited by Thomas Allen and Jennifer Blair, Wilfrid Laurier UP, 2015, pp. 209–222.

"Xylem." *OED Online*. Oxford UP, March 2022.

13
Learning Landguage

SISSEL M. BERGH

History is the fruit of power, but power itself is never so transparent that its analysis becomes superfluous. The ultimate mark of power may be its invisibility; the ultimate challenge, the exposition of its roots.
—MICHEL-ROLPH TROUILLOT,
  Silencing the Past: Power and the Production of History

IN MY ARTISTIC WORK, I investigate local history and land by collecting and combining different kinds of knowledges, emphasizing South Saami language as a key to understand what happened, to heal, and to try to re-establish the relationship to land. Saami histories have been gagged and shuffled away; they have been presented as unrelated, foreign, non-belonging, and erased.

To be able to understand these processes, we need to dive into the local and the specific. We need to stay as close as possible and attempt to arrive at the topics from many different angles.

I would like to show why art is a tool we need to be able to take a closer look at the production of history and the history of science.

We also need to relearn with the land. Many place names do not make sense in Norwegian language, but if we filter them through South Saami language, which is a very specific language when it comes to different kinds of rivers, forests, mountains, it's like coming home. The land responds and corresponds with the names given.

FIGURE 13.1 John K. Jåma testing the structure we had worked on.
(Photo by Anne Olive Karlsen, courtesy of the artist.)

Art can help shift the perspective, return the gaze, and give space to other voices. In this way, art can expose the roots of what is today considered "truth," and why it has become like that.

History is still being used to claim rights to exploit land, to create national pride, and, in our context, to erase Saami presence and the complexity of a multicultural past. When the new National Museum opened in Oslo on June

11, 2022, I contributed a work called *Hovren Gåetie* that aims to deconstruct the nation in the opening exhibition *I Call It Art*. The exhibition is a mishmash of works from artists living and working in the whole of this land at the moment, questioning hierarchy and museum. My contribution is an etymological study in physical form of the South Saami word for moose hide.

It is a sculpture based on a *gåetie*-structure, the wooden structure of the traditional Saami turf house (Figure 13.1). John Kristian Jåma has learned to build the traditional *gåetie* from his skilled father, Ingvald Jåma. He is now the keeper and teacher of these ancient traditions. He is a member of the *sijtie* of Åerjel Fovsen Njaarke, a reindeer owner of the southern Fosen in the western mountain chain, just across the fjord of Trondheim. We met in the Fovsen mountains to collect subjects for the structure. The four basic supporters in this kind of *gåetie*, the *otnerassh*, are based on birch trees growing in steep hills, which makes them grow into J-shapes. We walked the hilly birch forest and picked the most beautiful and functional supporters. All the different parts were taken by car all the way down to John and Anne's home by the fjord, and we worked on the pieces there. We removed all the bark. Later, after the pieces had dried over the winter, they were moved across the mountain to my studio by the sea, where I come from—to be transformed.

The South Saami *gåetie* has kept its traditional form with the ancient naming of the different parts, a micro-cosmos mirroring the greater world. You may say that the fireplace in the middle, the *aernie*, is the heart, mirroring the life-giving sun. The fireplace giving us warmth and life.

This *hovren-gåetie* is based on a traditional *gåetie*/house structure, but becomes a *låevtie*: a tent. The work investigates the etymology of the South Saami word *hovre/hovde*, the leather, the hide, the dermis of moose. The *r* and *d* may reflect a dialectic difference, but the sound is closer to the ð, in English *th(r)*. *Hovre/hovde* is, according to Minerva Piha, a Germanic loanword related to *haut/hud* and *hide*. According to Wiktionary online etymological dictionary, *hud* (skin) is connected to *hood* (covering), and has an Indo-European origin, *(s)kewH*.

The sculpture is made by more than ten dehaired, dried rawhide of moose, the biggest ungulate of our land, collected from different groups of hunters in the area, among them a first-time hunter, a nineteen-year-old woman from Røssvatnet, who shot a big moose an hour into the hunt (Figure 13.2).

FIGURE 13.2 Here, I am working on the salted, fresh hides.
(Photo by Sturla Leth-Olsen, courtesy of the artist.)

FIGURE 13.3 Freshly slaughtered moose hide, resembling the sky. (Photo courtesy of the artist.)

These days, rawhide would otherwise be wasted because there are only one or two places that use moose hides to make leather in this country, and the knowledge seems lost outside of Saami central areas. I have had to learn to prepare the skins from scratch because I do not have access to the knowledge of preparing hides. What kind of scraper is best to use? How to stretch and dry the hides? I have tried different scrapers made by a blacksmith on the Swedish side. The hides are huge and heavy. When I received them, they were full of leftover fats and meat. Some of them had big holes from the skinning and some had started decomposing with white larvae—which I stopped by using chalk. The hides were first laid in salt, then in water. When they are "ripe," you can pull the hairs off easily. I got some assistance from friends to stretch and scrape the skins. But I also stayed outdoors alone in the cold winter with winds from north, scraping to be able to finalize the work in time.

It is a cold and dirty work, but also very giving. The closeness to, and the smell of, the animal. The skins, almost like human skin—even with moles. It feels like connecting to many thousands of years of history.

The first temporary housing for nomads and semi-nomads may have been tents made of moose hides. The strong, big hides could be bathed in fish-liver oil or other fats to make them resistant to rain. The word *hovre/hovde* means hide/dermis from moose (and cow—but that seems like a later addition), but why are words for rainbow and thunder connected to the same word?

A hide from a freshly killed moose looks like the sky on the inside (Figure 13.3). It is clear blue like a summer's day with white clouds of fat. People must have seen and recognized the sky in the skin.

Maybe they would have kept the hairs on the hides when they made tents? Or it would for sure fall off after time and expose the transparent dermis and let the light in. And if they did dehair the dried skins for tents, the dwelling would be semi-transparent, which would make you wake up with the sun. And in cosmology, the tent cloth/skin would be the sky. The world is a tent. The tent is a world (Figures 13.4, 13.5).

The dried hides make pretty nice canvases: Did people paint their stories there? Maybe we have to imagine beautiful, decorated tents? But they probably made them soft, to be able to transport them easily.

The name of the thunder god in the southern part of Saepmie was Hovrengaellies, registered by the missionaries of the eighteenth century as Horagalles (Qvigstad). The mission towards the Saami was established in Trondheim in 1717 on the order of King Christian IV of Denmark-Norway. Hovrengaellies is depicted on many *gievrieh*, Saami spiritual drums with two hammers. The god of the sky, of thunder and lightning, the weather, oceans, and lakes. He rules over the life, health, and well-being of humans and animals.

Hovrengaellies protects the *nåejtie*, the spiritual guide of Saami communities, on his spiritual journeys to other levels of the world. The *nåejtie* uses the *gievrie* to contact the spirits and to predict the comings. The drums were taken by force by the apostle to the Saami, Thomas von Westen, to erase Saami cultural beliefs. The name Hovrengaellies occurs only in the south and directly translated it would be Leather Husband/old man, which doesn't really make

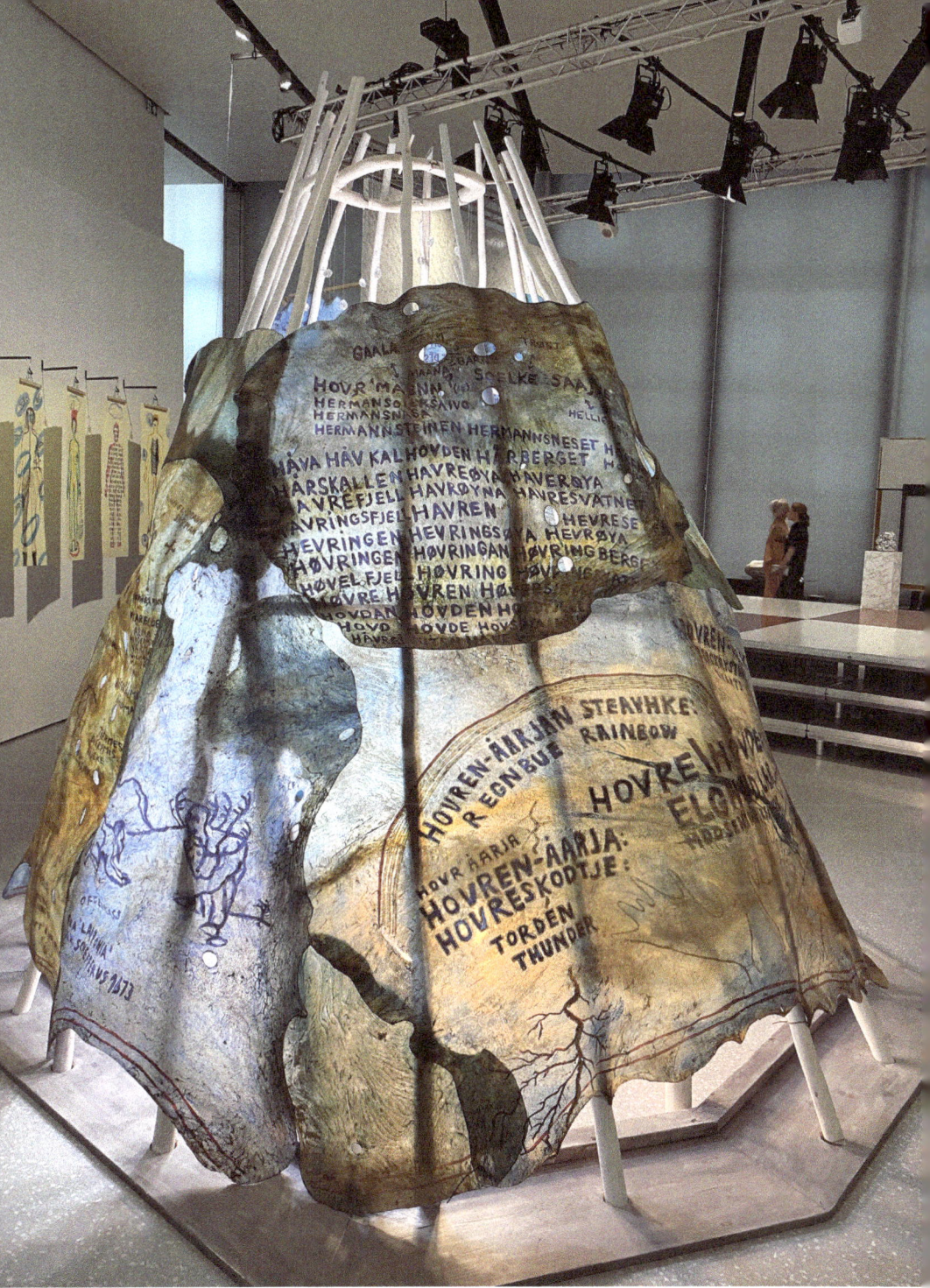

Figure 13.4 *Hovren Gåetie* at the newly opened National Museum of Norway.
(Photo courtesy of the artist.)

sense. The sky god has other names in the north, like Átja in Lulesaami, meaning grandfather. Early Nordic scholars, like the priest Randulf of Nærøy, who wrote about the local Saami after meeting with Thomas von Westen, noticed the similarities between Hovrengaellies and the Norse thunder god Thor. The notion that cultural adaptation only happens from the Norse to the Saami, and never the other way around, has been widely accepted. The contact between the South Saami and Germanic, and other tribes, occurred earlier in the south, which perhaps explains why also Saami scholars did not question Norwegian scholars' idea that the name was an adaptation from Norse. South Saami language is like an archive of different contact points in different times, and contains ancient loanwords from Indo-European, Indo-Persian, and Old-Germanic languages. But could it be that Thor, or Tor-kaillen (where *kaill* means old man) in Norwegian dialects, is a simplification of Hovrengaellies, where *gaellies* means husband/old man. In Saami culture, he was a protective force. It is known both among Saami and people considered Norwegians that they put a like-sided cross, the symbol of Hovrengaellies, on doors and items as a protective symbol.

Is it the same god as mentioned in Germanic sources? In an early Anglo-Saxon source, a baptismal vow found in a monastery in Mainz, Germany, from the ninth century, which renounces the evil as well as the heathen gods, he is called Thunaer (as in Germanic *donner*: thunder?): "I promise to forsake all the Devil's, Thunaer and Woden and Seaxnot, works and their followers" (Simek). The sky god has been a common denominator in many cultures. In old Turk languages, among the Khazars and others, "he" is called Tenri or Kök/Gök Tenri (Blue Sky). The Rus´ Vikings of the East had close contact with Turk tribes, according to early Middle Eastern sources, such as Ibn Fadlan's, in which he described the Viking tribe as traders in these multicultural towns (Hraundal).

In the upper ring of the *Hovren Gåetie*, there are several transparent quartz stones hanging, catching the light from the *aernie*. These stones are called *hovren-gierkie* (the latter term means stone) (Figure 13.6). This kind of stone has been found in graves and other archaeological sites. It has been used as jewellery, as protective talisman, magic arrows, and guides on the *gievrie*, the divination drum. Many *gievrieh* have been found hidden from the missionaries in the mountains, with all equipment almost intact. According to Norwegian scholar Birgitta Berglund, the *hovren-gierkie* (either a transparent or a milky one) could be used as a guide on the *gievrie*, when asking

FIGURE 13.5 *Hovren-gierkie* hanging from the *raejkie*—opening.
(Installation at Kunsthall Trondheim. Photo courtesy of the artist.)

FIGURE 13.6 *Hovren-gierkie* found in the ground of Tråante.
(Photo courtesy of the Museum of Science in Trondheim.)

FIGURE 13.7 Moose in rock art at Flatruet, Härjedalen.
(Photo courtesy of Wikimedia Commons.)

for guidance and divination by the drum. The *hovren-gierkie* was placed on top of the drum and moved around on the red ochre painted patterns as the user of the *gievrie* drummed rhythmically on the surface. The idea was that the stone's movement would predict future events or provide guidance about what to do.

Arrows made from *hovren-gierkie* have been found next to the large field of painted petroglyphs at Ruänden in Flatruet in the beautiful mountainous region of Härjedalen, the Saami reindeer husbandry district of Ruvhten Sijte on the Swedish side. Central in the petroglyphs are several depictions of moose (Figure 13.7). The archeologists of Jamtli Museum, one of them being Annabell Rahm, believe the arrows were shot at the painted animals during rituals. The site for the petroglyphs is next to Särvesjöen, a name that comes from the Saami word *Sarve*, which can be translated into English as Moose Lake.

Anders Fjellner was a South Saami priest and scholar born in the same area as the petroglyphs, in Tänndalen, Härjedalen in 1795. Today, this region is seen as the one of the most southern parts of Saepmie—land of Saami people. Four nations states are built on Saami land: Norway, Sweden, Finland, and Russia. One people in four countries. Fjellner's family originated from the Dovre Mountains on the Norwegian side, where they lived with and

FIGURE 13.8 The sky moose must never be killed.

(Installation at the National Museum of Norway. Photo courtesy of the artist.)

FIGURE 13.9 The fireplace is the heart.

(Installation at the National Museum of Norway. Photo courtesy of the artist.)

herded reindeer. Fjellner, who was an educated scholar in Uppsala, later lived and worked as a priest in the Swedish regions of Norrland and Västerbotten in central Saepmie. Inspired by other contemporary scholars such as Elias Lönnrot from Finland who compiled the Finnish tales of Kalevala, Fjellner recorded oral Saami myths and stories from both the southern and more northern part of Saepmie (Lundmark).

The starry night sky has been of great importance for all people moving on the sea and the wide mountain planes, both for directions and for stories. Every night, wrote Fjellner, the great sky moose, Sarve, moves across the sky for pasturing; and every night, Favdna, the hunter, arrives to hunt Sarve with his bow and arrow. There are other hunters, too. Among them, the three sons of Gaalla, the old man, whom we also find as a star in the sky. He, the (*Hovren?*) *gaalla* is there with the old woman, Båeries Aahka. But every night the polar star is in the way for the hunters. They don't dare to shoot Sarve, because if they hit the *noerhte naestie* (polar star), the whole world will end. The polar star is seen in other Arctic and Subarctic cultures as the (tent) pole that keeps the sky up. The hunt for Sarve must go on forever, and the great Sarve must never be killed (Figures 13.8, 13.9).

The Saami scholar Leena Gaebien talks about the creation myth from Byrkije, the Børgefjell mountains here in Southern Saepmie. This area is a very central place for reindeer husbandry from both sides of the Norway-Sweden border. In this story there is a sacred reindeer that has been sacrificed to create the land. The meat becomes earth, the bones mountains, the blood rivers, and deep down in the earth the heart is buried. This myth is similar to that which Swedish scholar Kerstin Kuoljok refers to in her book *Bilden av universum bland folken I norr*. Kuoljok cites a 1929 interview between the Siberian shaman Savelij Chutunka and the Russian anthropologists V.A. Avrorin and I.I. Kozminskij, where they discuss how the world is made of a sacred moose. Its spine is a mountain chain, etc. The reindeer of the Byrkije can be a transformation from moose to reindeer, as husbandry, not hunting, became the central part of the culture.

I imagine the ancient connection between *hovre*/moose skin and sky lies here. Maybe we are living inside Sarve; we look at Sarve's skin from the inside, just like when we sat inside our moose-hide tents. Sarve is our mother. Sarve is our world. There is a delicate balance to keep our world alive.

In a dictionary from 1780 by Swedish scholar Johan Ihre, the verb *saredh* is translated as "to create." His example is "Saraahka has created me." Saraahka, the most important deity in our South Saami area, alongside Hovrengaellies as documented by the eighteenth-century missionaries, would then actually mean creator-woman. *Sar-aahka.* Interestingly, today the word *saredh* means to split. In her 1992 book *Røros Samiske tekster*, Bergsland explains that in Saami they used to say a pregnant woman has two layers. She will split/give birth. I wonder if there is an ancient connection between the word *saredh* and *Sarve—Sar-ve*? The animal that is split to make the world.

The stories about Thor, the thunder god, like in the sagas "Trymskviða" (or "Hymiskviða"), written by Snorre Sturluson, seem like a mix between fairytales and parody. The authors were writing from a Christian point of view about heathen times. But there might be fragments and remnants of what the "heathen people" believed if we look closer. The Icelandic sagas are a collection of manuscripts mainly written during the thirteenth century about events that happened two to five hundred years earlier in Iceland, England, Denmark, and Norway—and even other places. Sturluson emphasizes that his text is written in "Danish tongue."

The oldest saga is the ancient poem called "The Poetic Edda" or "Voluspá"—the prophecy of the Volve/The Sibyl's Prophecy. It is believed to be based on an oral tradition dating back before the 700s. It is about the beginning and the end of the world. There is no clear author of the poems. The poem is also known as "Saemundar Edda," which has made some suggest it was written by an author named Saemund. According to Elsa-Brita Titchenell in *The Masks of Odin*, Edda means great-grandmother in ancient Icelandic. In North Saami, *Èadni* means mother/*Eadnan* earth. In South Saami, *Ietnie* means mother; *Eatneme* means earth; *Ietnie-maa* means motherland. Perhaps we can envision that Saemundar is a garbled naming of the *Saemien* (in South Saami)—the Saami Edda, or the Saami motherland, or what we today call Saepmie. The envisioner who speaks about the future in the Edda poem is a volve. In South Saami, we have the verb *volvedh*: to have a vision in dream. A *volverimmie* is the vision in the dreams. There are no such words in Icelandic, Norse, or Norwegian/Swedish languages.

Sturluson wrote the second Edda, the "Prose Edda," around 1222, a teaching about how to write poetry, and about the ancient mythology, maybe because the oral traditions were disappearing with Christianity. In the introduction "Gylfaginning," Gylfa meets three of the gods, and, in a conversation, he learns about the gods and the Ragnarök, the end of the world. We hear about the god Thor who came to a farm and asked to stay overnight with his companion Loke. He was travelling with his carriage dragged by his two bucks. ("The bucks" is translated as sled goats. But does it anywhere write what kind of bucks? No one has ever used goats to drag a wagon, but the use of reindeers— a Saami tradition—is well documented way back.) In the night, he slaughters his two bucks, cooks them, and invites the family to join him for the meal. He tells them not to break the bones of the animals while eating, but to leave them intact on the slaughtered skins. (To regenerate the animals' life by keeping all the bones intact is a ritual tradition in Saami culture, documented in the bear burials, an ancient tradition existing almost up to our time.) The son in the house, Tjalve, wants to eat the marrow and breaks one bone. In the morning, Thor/Hovrengaellies uses his hammer, *Mjollne*, to call the bucks back to life. He realizes that one of the bucks is limping, and Thor gets furious. The story ends with Thor being given both of the children, Tjalve and Röskva, to serve him, as an apology.

Is it a coincidence that the word for hard, dried, stiff leather—*hovre*— is *Tjalhve* or *Tjalhven-hovre* in South Saami? And that the word for a subject from which to make a soft fur is called *Rååvkese*? Two aspects of moose hide, one hard ("masculine") and one soft ("feminine"). I don't think this is a coincidence.

According to the *Norwegian Academic Dictionary*, the ritual places for the gods in heathen time in the Nordic area were called *Horg* and *Hov*, as mentioned in the sagas. In "The Poetic Edda," *Horg* and *Hov* are mentioned as connected to high places. The *Norwegian Academic Dictionary* differentiates the two words *Horg* and *Hov* as outdoor and indoor ritual places. In South Saami language, you can transform a subject in many ways. *Hovrege* is *hovre* + *-ege*. The *-ege* ending is the state of or the qualities of the subject. If we consider the concrete meaning of *hovrege*, it would be the skinlyness of the skin, or to be skin-like. If we think of the skin as the sky, would it be the sky-ness or the closeness to the sky, the sky forces? (Figure 13.10). *Hovr´ -* is a short form of *Hovren*, and would be used in a sentence in connection with another word— like in *Hovr´ åarja-* (thunder and lightning): the *åarja* of the *Hovre* (the blood vein of the skin). It is a short form of *genitiv*. *Hovr´* thus means that which belongs to *Hovre*, that which belongs to the sky (Figure 13.11).

I believe that we find these words in place names such as Hov, Hovd, Hovden, Høvren, Havren, Høvringen, Hårberg, Hårskallen, Hovmannen, etc.

FIGURE 13.10 Hovrengaellies is the sky deity.

(Installation at Kunsthall Trondheim. Photo courtesy of the artist.)

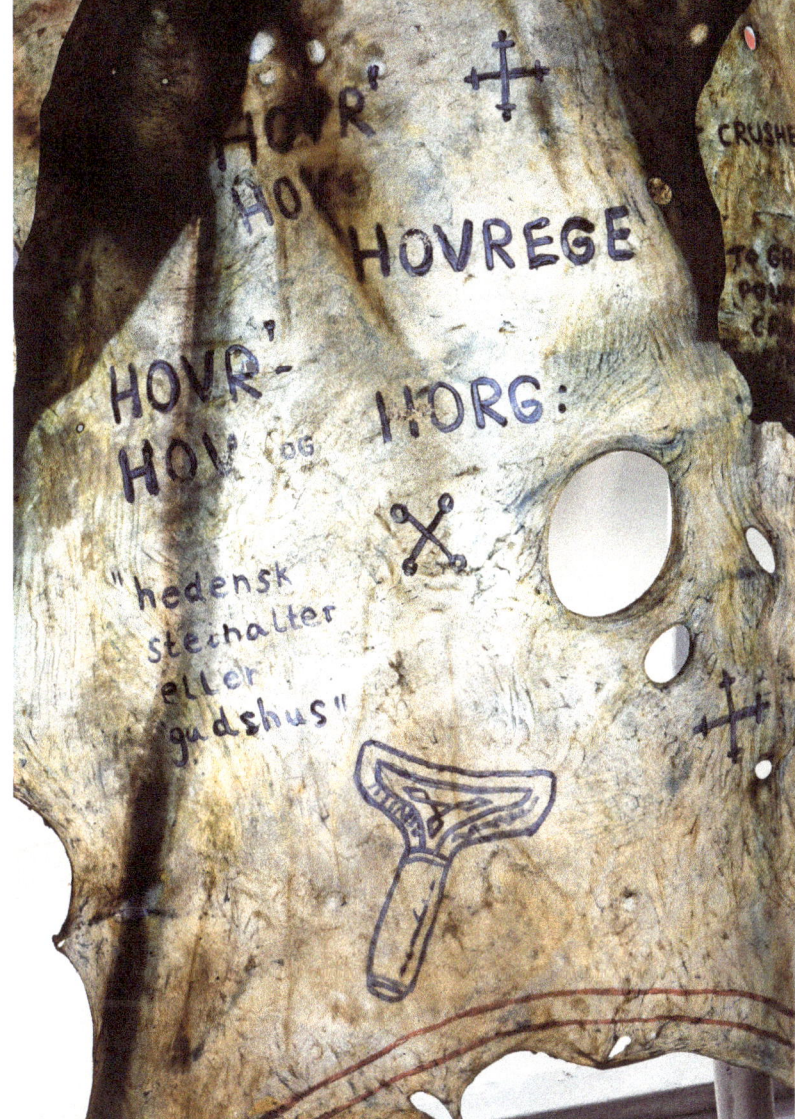

FIGURE 13.11 *Hovre* connected to places of connection, of "worship." (Installation at Kunsthall Trondheim. Photo courtesy of the artist.)

All these places are higher topographic areas, some in proximity to the sea, or dwelling places—but always on some height on the land. Maybe we can look for *Hov* and *Horg* in these places? Places of worshiping, asking for help, giving thanks to the sky, the weather man, the thunder man, the wind, the forces of the sky. In Valdres a local man found a ruin of stones in the shape of the sun on a lower mountain called Kvålshovd. It is a place easy to climb, close to the lake, with a very wide view. The archaeologist Jostein Bergstøl was there, among other archaeologists, to study the finding, but they could not conclude of what this is. When I asked him about it during an online conversation, he wondered whether this is one of the *Hov/Horg* mentioned in the sagas.

Sometimes it is necessary to return to what is considered source material for our history. Who made the sources collected in archives? Who is interpreting them? Can we find the beginning of the tale? There are not that many written records from our area, Trøndelag.

And perhaps we should start by calling it—in South Saami language—Tråantelahkan. The name of the city of Tråante/Trondheim comes from the name of the area, or vice versa. The earlier mentioned South Saami priest and scholar Anders Fjellner wrote that the first word, part of the word *Tråant*, comes from rough and intractable land. There is a verb *Tråannedh* that means aggressive or angry (maybe as intractable, not easily controlled, stubborn, obstinate). The second part, *lahkan*, means an undefined area of land. According to Norwegian scholars, *Trøndelag* should mean "The law of the Trønders," where the Trønders is an ancient Norse, a North Germanic people and this a land ruled by their laws.

If you are trying to reach Tråante from southern Norway by land, you have to cross the harsh mountainous region of Dovre. Even from the Swedish side, you have to cross dangerous mountains such as Sylane or Sul to reach the area. There were just a few known difficult mountain passes to enter the area, wrote the Swedish clergyman Olaus Magnus in his 1555 *Historia de gentibus septentrionalibus* (Granlund). Even from the sea, you have to cross the harsh stretches of sea, like the Stadt Ocean, with no protective outer line of reefs. A lot of shipwrecks have happened there.

So, for a long time, it was an intractable land for outsiders.

One of the major sources about the history of Trøndelag is a travelogue written by Gerhard Schøning from 1773 to 1775 (*Reise*). This diary has been seen as the first scientific registration of places and cultural heritage in Tråantelahkan, a source of Genuine Facts. But we need to look at his words with this in mind—that Schøning had a greater purpose for his journey. He wanted to document the Germanic peoples' cultural heritage. We need to take a closer look at the context and start with the biographical story of this man, who is regarded as one of Norway's first historians and scientists. Schøning was born in 1722 from a family in Lofoten in the north. His grandfather came from Ebeltoft in Denmark to Lodek/Lødingen in Nordland around 1670. The father of Gerhard was a tradesman with tenth rights—the king's right to tax his subordinates by a tenth of their income. Schøning grew up among the privileged in a society where Saami people were present. It is well documented that he regarded the Saami with contempt, as inferior people. At seventeen years old, he travelled to Tråante to study at the Cathedral school. Later he received a two-year stipend to study in the capital of Denmark-Norway. The grant came from a foundation built on huge forest properties by one of the wealthiest men in Norway, Thomas Angell, who was born in 1692. His grandparents also immigrated from places in Denmark, Germany, England, and the Netherlands, to Tråantem, the northern trading port. They had been given letters of privileges from the king in Copenhagen that enabled them to do lucrative businesses from the natural resources. (This foundation continues even today, owning huge areas of land south of Tråante.)

In 1751 Schøning was enrolled as a member of the Royal Danish Academy of Science and Letters. He was asked to work on a historical publication—*Inquiry into the Ancient Geography of the Nordic Countries, Particularly Norway* (Figure 13.12)—as he was called back to Tråante by his former headmaster who wanted Schøning to replace him as the new headmaster of the Cathedral school. The book, which was published the same year, declares its purpose: to show that the widespread perception of the Saami as the indigenous people of Norway is wrong, and that the true inhabitants of the north are the Germanic people. Schøning wanted to show that this was the Germanic people's homelands, and he portrayed the Saami people as late invaders, "Samojeds from the Siberia," long after the Germanic peoples arrived. He invented a theory of the arrival of the Germanic people through a northern bridge and used the biblical story of the sons of Noah as facts of origin. This work was given great public and political interest. There was no coincidence that the "inquiry" was published the same year as the border treaty between Sweden and Denmark-Norway was signed.

For nine years, the Danish-Norwegian mayor Peter Schnitler had been investigating "a natural border" between the two countries from Trøndelag and up northeast. The border treaty was signed with an addition, the so-called Lapp Codicil, which declared and acknowledged the rights of the Saami people, as a separate people living in both countries, to continue their ancient use of land on both sides of the newly established border. It

FIGURE 13.12 Front cover of Schøning's first attempt of history revision.
(Photo courtesy of the National Library of Norway.)

also stated their fishing and hunting rights, rights to their old dwellings, and their rights to travel with their reindeer between the mountains and the coast. For a man of privileges of the north such as Schøning, this might have felt like a real threat. Something needed to be done to undermine the idea that the Saami had ancient rights to the land.

Schøning arrived in Tråantem during the summer of 1751 with his friend, the Danish nobleman Peter Fredrik Suhm, who came along to the north to marry the niece of the wealthy Mr. Angell. In his opening speech at the Cathedral school, he emphasized the lack of scientific research in Norway and the need to write a history of both Norway and Denmark. This became his life project. In 1760 Schøning, Suhm, the councillor of state, together with the newly arrived Bishop Ernst Gunnerus, started a society for scholars, the Trondhjem Society, and shortly after started to publish a series of scientific scriptures. In 1767 the society came under the protection of the king and was renamed the Royal Norwegian Society of Science and Letters.

Schøning's book of 1751 was one of the first attempts to revise the history of Norway and the first attempt to erase the Saami presence in this history. This easily refuted theory about the north as the Germanic peoples' homeland was later continued and promoted by other historians, especially through the Royal Norwegian Society of Science and Letters. For example, the Norwegian folklorist Ivar Aasen, as documented in letter correspondence, was appointed to look for traces of the Germanic invasion from the north as late as in the 1840s, as he was travelling the country studying the Norwegian dialects.

The priest and linguist Knud Leem had his education as a missionary at the first seminar for priests and missionaries towards the Saami established by Thomas von Westen in Tråante from 1717 to 1727. For many years, Leem had been working as a missionary in Finmark. In 1751 the bishop approved a request from the mission board to reopen the mission for the Saami. It was regarded of such great importance for the king that he secured the finances directly. When the border treaty had been signed, it was important to win the Saami people to the Danish-Norwegian side. Leem was appointed professor *lingvæ lapponiæ*, head of the Seminarium Lapponicum Fridericianum that opened in March 1752. The first professor in Norway was of Saami language and culture! Already in 1748 he had made a grammar study based on the dialect of mountain Saami of Porsanger fjord, published in Copenhagen. Anders Porsanger, a Saami from Finmark, was hired as a language scholar for the mission, and he was admitted to the school to study. Schøning made

FIGURE 13.13 Centre of the world.
(Installation at Kunsthall Trondheim. Photo courtesy of the artist.)

use of his position, as he was not pleased that Saami people, whom he regarded as inferior, were to be at the same study class as everyone else. He made a very public statement by withdrawing his nephew from the school.

Schøning was of the opinion that Saami people were to learn Danish, and no mission should be in Saami language. Leem was supported by Bishop Nannestad and his successor Ernst Gunnerus to continue the seminarium. He had time to continue his studies of Saami language and culture. In 1756 he published a Danish-Norwegian grammar and lexica in Tråante. This year Schøning and his companions managed to install an arrangement that determined that only boys who could read and write Latin could attend the school. It made it more difficult to admit Saami pupils (Anders Porsanger, however, did well at school and in 1758 he went to study in Copenhagen). From 1763 to 1767, Leem was the editor of two important primers for school and tuition, a catechism and an ABC in Saami, made by the seminarists. In 1767 he published his most famous work, *Description of the Saami of Finnmark*, which was published in a shortened manuscript in both German and Latin. In 1768 the first part of his greatest work, *Lexicon lapponicum bipartitum,* was published. It was a detailed ethnographic and linguistic work of more than six hundred pages and with colourful illustrations of clothes, housing, tools, culture, and so on. At the time of his death, he had arrived at the letter *S*, but Leem was never admitted as a member of the Royal Norwegian Society of Science and Letters. The first scientific society of Norway had no interest in promoting and highlighting anything about the Saami.

From the early 1770s onward, the scientific society was given a purpose by the Crown Prince Fredrik: to promote the development of agriculture in Norway. This was the beginning of an era of intense privatization of land, of farmers taking over the fertile grounds of reindeer-gatherings in the mountains, chasing the Saami reindeer herders off the land. And this was the beginning of capital *S* Science in Norway. A science that, in the next two hundred years, spent a lot of energy trying to prove the Norwegians as superior and Saami people as foreign to these lands.

The *Hovren Gåetie* is glowing in the dark, enlightening the mirrored letters written on the inside of the leather from within, materializing other knowledges and believes, or another history all together (Figure 13.13).

Works Cited

Bergh, Sissel M. *Hovren Gåetie. Jeg kaller det kunst*, 11 June 2022–11 Sept. 2022, National Museum, Oslo, Norway.

Bergh, Sissel M. *Kunna Guanna Concha*, 8 Dec. 2022–12 Mar. 2023, Kunsthall Trondheim, Norway.

Berglund, Birgitta. *Samisk runebomme, Røyrvik*. Spor, 2011.

Bergsland, Knut. *Røros samiske tekster*. Norsk folkemuseum, 1992.

Gaebien, Leena. Lecture at project *Raanen vuodna,* seminar at library, Mo i Rana, 2018.

Granlund, John. *Magnus, Olaus: Historia om de Nordiska Folken* (1555). Gidlunds, 1979.

Hraundal, Thorir Jonsson. *Rus in Arabic Sources: Cultural Contact and Identity*. 2013. University of Bergen, PHD dissertation.

Ihre, Johan, Lindahl, et al. *Lexicon Lapponicum/Latino/Svecanum eller Lapsk ordbok med ordförklaringar på Svenska och Latin*. Stockholm, 1780. Digitized by Nordstedt, Gudrun 2015.

Jamtli Museum. "Hällmålningarna på Flatruet." *YouTube*, 2019, https://www.youtube.com/watch?v=lbsGbZ07-zw.

Kuoljok, Kerstin Eidlitz. *Bilden av universum bland folken i norr*. Carlssons, 2009.

Leem, Knut. *Beskrivelse over Finmarkens Lapper, deres Tungemaal, Levemaade og forrige Afgudsdyrkelse, oplyst ved mange kaabberstykker.* Tryft af G.G. Salikath, 1767.

Lundmark, Bo. *Anders Fjellner, samernas Homeros och diktningen om solsönerna.* Västerbottens läns hembygdsförening, 1979.

Piha, Minerva. "Archaeological and Lexical Perspectives on Indigenous South Saami Religion." *Entangled Beliefs and Rituals: Religion in Finland and Sápmi from Stone Age to Contemporary Times*, edited by Tiina Aikas and Sanna Lipkin, Archaeological Society of Finland, 2020, pp. 111–157.

Qvigstad, Just. *Kildeskrifter til den lappiske mythologi* (1723). Aktierykkeriet, 1903.

Simek, Rudolf. "Saxon Baptismal Vow." *Dictionary of Northern Mythology*. Translated by Angela Hall, D.S. Brewer, 1993.

Schøning, Gerhard. *Forsøg til de nordiske landes, særdeles Norges, gamle Geographie* (Trans. *Inquiry into the ancient geography of the Nordic countries, particularly Norway*). Copenhagen, 1751.

Schøning, Gerhard. *Reise som giennem en Deel af Norge i de Aar 1773, 1774, 1775.* Adresseavisen, 1910.

Sturluson, Snorre. *The Prose Edda (Gylfaginning), Sæmundar Edda, or The Poetic Edda.* 1220.

Titchenell, Elsa-Brita. *The Masks of Odin: Wisdom of the Ancient Norse.* Theosophical UP, 1995.

Trouillot, Michel-Rolph. *Silencing the Past: Power and the Production of History.* Beacon Press, 1995.

An Envoi from the Editors

MARIE CARRIÈRE AND AMANDA FAYANT

FEMINIST WRITING, ART, AND CRITICISM have always been a question of ethics—from Sappho's poetry in antiquity, to Christine de Pisan's political theory in the Middle Ages, or Simone de Beauvoir's twentieth-century existential philosophy. The same is true of the heady so-called second-wave manifestations of Black, intersectional, anti-colonial, ecological, lesbian/queer, and Indigenous feminisms of the 1970s and early '80s. The postmodern, transnational, and posthuman feminist praxes that followed also make ethics one of their ultimate concerns. At the start of the current millennium, Misha Kavka argued what is also still the case today, more than twenty years later: that feminism has "moved well beyond the mother term, already fractured at its origin," producing "innumerable modes of doing—whether activist, practical, theoretical, or just 'quiet'" ("Introduction" xi). This volume is full of such doing, for instance in the building of the Nokom's House that Kim Anderson, Amina Lalor, Sheri Longboat, and Brittany Luby define as "a place of purpose, belonging, creativity, and knowledge sharing among all our relations." It is in the uncovering of stories in Sissel M. Bergh's work as it represents a whole community of "doers" who find, research, and share knowledge that revisualizes the presence of the Sámi people that has been erased by colonial actions and Norwegianization. It is in Rita Wong's feminist ecopoetry and the valuable "learning with" the Tsleil-Waututh, Musqueam, Squamish, and Stó:lō Nations that Stephanie Oliver brings to light also in this volume. It is, moreover, in the emblematic care of a friend in need that Erin Soros describes. In fact, whether feminism is understood in terms of theory, praxis, or aesthetics, perhaps today, especially today, and in light of the global environmental emergency and ongoing ravages of settler colonialism, gender- and race-based violence, we need all the feminisms and all the modes of doing that address these problems in non-exclusive, intersectional, and care-oriented ways. "*Nous avons besoin de tous les féminismes*," recalls in this vein Québécoise poet Louise Dupré (292), which this collection again highlights in droves. We believe there is strength in such connections and hope in community.

As when Kavka wrote about the "mother term," our current time is also one of incredible backlash where feminist practices and 2SLGBTQQIA+ and women's rights are concerned. Generally, there is a backlash against all movements for equality, with what seems like never-ending attempts to grip onto systems that the privileged benefit from and that favour the control of women, whether it is their bodies, minds, or definitions of what it means to be a woman. Women are still being told by far too many institutions and systems that they cannot be trusted to live in their own bodies. Susan Faludi and bell hooks have both written about ongoing misogyny and feminist backlash, while Lauren McKeon's *F-Bomb: Dispatches from the War on Feminism*, or Lindy West's writing on her experiences with violent Twitter trolls as a reporter on sexist and fat-shaming culture, are among several works having dealt with the ill effects of anti-feminism. Meanwhile, at our time of writing in spring 2023, the stripping of abortion rights and now possibly the criminalization of birth control in some parts of the United States are setting hard-won battles back an entire half century. As far as gender-based violence is concerned, the scope is appalling. The Canadian Women's Foundation reports increases, not decreases, of women and girls killed by violence between 2020 and 2022, and we also know that hate crimes against transgender people have been on the rise "even in Canada" (Curlew). We know that "Indigenous women and girls are 12 times more likely to be murdered or missing than any other women in Canada, and 16 times more likely than white women" (Canadian Women's Foundation); according to Amnesty International, between 1980 and 2012 alone, the homicide rate of Indigenous women and girls was "roughly 4.5 times higher than that of all other women in Canada."

These grim statistics can make it difficult to gauge feminism's transformative potential in the world. However, the revitalization of feminist movements since the early 2000s (from the Arab Spring, One Billion Rising, to the global #MeToo movement), although seemingly waning these past few years, can still give us hope. As Rebecca Solnit designates this important affect of hope as "an embrace of the unknown and the unknowable, an alternative to the certainty of both optimists and pessimists," we might look again to Kavka who finds hope in the particular temporalities of feminism itself. She finds feminist time to be outside the normative constraints of linear time, "for the very reason that [feminism] embodies dispersed and often conflicting sites of past and present historical struggle determined by class, race, location, and sexual identities—just as it is presently, as well as historically, motivated by an unknowable future of social transformation" (Carrière 33). As Kavka herself writes, "feminism is out of time because it is always as much a manifest, or promise of justice to come, as it is a past and present historical struggle" ("Feminism" 36). In this temporal collapse lies feminism's futurity as it draws from both its past and present limitations and accomplishments, and looks to its ongoing potential for creating change and social betterment for women and 2SLGBTQQIA+ people, and also children, men, and the non-human environment.

Feminism's ongoing potential for change, we would suggest, lies in, and maybe even depends on, the transfeminist critical ethos that we believe characterizes this volume and its future-oriented imperative, its ultimate hopefulness. Stepping outside of the present volume, we could recall the now global Idle No More movement as one founded by such a transfeminist impulse of four women from Saskatchewan—Indigenous activists Nina Wilson, Sylvia McAdam, Jessica Gordon, and non-Indigenous ally Sheela McLean—calling for Indigenous sovereignty and environmental protection. In Norway, Sámi women activists, particularly from the National Sámi Youth Federation and the Nature and Youth Organization, brought various people together to stand up for Indigenous land rights and protect the environment from a wind turbine project that is built on Sámi land. The peaceful demonstrations and calls to action were built upon the work and leadership of three women: Ella Marie Hætta Isaksen—strategist, spokesperson, and artist/actress; Elle Nystad—spokesperson and leader of the National Sámi Youth Federation; and Gina Gylver—organizer, strategist, and leader of the Nature and Youth Organization. In turn, Kim TallBear, a Sisseton-Wahpeton Oyate scholar, draws the relationships between Idle No More, the international activist movement Black Lives Matter (in turn founded by three Black women organizers in response to the acquittal of Trayvon Martin's murderer), and the Standing Rock Resistance, highlighting Black Lives Matter's "powerful acts of (queer) women-led governance" (15), and how these movements address other vulnerable communities and criminal justice reform more broadly.

In this collection, Indigenous, women of colour, white, emerging and established artists, practitioners and scholars, from across Canada, Norway, and the United Kingdom, have in turn come together to learn with one another, staging a living with, through this collection, their thoughts, interpretations, and experiences of some of the biggest challenges and issues of our contemporary era. Together their contributions and summoning of community reflect upon, and from, their oft multifaceted position in what Adrienne Rich called this "atlas of a difficult world." As co-editors of this volume, we too have tried to keep in mind our positions as multifaceted. I, Marie, am a white, abled francophone settler living on Treaty 6 territory and in Métis Nation Region 4. I am privileged in my race and French European lineage, middle-class upbringing and education, work as a full-time, tenured university professor, and mother of two daughters with similar social advantages. Working at the cross-border that Dominique and Libe evoke in their opening letter, I consider that a significant part of my work requires me to listen, truly and closely, to my Black, Indigenous, and women of colour colleagues, students, and friends; learn what they may be willing to share with me; and not assume that all forms of feminism are commensurable. Although I join Amanda in this writing space to contemplate past, present, and future directions for feminist engagement, I do not claim to know her learning, her ancestors, or her life, but rather try to live with, learn from, and write alongside it.

Drawing from Sean Wilson's *Research Is Ceremony*, Natalie Clark reminds us that "protocol within many Indigenous communities requires a person to situate themselves and their relationships to the people and the land" (1). I, Amanda, am an Indigenous artist, writer, and researcher. I use the last term with much confliction or trepidation. Too often the history of research seems to be in opposition to the work I am trying to do. A better word for myself would be *storyteller*, as I endeavour to find and tell the stories of my ancestors and my family. I want to represent their presence and impact in the places they lived and the communities they created for themselves. However, I am also writing from the perspective of an immigrant living in Sápmi, Sámi land within the colonial state of Norway. I immigrated here many years ago and have struggled to find spaces of belonging, or spaces to live and learn with. This is because identity is a puzzle I am still working on. By this I mean that I have always spent a lot of time reflecting on my identity as a Métis person, as a Cree/Saulteaux person, and as a French Canadian person. All of these identities hold long histories, and finding connections between them and my identity is a large part of why I want to tell our stories. When I learn about my ancestors and family, I am also living with them. Their stories become a part of me and part of who I am. I am situated in Treaty 4 in my heart and situated in Norway with my body.

I, Amanda, strive to connect across communities and feminisms because of all of my experiences as an immigrant and Indigenous woman. This kind of living and learning with expresses an Indigenous perspective of kinship. Tasha Hubbard explains in her doctoral thesis that "revival of the importance of kinship within Indigenous literary criticism means a renewal of relationships to self and others" (11). For I also stretch across boundaries, across land and water, and across international borders. My body and story reach out to seek connections in feminism and Indigeneity. As Neal McLeod explains in *Cree Narrative Memory*, "through relations, we are able to create the web of understanding of our embodied locations and stretch it outwards to a wider context of collective historicity" (112). The Indigenous feminism I strive to embody reaches out to form alliances with fellow immigrant communities, with Sámi communities, and with Indigenous communities at home. In these connections I am struck by the strength and solidarity that reveal themselves through the sharing of stories and knowledge. Here I am reminded of Margaret Kovach when she writes, "the ability to craft our own research stories, in our own voice, has the best chance of engaging others" (60). The essays contained within this collected edition reach beyond the limits of the text and plant seeds of relationships, community, and art as means of connection. As a Métis person, I am reminded of Louis Riel when he said, "my people will sleep for one hundred years, but when they awake, it will be the artists who give them their spirit back" (by oral tradition attributed to Louis Riel).

We end this envoi with Chandra Talpade Mohanty's understanding of borders in terms of limits and openings, and thus as a potential ethical site:

> Borders suggest both containment and safety, and women often pay a price for daring to claim the integrity, security, and safety of our bodies and our living spaces. I choose "feminism without borders," then, to stress that our

most expansive and inclusive visions of feminism need to be attentive to borders while learning to transcend them. Feminism without borders is not the same as "border-less" feminism. It acknowledges the fault lines, conflicts, differences, fears, and containment that borders represent. It acknowledges that there is no one sense of a border, that the lines between and through nations, race, classes, sexualities, religions, and disabilities, are real—and that a feminism without borders must envision changed and social justice work across these lines of demarcation and division. (1–2)

To return to Dominique and Libe's opening letter, this is how we, Amanda and Marie, also dare to imagine new relations and ways of being that can be truly equitable, diverse, and inclusive. These will not always be easy to nurture or sustain, and we must remain critical of calls for solidarity when working from within a system—any system, including educational or socially minded ones. Our suspicion is part of protecting and encouraging an ethics of ongoing resilience and resistance to reverting to a status quo. This balance of being critical and staying connected is part of living and learning with. Learning comes from being critically vigilant and connection comes from living in community and forming relationships across feminisms. While we understand that ethics may not solve everything, ethics, as a way of working, thinking, and creating, can be a useful tool in fighting oppressive systems. It is at the juncture of potential alliances where we recognize that some borders can be crossed while others cannot; where we are willing to risk a very wide, challenging, and also potentially productive sense of renewed feminist solidarity.

Works Cited

Amnesty International. "Missing and Murdered Indigenous Women and Girls: The Facts." *Amnesty International Blog*, 29 Jan. 2021, https://amnesty.ca/blog/missing-and-murdered-indigenous-women-facts/#:~:text=According%20to%20the%20report%2C%201%2C017,all%20other%20women%20in%20Canada.

Canadian Women's Foundation. "The Facts about Gender-Based Violence." *Canadian Women's Foundation*, 2022, https://canadianwomen.org/the-facts/gender-based-violence/. Accessed 2 Apr. 2023.

Carrière, Marie. *Cautiously Hopeful: Metafeminist Practices in Canada*. McGill-Queen's UP, 2020.

Clark, Natalie. "Shock and Awe: Trauma as the New Colonial Frontier." *Humanities* 5, no. 1 (2016): 1–16.

Curlew, Abigail. "Transgender Hate Crimes Are on the Rise Even in Canada." *The Conversation*, 20 Aug. 2019, https://newsroom.carleton.ca/story/transgender-hate-crimes/.

Dupré, Louise. "Des fantômes dans les yeux." *All the Feels: Affect and Writing in Canada / Tous les sens: Affect et écriture au Canada*, edited by Marie Carrière, et al., U of Alberta P, 2021, pp. 283–297.

Faludi, Susan. *The Terror Dream: Myth and Misogyny in an Insecure America*. Henry Holt, 2007.

hooks, bell. *Feminism Is for Everybody: Passionate Politics*. Routledge, 2014.

Hubbard, T. *The Call of the Buffalo: Exploring Kinship with the Buffalo in Indigenous Creative Expression*. 2016. University of Calgary, PHD dissertation, http://hdl.handle.net/11023/3272.

Kavka, Misha. "Feminism, Ethics, and History, or What Is the 'Post' in Postfeminism?" *Tulsa Studies in Women's Literature*, vol. 21, no. 1, 2002, pp. 29–44.

Kavka, Misha. Introduction. *Feminist Consequences: Theory for the New Century*, edited by Elizabeth Bronfen and Misha Kavka, Columbia UP, 2001, pp. ix–xxvi.

Kovach, Margaret. *Indigenous Methodologies: Characteristics, Conversations, and Contexts*. U of Toronto P, 2009.

McKeon, Lauren. *F-Bomb: Dispatches from the War on Feminism*. Gooselane Editions, 2017.

McLeod Neal. *Cree Narrative Memory: From Treaties to Contemporary Times*. Purich Pub, 2007.

Mohanty, Chandra Talpade. *Feminism without Borders: Decolonizing Theory, Practicing Solidarity*. Duke UP, 2003.

Rich, Adrienne. *An Atlas of the Difficult World: Poems 1988–1991*. W.W. Norton & Company, 1991.

Solnit, Rebecca. "Hope Is an Embrace of the Unknown." *Guardian*, 15 July 2016, https://www.theguardian.com/books/2016/jul/15/rebecca-solnit-hope-in-the-dark-new-essay-embrace-unknown.

TallBear, Kim. "Badass Indigenous Women Caretake Relations: #STANDINGROCK, #IDLENOMORE, #BLACKLIVESMATTER." *Standing with Standing Rock: Voices from the #NoDAPL Movement*, edited by Nick Estes and Jaskiran Dhillon, U of Minnesota P, 2019, pp. 13–18.

West, Lindy. "I've Left Twitter. It Is Unusable for Anyone But Trolls, Robots and Dictators." *Guardian*, 3 Jan. 2017, https://www.theguardian.com/commentisfree/2017/jan/03/ive-left-twitter-unusable-anyone-but-trolls-robots-dictators-lindy-west.

Contributors

KIM ANDERSON (Métis) holds a Canada Research Chair in Indigenous Relationality and Storied Practice and is Professor in the Department of Family Relations and Applied Nutrition at the University of Guelph. Dr. Anderson has published seven books, along with numerous articles and book chapters on gender and Indigeneity, Indigenous health and well-being, Indigenizing the academy, and Indigenous knowledge transfer in urban settings. She is the author of *A Recognition of Being: Reconstructing Native Womanhood* (2nd ed., CSPI, 2016) and *Life Stages and Native Women: Memory, Teachings and Story Medicine* (University of Manitoba Press, 2011). Dr. Anderson's latest book publication is a co-produced memoir with Anishinaabe artist Rene Meshake, titled *Injichaag, My Soul in Story: Anishinaabe Poetics in Art and Words* (University of Manitoba Press, 2019).

ALEXANDRE BARIL is Associate Professor at the University of Ottawa. His work is situated at the crossroads of gender, queer, trans, disability/crip/Mad studies, critical gerontology, and critical suicidology. His commitment to equity has earned him awards for his involvement in queer, trans, and disabled communities, including the Canadian Disability Studies Association Tanis Doe Francophone Award, and the Equity, Diversity and Inclusion President's Award at the University of Ottawa. A prolific author who won the Young Researcher Award from the Faculty of Social Sciences at the University of Ottawa (2023), he has given over two hundred presentations at the international level and has over eighty publications. He is the author of *Undoing Suicidism: A Trans, Queer, Crip Approach to Rethinking (Assisted) Suicide* (2023) available in open access on the Temple University Press website.

SISSEL M. BERGH is an artist from Southwest Sapmi/Norway. In 2020 she was part of *Nirin*, the 22nd Biennale of Sydney. In 2019 she was part of *Gøteborg International Biennale of Contemporary Art*. Recent exhibitions include *Speaking Back* at Kunsthaus Hamburg, *Kunna Guanna Concha* at Kunsthall Trondheim, *Jeg kaller det kunst* at the National Museum in Oslo, Norway, and *Alakkaajut* at Urban Shaman gallery, Winnipeg, Canada. Bergh is educated at the Oslo National Academy of the Arts and University of Technology in Durban, South Africa. She was based in Lusaka, Zambia, for several years before she returned to Traante/Trondheim in 2009.

MARIE CARRIÈRE (she/her) is Professor of English and Vice Dean (Research) in the Faculty of Arts at the University of Alberta. A French Canadian settler born in Ottawa on the unceded territory of the Anishinaabe Algonquin Nation, Carrière has authored several books and articles on feminist thought, cultural theory, and contemporary literatures written in English and French. Her monographs include *Cautiously Hopeful: Metafeminist Practices in Canada* (McGill-Queen's University Press, 2020); *Médée, protéiforme* (Presses de l'Université d'Ottawa, 2012); and *Writing in the Feminine in French and English Canada: A Question of Ethics* (University of Toronto Press, 2002). She is the editor, with Kit Dobson and Ursula Mathis Moser, of *All the Feels: Affect and Writing in Canada / Tous les sens: Affect et écriture au Canada* (University of Alberta Press, 2021), and, with Patricia Demers, of *Regenerations: Canadian Women's Writing / Régénérations: Écriture des femmes au Canada* (University of Alberta Press, 2014). Her current research focuses on feminist ecologies, with a recent article on the ecopoetry of Katherena Vermette and Rita Wong appearing in *Ariel* (2023).

ÉLISE COUTURE-GRONDIN completed her PHD in comparative literature at the University of Toronto and a Fonds de recherche du Québec—Société et culture (FRQSC) postdoctoral fellowship at Simon Fraser University and Concordia University. She teaches and does research on Indigenous literatures of Québec and Canada. As a settler scholar, her work explores possibilities for ethical readings of Indigenous women's life-writing. She has published in *Studies in American Indian Literatures*, *Studies in Book Culture*, *Arborescences*, *Voix plurielles*, and *Transitional Justice Review*.

JUNIE DÉSIL is a poet. Born of immigrant (Haitian) parents on the Traditional Territories of the Kanien'kehá:ka in the island known as Tiohtià:ke (Montréal), raised in Treaty 1 territory (Winnipeg). Junie's debut poetry collection *eat salt | gaze at the ocean* (Talonbooks, 2020) was a finalist for the Dorothy Livesay Poetry Prize. Junie currently lives on the traditional territories of the Homalco, Tla'amin, and Klahoose, where she is currently working on a forthcoming (spring 2025) poetry collection titled *allostatic load*.

AMANDA FAYANT (she/her) is a Cree/Métis/Saulteaux artist (BFA, film production) and researcher MPHIL (Indigenous studies) based in Trondheim, Norway. Amanda is originally from Regina, Saskatchewan, Treaty 4 land. Amanda's art practice deals with the complexities of identity, exploring Indigenous feminisms, and confronting the colonial history in Canada through various mediums. Amanda's research focuses on Indigenous research methodologies and Indigenous feminist perspectives in art and education. In addition to several group art shows in Canada, Trondheim, Oslo, and Prague, Amanda has also shared artistic and research work with *ArtLeaks Gazette*, *Canadian Literature*, and the University of the Underground and the Regeneration collaborative project between Czech Republic, Iceland, and Norway. Amanda's master thesis, "Thunderbird Women: Indigenous Women Reclaiming Autonomy through Stories of Resistance," has been shared at several conferences and workshops. Amanda actively works as a guest speaker and moderator at schools, universities, art institutions, and conferences.

MYLÈNE YANNICK GAMACHE is a Franco-Métis assistant professor cross-appointed in Indigenous Studies and Women's and Gender Studies at the University of Manitoba. Red River Métis by her mother line with Carrière relations in St. Pierre-Jolys, Manitoba, and Beauchemin relations in Îles-des-Chênes via Grande Pointe, St. Vital, and St. Boniface, Manitoba, she is a member of l'Union Nationale Métisse Saint-Joseph du Manitoba and a registered citizen of the Manitoba Métis Federation. Her recent research engages Indigenous literacies of the unknown, Freudian psychoanalysis, and critical borderland studies through collaborative engagement with Iron Alliance historiographies as one of five founding members of the SSHRC-funded Iapi debwewin aansaamb co-lab. Her work is published in *Feminist Review, The*

Oxford Literary Review, *English Studies in Canada*, *Australian Feminist Studies*, and *Métis Coming Together: Sharing Our Stories and Knowledges* (Peter Lang).

LIBE GARCÍA ZARRANZ (she/her) is Associate Professor of Literature in English in the Department of Teacher Education at the Norwegian University of Science and Technology (NTNU, Norway). Her research sits at the intersection of Canadian literature and visual cultures, affect studies, with a focus on feminist and queer approaches, and trans studies. She is the author of *TransCanadian Feminist Fictions: New Cross-Border Ethics* (McGill Queen's University Press, 2017) and the co-editor of a special issue on affect and feminist literary production for *Atlantis: Critical Studies in Gender, Culture and Social Justice* (2018). Her latest research has been published by Palgrave Macmillan (2023), *Capacious: Journal for Emerging Affect Inquiry* (2022), and *The Year's Work in English Studies* (2022). She leads the research group TransLit: Sustainable Ethics, Affects and Pedagogies at NTNU, and is a member of the international research project Communitas/Immunitas: Relational Ontologies in Atlantic Anglophone Cultures of the 21st Century, funded by the Spanish Ministry of Science and Innovation.

DOMINIQUE HÉTU (she/her) is Assistant Professor in the Department of Francophone Studies and Languages at Brandon University, on Treaty 2 territory. She is a bilingual Canadian (French-English) scholar trained in literatures from Québec and Canada. She examines the functions and responses of contemporary literary and cultural production to interpersonal and sociopolitical struggles with a focus on vulnerability narratives, poetics of care, and representations of belonging, responsibility, and relationality, critical notions for thinking through minoritized and vulnerable experiences. She has published on those topics in several articles and book chapters, such as in the special issue *Women's Writing and Models of Care*, which she edited for *Studies in Canadian Literature*, and in the online volume *Souci de l'autre, souci de soi et création, Pour une littérature du care*. She is currently finishing a monograph, in French, on the transformative and damaging manifestations of care in contemporary literature from Québec.

LARISSA LAI (she/her) is the author of nine books, including *Slanting I, Imagining We: Asian Canadian Literary Production in the 1980s and 1990s*, *The Tiger Flu*, *Salt Fish Girl*, and most recently *The Lost Century*. Recipient of the

Jim Duggins Novelist's Prize, the Lambda Literary Award, the Astraea Award, and the Otherwise Honor Book, and twice finalist for the City of Calgary W.O. Mitchell Award, she has also been a finalist for the Books in Canada First Novel Award, the Lambda Award, the Sunburst Award , the bpNichol Chapbook Award, the Dorothy Livesay Prize, the ACQL Gabrielle Roy Prize for Literary Criticism, and a Governor General's Award. She has held a Canada Research Chair in Creative Writing at the University of Calgary, and a Maria Zambrano Fellowship at the University of Huelva. She is currently the Richard Charles Lee Chair of Chinese Canadian Studies at the University of Toronto.

AMINA LALOR (she/her) is a mixed Vietnamese Irish Métis designer, artist, researcher, and educator currently based in N'Swakamok (Sudbury, Ontario). Her Métis roots are from the Red River Settlement, and she is a member of the Métis Nation of Ontario. Amina is an Assistant Professor at the Laurentian University McEwen School of Architecture and is also a candidate for a master of Indigenous Land-based Education at the University of Saskatchewan. She holds a bachelor of architectural studies and master of architecture from the University of Waterloo. Since 2018 she has been working as a researcher at the University of Guelph to help create Nokom's House and is also a collaborator on Where the Rivers Meet: Decolonizing Place Narratives in the City, a project aiming to challenge the settler colonial erasure of Indigenous presence and relationships to land in the City of Guelph.

SHERI LONGBOAT (she/her) is a mixed Mohawk Ukrainian, and band member of the Six Nations of the Grand River. An associate professor in the Department of Geography and Environmental Studies, Faculty of Science, at Wilfrid Laurier University, and an adjunct professor in Rural Planning and Development at the University of Guelph, she has over twenty-five years of practical experience working with and within First Nations communities. Her teaching and collaborative interdisciplinary research focuses on water planning, management, and governance, in the context of security, sustainability, justice, and change. She has published over thirty articles and reports and recently co-edited the book *Local Communities and the Mining Industry: Economic Potential and Social and Environmental Responsibilities* (Routledge, 2023) and co-authored the chapter "Gender, Indigeneity and Mining."

BRITTANY LUBY, of Anishinaabe and mixed European descent, was raised on Treaty 3 Lands in what is now known as Northwestern Ontario. She has been trained by Elders at her ancestral community, Niisaachewan Anishinaabe Nation, to raise awareness of Crown-Anishinaabe relations. As an associate professor of history at the University of Guelph, Luby stimulates public discussion of Indigenous issues. Her picture books include *When the Stars Came Home* (Little, Brown Books for Young Readers, 2023), *Mnoomin maan'gowing / The Gift of Mnoomin* (Groundwood Books, 2023), *Mii maanda ezhi-gkendmaanh / This Is How I Know* (Groundwood Books, 2021), and *Encounter* (Little, Brown Books for Young Readers, 2019). Her monograph *Dammed: The Politics of Loss and Survival in Anishinaabe Territory* (University of Manitoba Press, 2020) received the 2021 Governor General's Award for Scholarly Research. Luby's first co-edited anthology, *Manomin: Caring for Ecosystems and Each Other* (University of Manitoba Press, 2024), has received advanced praise as "a blessing of teachings and acknowledgement for the great gift of Manomin."

STEPHANIE OLIVER is an associate professor of English at the University of Alberta–Augustana, where she teaches Canadian, postcolonial, and diasporic literatures. Her research interests include literary representations of smell and diaspora, sensory encounters with oil, the poetics and ethics of breathing in settler atmospheres, and the scholarship of teaching and learning. Most recently, her article "'Stinking as Thinking' in Warren Cariou's 'Tarhands: A Messy Manifesto'" appeared in the *Poetics and Extraction* special issue of *Canadian Literature*, and her essay "'Literary Biodiversity and You!': Restorying Biodiversity through Bitumen" appeared in a *Canadian Literature* Reader's Forum on "Literary Biodiversities." She has also co-edited (with Kit Dobson) the special issue *Everything Is Awful? Ecology and Affect in Literatures in Canada* for *Canada and Beyond: A Journal of Canadian Literary and Cultural Studies*. She is currently working on a manuscript about smell in recent Canadian literature.

ANNE QUÉMA teaches at Acadia University and has written about experimental poetry, queer studies, historiography, Gothic fiction, modernism, the visual arts, law, and literature. Publications include *Power and Legitimacy* (University of Toronto Press, 2015) as well as contributions to *Sensing Law, Gothic Kinship, The Canadian Modernists Meet,* and *Wider Boundaries of*

Daring. Articles have appeared in *Contemporary Literary Criticism, Philosophy and Literature, West Coast Line, Gothic Studies,* and the *International Journal of Law in Context*. Recent publications on poetry include essays on Dionne Brand's *Ossuaries* (*Canadian Literature*, 2014); M. NourbeSe Philip's *Zong!* (*Journal of Law and Society*, 2016); Erín Moure's *The Unmemntioable* (*Studies in Canadian Literature*, 2021); Oana Avasilichioaei's *Limbinal* (Falschrum Books, 2021); and Erín Moure's *Secession by Chus Pato with Insecession by Erín Moure* and Louise Dupré's *Plus haut que les flammes* (*Canadian Jewish Studies*, 2021).

VERONIKA SCHUCHTER completed a PHD on supermodernity and contemporary British and Canadian women's writing in 2020. Since then, she has worked on a project that studies the menopause as a literary trope in fiction, auto-fiction, and poetry by selected women writers publishing in English in the twenty-first century and develops a new critical ethical framework for medical humanities researchers. Her recent publications include "Rich Women in Literature and Film" (*Text Matters*, 2019), "Toward a Feminist Archival Ethics of Accountability: Researching with the Aritha van Herk Fonds" (*Studies in Canadian Literature*, 2019), and "Long Thoughts with Aritha van Herk: An Interview" (*Contemporary Women's Writing*, 2020).

ERIN SOROS teaches at Emily Carr University and writes fiction, nonfiction, poetry, and critical essays. She researches psychosis and the psychiatric and police response to it. She has been a postdoctoral fellow at Cornell University and the University of Toronto and a visiting writer at Cambridge University. Recent essays have appeared in *Carte Blanche, English Studies in Canada, Topia: Canadian Journal of Cultural Studies,* and *Sociologica: International Journal for Sociological Debate.* New essays on psychosis are forthcoming in *Futures of Neurodiversity, MLA,* and in *Palimpsest: A Journal of Women, Gender, and the Black International.* Her poetry received the Malahat Review Long Poem Prize and was included in *Best Canadian Poetry 2020.* Her nonfiction received the Writers' Union of Canada Short Prose Award and won Gold at the 2021 National Magazine Award for "One of a Kind Storytelling." Her fiction received the CBC Literary Award and the Commonwealth Award for the Short Story.

ERIN WUNKER teaches, researches, and writes in Mi'kma'ki where she is an associate professor in the Department of English at Dalhousie University. Her areas of interest include feminist theory, poetry, and poetics as well as literary and cultural production in Canada. She is the author of *Notes from a Feminist Killjoy: Essays on Everyday Life* (Book*hug, 2016) and *The Routledge Introduction to 20th and 21st Century Canadian Poetry* (Routledge, 2022). She is also the co-editor of *Avant Desire: A Nicole Brossard Reader* (Coach House, 2020), with Sina Queyras and Geneviève Robichaud; *Public Poetics: Critical Issues in Contemporary Canadian Poetry and Poetics* (Wilfrid Laurier University Press, 2015), with Bart Vautour, Travis Mason, and Christl Verduyn; and *Refuse: CanLit in Ruins* (Book*hug, 2018), with Hannah McGregor and Julie Rak.

Index

Page numbers in *italics* indicate images.

Abel, Jordan, 174
accompaniment logic, 72–74
acedia, 48–49, 51–52, 54
activism, 67–68, 131, 153–164, 211
    See also feminist pedagogical praxis
Adorno, T.W., 57
Afropessimism, 33
Agamben, Giorgio, 49
Age Matters, 99–100
ageism, xviii–xix, 97–101, 108–109
Ahmann, Chloe, 201, 209
Ahmed, Sara
    The Cultural Politics of Emotion, 49, 51
    Living a Feminist Life, 149n9
    A Mess as a Queer Map, 155–156
    The Promise of Happiness, 209
Akiwenzie-Damm, Kateri, 21
All My Relations, 117
Allooloo, Siku, 18

Anderson, Kim
    building Nokom's House, 1–3, 6–8, 11–13
    learning to be a good relation, xvi, 1–2, 4–6, 9–13
    spirit work, 2, 5–6, 12
Angel, Buck, 103–104
Angell, Thomas, 233, 235
Annharte, 182
anthropocentrism, xv, xxi, 120, 194–195, 197, 201, 204–206
    See also posthumanism
Archibald, Jo-ann, 19
architecture as tool
    for decolonization, 4, 8–9
    for storytelling, 217
    for teaching, 4, 11
archives
    as colonial institutions, 33, 52, 232
    of the ordinary, xix, 61n1, 154–156, 162
    shadow archives, 33
Armstrong, Jeannette
    feminist activism, 117
    land learning, 23

"Land Speaking," 23
Looking at the Words of Our People, 21
art, xx, 167–189, 215–238
  See also feminist pedagogical praxis
assisted death, 72–73
atmospheric futurities
  See environmental futurities; futurities
Aunties as teachers, xvi, 2, 13
Avrorin, V.A., 227

Badiou, Alain, 50
Baker, David, 53
Baldwin, James, 158
Bambara, Toni Cade, 162
Barad, Karen
  Meeting the Universe Halfway, 54, 57
  on response-ability, xiii–xiv, 50–51, 60
  On Touching, xiii–xiv
Barbeau, Marius, 174
Baril, Alexandre
  critical suicidology, 64–69
  ethical suicide accompaniment, xviii, xx, 71–74, 78
  life-affirming suicide approaches, xviii, 71–74
  transformative justice approaches to reducing violence, 74–78
  Undoing Suicidism, 65
  violence of suicide prevention, 63–64, 69–71

Battiste, Marie
  Decolonizing Education, 19
  the process of "unlearning," 22, 25
Baudelaire, Charles, 49
Bearing Witness While Black, xvii, 33–34, 36
Beauvoir, Simone de, 99–100, 239
Behind the Book, 43–44
Belcourt, Christi, 188–189,
  This Painting Is a Mirror, 189
Belleau, Lesley, 19–20
Belmore, Rebecca
  Fringe, 176, 176, 186
  The Named and the Unnamed, 182–183
  Speaking to Their Mother, 184
  tarpaulin, 178, 179, 180
  Tower, 179
  Wave Sound, 183, 184, 185
Benjamin, Walter, 49
Bergh, Sissel M.
  decolonizing language, xxi, 215–220, 222
  Hovren Gåetie, 217, 221, 222, 223, 225, 226, 230, 231, 236
  hybrid form of art and language, xv
  reclaiming Sámi history, 220, 222, 224, 227–229, 231–237, 239
Berglund, Birgitta, 222
Bergsland, Knut, 228
Bergstøl, Jostein, 232
Berlant, Lauren, ix, xii, 51
Betasamosake Simpson, Leanne
  body of work, 180

"Idle No More and Black Lives Matter," ix–xii
"Indigenous Queer Normativity," 24
"Land Pedagogy," 169
"Restoring Nationhood," 205
As We Have Always Done, 24, 169
Biden, Jo, 39
Bishop of Laval, 122
Black deaths
 as consumable media, 33–34, 160
 extrajudicial cases, 32, 38, 40, 84, 195–196
 Floyd, George, 32, 39–40, 195–196
 Garner, Eric, 40, 196
 as invisible, 34, 37, 69–70
 Louima, Abner, 40
 mourning, 41
 as part of climate, xiv, 36–37, 42, 156, 194
 as a tool of colonialism, 134, 136, 142
 witnessing, xvii, 31, 33–34, 36, 40–42, 159–160
Black futurities, 35–37, 43–44, 147–148, 159–160, 163–164
 See also futurities
Black lives, celebrating, 36, 42–44, 132, 158–164
Black people as figure of "living dead," xvii, 31, 36
"Black witnessing," 39–40
Blaeser, Kimberly M., 168–169
Blain, Cicely Belle, xi, xiin1
Blais, Marie-Claire, 115–116

Boast, Hannah, 202, 205, 207, 209
Bollas, Christopher, 88–89, 92
Bourgault, Sophie, 68, 72
Brand, Dionne
 body of work, 164n3
 At the Full and Change of the Moon, xix, 132, 135–137, 147
 A Map to the Door of No Return, 160
Brennan, Teresa, 49, 51
The Brief Reincarnation of a Girl, xvii–xviii, 47–60
Browne, Victoria, 98
Burelle, Julie, 117
Butler, Judith, 71, 163
Butler, Octavia, 160

Calasanti, Toni M., 99–100
call centers
 See hotlines
Campbell, Maria, 2, 8, 10
Campbell, Mark V., 36
care ethics, x, 71–72, 91, 156
care webs, xi–xii, 4–5, 9–10, 51, 158, 197, 201, 243
"Caribou People" teaching, 18
Cariou, Warren, xvi, 149n10, 252
Carr, Marina, 52
Carrière, Marie, 239–242
Cartesian theory, 167–168, 174, 181–182, 186
Cassian, John, 48–49
Catch Them Before They Fall, 88–89
Cawthorne, Jane, xviii–xix, 96–97, 101–104, 106–109
ceremony as performance, 2

research, xvi, 1–14, 242
source of knowledge, 3, 186
transformative, 180–181, 208
Chopik, William J., 97
Christakos, Margaret, 167
Christian, Dorothy, 131–132
Chutunka, Savelij, 227
citation as dialogue with
    Indigenous authors, xx, 167–189
    See also feminist pedagogical praxis
Clark, Natalie, 242
Closse, Lambert, 122
Coates, Ta-Nehisi, 33
co-learning in colonialist
    institutions, xii, xvii, 15–27
colonial management, 142, 149n11
"The Coming of Anontaks," 19
Compton, Wayde
    on monstrous figures, 36
    The Outer Harbour, 145–146, 147
"Considering Wenonah, Considering Us," 24
contaminated waterways, 15–16, 160, 172, 178, 194, 196, 200–201
Cook, Katsi, 19
Coriolan, Pierre, 84
Coulthard, Glenn, 145, 168, 171
Couric, Katie, 54–55
Couture-Grondin, Élise
    biographical sketch of Marchessault, 113–114
    constructing self-identity, xix, 115, 118–121
    critiquing colonialism, xix, 114–117, 121–124
    positionality, 115, 116–117
    storytelling as witnessing, xix, 115–117, 125–126
COVID-19 pandemic, 10, 12, 15–16, 24, 32, 41, 64, 153, 155, 195, 211
Coyote, Ivan
    body of work, xix–xx, 61n1, 153, 156–157, 159, 162–163
    Care Of, 154–158, 160, 163–164
    One in Every Crowd, 156
    Rebent Sinner, 157
    Tomboy Survival Guide, 156–157
creation stories, 4–5, 119, 227
Cree Narrative Memory, 243
crip theory
    See queercrip theory
crisis as moment for
    accompaniment, 73–74, 89, 91–92
crisis lines
    See hotlines
critical literacy, 15–27, 70, 113–116, 124, 168–169
    See also feminist pedagogical praxis
critical scholarship, 67–68, 72, 131–132, 147, 241
    See also feminist pedagogical praxis
Culhane, Dara, 134

decolonization
    architecture, 4, 8–9
    education, 15–27
    language, 217, 220

Decolonizing Education, 19, 22, 25
decolonizing etymology, 217, 220
Depression, 47–49, 51
Descartes, Rene, 167–168, 170, 174, 181–182, 186
Désil, Junie
    "alongé," 38
    eat salt | gaze at the ocean, 31–32, 38
    "ethical wake work and witnessing," 41–42
    "except your dad isn't dead," 38–39
    "And have you put our weight behind its glass door to keep the ocean out? All of it?" 40–41
    "How do you mourn again when you actually never even stopped," 41
    on opacité, 35–37
    on poethics, 34–35
    "a prayer," 37
    on the Zombie as a symbol of Black life and death, xiv–xv, xvii–xviii, 31–37, 44
Diamond, Elin, 57
Dickinson, Emily, 35
Diehl, Lindsay, 139
documentary long poem, 51–52
Dotson, Kristie, 70
Dumont, Gabriel, 2
Dumont, Marilyn, 175, 189
Dunn, Steven, 44
Dupré, Louise, 240
Dzama, Marcel, 50

Edmonds, Pamela, 36
Elliott, Alicia
    "The Colonialism-Depression Link," 28n3, 148n5
    A Mind Spread Out on the Ground, ix, 24–25, 168
embodied experience
    of acedia, 48–49, 51
    of being othered, 155
    of colonial violence, 137–138, 176
    of loneliness, 83, 93
    of menopause, 98, 104–107
    of racism, 38, 41–42, 149n9, 156
    of storytelling, 154–155
    through poetry reading, 198–200, 202, 208
Eng, David, 49
Enorm-ality, 118–119, 123
environmental futurities, 8, 13–14, 209–210
    See also futurities
Episkenew, Jo-Ann, 169
epistemic oppression of the suicidal, 69–78
epistemic violence, xx, 69–70, 168, 173
ethical accompaniment, xviii, 83–93
ethical engagement, xii–xiii, 101
ethical loneliness, 83, 86
ethics
    of care, 71, 74, 210
    of witnessing, xiv–xviii, 31, 36–37, 40–41, 51
extractive practices
    bitumen extraction, 199–201

cultural extraction, xvii, 17, 177–178, 182, 203–206
resource extraction, xvii, 11, 15, 23–24, 160, 170–171, 178, 180, 182, 193, 197, 209–210

Faludi, Susan, 240
Fanon, Frantz, 145
Farrell-Racette, Sherry, 2–3
Fayant, Amanda, xix, 239–242
F-Bomb, 240
feminism
    intersectional, xviii, xxii, 72–73, 100, 126, 239–240
    transgenerational, 96–98, 100–103, 108–109
    trans-inclusive, xix, 104, 163, 242–243
Feminism, Time, and Nonlinear History, 98
feminist investigative lyric poetry, 51–54
feminist methodologies, xii–xiii, xv, xxiii, 22, 24, 102, 168, 172, 206
feminist pedagogical praxis
    activism, 67–68, 131, 153–164, 211
    art, xx, 167–189, 215–238
    critical literacy, 15–27, 70, 114–115, 124, 168–169
    critical scholarship, 67–68, 72, 131–132, 147, 241
    experimental citation, xx, 167–189
    life-writing, xix, 96–97, 101–103, 105, 113–116, 118–121, 126, 143, 162–163
    speculative fiction, xix, 131–148

unlearning, xx, 25, 103, 157, 186
feminist waves, 97–102
Figuring Age, 99–100
Fjellner, Anders, 224, 227, 232
Floyd, George, 32, 39–40, 195–196
Follett, Alec, 198, 200
Fortun, Kim, 201
French texts
    Aimititau! Parlons-nous! 117
    Femmes autochtones en mouvement, 117
    Recherches féministe, 117
Fricker, Miranda, 70
Friedan, Betty, 99–100
"The Future is Menopausal," 95
futurities
    Black, 35–37, 147–148, 159–160, 163–164
    environmental futurities, 8, 13–14, 209–210
    Indigenous, 2, 6, 123, 147–148
    menopause, 97–102, 108–109
    queer, 156–157, 163–164, 241

Gaebien, Leena, 227
Gage, Carolyn, 107
Gamache, Mylène Yannick
    building anti-oppressive curricula, xx, 15–16, 20–23
    co-learning, xvii, 16, 18–20, 23–26
    limits of co-learning, 23–25
    positionality, 17–18, 20
García Zarranz, Libe
    archives of the ordinary, xix–xx, 61n1, 153–154, 159, 162

on Ivan Coyote, 154–158, 163–164
poetics of Black aliveness, 160–162
positionality, 154
on Syrus Marcus Ware, 158–164
trans-aliveness as feminist praxis, xv, xx, 156–159, 162–163
Garner, Eric, 40, 196
Gay, Ross, 44
generous listening, xviii, 68–69, 71–74, 75, 77–78, 89–90
Geniza, Keet, xix, 96, 102–103
Gill, Marie-Andrée, 126
Glissant, Édouard, xvii, 35–37
Godard, Barbara, 115–116
González-Díaz, Isabel, 156–157
Gordon, Avery, 136
Gordon, Jessica, 241
Gould, Janice, 120–121
Goyette, Sue, xvii–xviii, 47–60
Grannies
　See Aunties as teachers
Green, Kim, 136
Greer, Germaine, 99–100
Gunn Allen, Paula, 113–114
Gunnerus, Ernst, Bishop, 235–236
Gylver, Gina, 241

Halfe, Louise Bernice, 20, 183
Hargreaves, Allison, 20–21
Hegel, G.W.F., 131
Hello I Want to Die Please Fix Me, 65–66, 69, 74, 77–78
helplines, 63, 69, 85, 87
Hemmings, Clare, 98

Hernandez, Catherine, 158
Hétu, Dominique, 154, 242, 244
Hill, Rick, 13
"Hold This for Me," 136
hooks, bell, xvi–xvii, 163, 240
hormone treatment, 95, 102, 104
　See also HRT (Hormone Replacement Therapy)
hotlines, 63, 69, 85, 87
Hovrengaellies, 220, 222, 228
hovren-gierkie, 222–224, 223
Howard, Liz
　Infinite Citizen of the Shaking Tent, xx, 167–178, 180–189
　"Neural Cascade," 174
　"Steinian Aphasia," 174
HRT (Hormone Replacement Therapy), 95
　See also hormone treatment
Hubbard, Tasha, 24, 243

I Call It Art (National Museum of Norway exhibit), 216–217, 221, 225–226
I Ching, 132, 144–145, 147
　See also Lai, Larissa
I Hope We Choose Love, 69, 75–77, 162
I Promise, 158
Ihre, Johan, 227
"Imagining the Other?" 101
Indigena Awry, 182
Indigenous and Decolonizing Studies in Education, 19–20, 23, 171
Indigenous futurities, 2, 6, 11, 26–27, 123, 147–148
　See also futurities

Indigenous joy, 26–27
Indigenous Literary nationalism, 22, 118
Indigenous Storywork, 19
"Insurgent Utopias," xiv, xix–xx, 146
intersectional feminism
    See feminism
Intimacies of Four Continents, xix, 131–133, 135, 137, 140, 142
Isaksen, Ella Marie Hætta, 241

Jåma, John Kristian, 216, 217
Janvier, Alex, 186–187,
    Untitled, 187
Jaworski, Katrina, 68, 71
Johnston, Basil, 4, 20
"Jumping Generations," 98

Kanapé Fontaine, Natasha, 126
Karcher, Stephen, 132
Karpinski, Max, 202–203, 210
Kavka, Misha, 239–241
Kay, Andrew, 197
Kazanjian, David, 49
Keeshig, Lenore, 177
Kenner, Alison, 201, 209
Kimiko Does Cancer, xix, 96–97, 101–108
kitchen, significance to Indigenous peoples, 2–3, 11
Kovach, Margaret, xi–xii, 20, 243
Kozminskij, I.I., 227
KT (kitchen table) lab, 2–3
    See also Nokom's House
Kuokkanen, Rauna, 19
Kuoljok, Kerstin, 227
Kwan, Vanessa, 160

Lai, Larissa
    creation of settler-Canadian identities, 132–142
    creative, critical uptake of the I Ching, 144–145, 147
    "Insurgent Utopias," xiv, xix–xx, 146
    poethics for writing and relationality, 131–132
    speculative Taoist poethics, 132, 144, 147–148
Lalor, Amina
    building Nokom's House, 1–3, 6–8, 11–13
    learning to be a good relation, xvi, 1–2, 4–6, 9–13
    positionality, 4
Lamothe, Ethel, 18
land acknowledgments, 16
Land Literacies, 171
"Land Speaking," 23
land-based learning, xvi, 1–14, 20, 27, 215
LaRocque, Emma, 20–21, 27n4, 180
Lauro, Sarah J., 31–32
Learn, Teach, Challenge, 168
learning in dark times, 23–25
"Learning to Live with Wanting to Die," 69, 78
learning with acedia, 48–50
Leem, Knud, 235–237
LeGuin, Ursula, 132
LeMenager, Stephanie, 205, 209
life-writing, xix, 96–97, 101–103, 105, 113–116, 118–121, 126, 143, 162–163

See also feminist pedagogical praxis; relationality, tools for
Linton, Jamie, 195, 199
listening
    as accompaniment, 68–69, 71–74, 75, 77–78, 89–92
    as witnessing, 91
"Literacies of the Land," 19–20, 23, 171
Livesay, Dorothy, 51–52
living with
    acedia, 47–48
    complicity, xvii, 60, 198–201, 203
    marginality, 124, 176
    ongoing death of Black people, xvii, 31–44
    suicidality, 78
    uncertainty, 12–13
Locke, John, 134, 137
loneliness of mental health crisis, 76–77, 83–85
Longboat, Sheri
    building Nokom's House, 1–3, 6–8, 11–13
    learning to be a good relation, xvi, 1–2, 4–6, 9–13
    positionality, 6
Longfellow, Henry Wadsworth, 177–178, 189
Lönnrot, Elias, 227
Looking at the Words of Our People, 21
Lorde, Audre, 158
Louima, Abner, 40
Love after the End, 26
Lowe, Lisa, xix, 131–133, 135, 137, 140, 142

Luby, Brittany
    Anishinaabe-Aki creation story, 4–5
    building Nokom's House, 1–3, 6–8, 11–13
    learning to be a good relation, xvi, 1–2, 4–6, 9–13
Lyons, Oren, 13
"Lyric Poetry and the Problem of Time," 53

Magnus, Olaus, 232
Mahony, Martin, 203
Malatino, Hil, x, xiv, 153, 156, 158
"Man with a Vagina," 103–104
Mance, Jeanne, 114, 122
Maracle, Lee
    "Goodbye Snauq," 22–23, 193
    Memory Serves, 117, 145
    "Polka Partners, Uptown Indians and White Folks," 146–148
Marchessault, Jovette
    Comme une enfant de la terre, 113
    "Entrevue," 113, 118
    La mère des herbes, 114
    Like a Child of the Earth, 126n3
    "The Moon of the Dancing Suns," 117–118
    Mother of the Grass, xix, 114–126
Marshall, Albert, 172
Martinis Roe, Alex
    To Become Two, 98, 101–102
    "Forging Feminist Futures," 98–99
    "Solidarity in Difference," 108–109

Marx, Karl, 131, 145
Mbembe, Achille, 171
McAdam, Sylvia, 241
McKegney, Sam, xii–xiii
McKeon, Lauren, 240
McKittrick, Katherine, 162–163
McLean, Sheela, 241
McLeod, Neal, 243
Medina, José, 70
Mehler Paperny, Anna, 65–66, 69, 74, 77–78
menopause, xviii–xix, 95–109
menopause futurities, 97–102, 108–109
    See also futurities
Merola, Nicole M., 203
Meshake, Rene, 12
Miki, Roy, 196
Milne, Heather, 51, 194, 198, 210–211
Missing and Murdered Indigenous Women and Girls (MMIWG), 20, 85–86, 90, 176, 182, 208, 240
    See also ongoing legacy of settler colonialist violence; violence against women
Mohanty, Chandra Talpade, xxii, 243–244
Monkman, Kent, 178
Moon of the Crusted Snow, 171
Moore, Thomas, 146
Morali, Laure, 117
Morgan, Jas M., 19
Morin, E.D., xviii–xix, 96–97, 101–104, 106–109
Morra, Linda M., 168
Morrisseau, Norval, 180–181, 186

Moure, Erín, 132, 167
Moylan, Tom, 132
Munro, Alice, 93
murders of women in Vancouver's Downtown Eastside
    See ongoing legacy of settler colonialist violence; violence against women
Murphy, Michelle, 206, 208

Nærøy, Randulf, 222
Naylor, Paul, 51–52
necropolitcal logic, 136, 148n5
Neumann, Ann, 95
A New Life, 95
Ngai, Sianne, 50
"Niibinabe," 19–20
Nîtisânak, 19
Nixon, Rob, 194, 206–207
Nokom's House, 1–14, 239
Nystad, Elle, 241

Oliveira, Cindy, 15–16
Oliver, Kelly, xiii–xiv
Oliver, Stephanie
    decolonizing atmospheres, 206–209
    poetical critiques of colonialism, xx, 193–196
    positionality, 194
    pulmonary commons and hydrocommons, 197–201
    relational futurities, xx, 209–211, 239
    relationality and extractive practices, 204–206

settler-colonial atmospheres, 201–204
Oluo, Ijeoma, 43–44
ongoing legacy of settler colonialist violence, xiv, 4, 11, 85–91, 114–115, 120, 121–122, 124, 125, 148, 168–178, 194–195, 208
online learning, 23–25
opacité, 35–37

pedagogical tools for feminism
    activism, 67–68, 131, 153–164, 211
    art, xx, 215–238
    critical ethos, 241
    critical literacy, 15–27, 70, 114–115, 124, 168–169
    critical scholarship, 67–68, 72, 131–132, 147
    life-writing, xix, 96–97, 101–103, 105, 113–116, 118–121, 126, 143, 162–163
    self-inscription, xix, 113–126
    speculative fiction, xix, 131–148
    unlearning, xx, 25, 103, 157, 186
Peers, Danielle, 153
The Pemmican Eaters, 175
Pésémapéo Bordeleau, Virginia, 126
Philip, M. NourbeSe, 167
Piepzna-Samarasinha, Leah Lakshmi
    body of work, 158
    Care Work, x, 64, 66–68, 78
pipelines, 15, 210
The Poethical Wager, xi, 34–35, 58, 132, 144–145
poethics, xi, xx, 34–35, 58, 131, 144
Poetic Investigations, 52

poetics and aesthetics of trans aliveness, 154–156
poetics of Black aliveness, 160
poetry as witnessing, 55–58
Polytechnique Montréal shooting
    See violence against women
Porsanger, Anders, 235–236
positionality, xi–xii, 4, 6, 17–18, 20, 101, 115, 116–117, 132, 154, 194, 242–243
    See also individual contributors
posthumanism, xv, xxi, 120, 194, 197, 201, 204–206
    See also anthropocentrism
production of race, 132–134, 135–136, 142
project management, 8–10
psychiatric refusal to listen, 69–71, 93
pulmonary commons
    See Oliver, Stephanie
pulmonary commons as environmental pedagogy, 193–211

Quashie, Kevin, 160
queer
    futurities, 156–157, 163–164. *See also* futurities
    witnessing, 156
queercrip theory, x, 65–66, 68, 72–74, 78
Quéma, Anne
    art as an Indigenous literature, 176–189
    citation as centering Indigenous relationality, 169–170

critical approaches to
Indigenous literature, 168,
173–175
experimental citation, xx, 167–
168, 169, 186–189
experimental writing, 167, 175,
180–184
history as reiterative and
violent, 170–172
land literacies, 171–172
Queyras, Sina, 52, 54, 57–59

Rahm, Annabell, 224
reading as self-inscription, 116
re-citing as disturbing literary
colonialism, 168, 173
Reder, Deanna, xii, 168
"Reflections on Indigenous Literary
Nationalism," 21–22
relationality
ethical accompaniment as a
form of, xvii, 83–93
with the non-human world, 7–8,
13–14, 120–121, 170–171, 197,
201
relationality, tools for
experimental citation, 167–168,
186–189
life-writing, xix, 96–97, 101–103,
105, 113–116, 118–121, 126, 143,
162–163
speculative fiction, xix, 131–148
rematriation, 10–11
Research Is Ceremony, 242
resistance
against colonial encroachment,
120

Indigenous, xi, 169, 209
justice movements as forms of
ordinary, 153, 156–157
opacity as a form of, 36
poetry as a form of, 172–173
zombie as figure of, 32
response-ability, xiii–xiv, 50–51, 60
Retallack, Joan, xi, 34–35, 58, 132,
144–145
Rice, Carla, 101
Rice, Waubgeshig, 171
Rich, Adrienne, 242
Richardson, Allison, xvii, 33–34, 36
Right Before I Go, 64, 66
Riley, Rebecca, 50–51, 54
Rimbaud, Arthur, 175
Roberts, Gillian, 199
Robertson, Lisa, 52, 167
Ruffo, Armand Garnet, 180–181,
185, 186
rupture events, 50

The Sacred Hoop, 113–114
Sâkêwêwak Storyteller's Festival, 3
Scandinavian texts
*Description of the Saami of
Finnmark*, 235–237
*Historia de gentibus
septentrionalibus*, 232
Lexicon lapponicum bipartitum,
237
The Masks of Odin, 228
Norwegian Academic Dictionary,
229
"The Poetic Edda," 228
Røros Samiske tekster, 228
"Saemundar Edda," 228

"Voluspá," 228
Schnitler, Peter, 233
Schøning, Gerhard, 232–237, 234
Schuchter, Veronika
 exclusionary imaginings of menopause, xix, 104, 106–107
 induced menopause, 104–105, 107
 menopause futurities, 97–102, 108–109
 positionality, 101
 the rise of menopause literature, 95–96
 unlearning discourses relating to menopause, xvi, xviii–xix, 102–109
Scott, Corrie, 117
Scott, Gail, 167
self-inscription as decolonial feminist pedagogical praxis, xix, 113–126
self-silencing by the suicidal, 69–71
sensationalized journalism, 54–55
Seven Fallen Feathers, 24
shadow archives, 33
Shaiye, Said, 44
Sharpe, Christina, xiv–xv, xvii, 31, 37, 153, 160, 194, 196
Silcott, Jane, 106, 109
Silencing the Past, 215
Silva, Denise Ferreira da, 35
Simmons, Kristen, 194–195, 207
Simpson, Audra, 194
Slevin, Kathleen F., 99–100
Smith, Linda Tuhiwai, 20
Smith, Sidonie, 116
Solnit, Rebecca, 241

The Song of Hiawatha, 177–178, 189
Sontag, Susan, 99–100
Soros, Erin
 accompaniment through suffering, 87–90, 91–93
 current medical model for mental health treatment, 87–89, 90
 personal experiences of crises, 85, 87–93
 public witnessing of mental health crises, 84–85, 91
 suffering alone, 83, 90
 violence against women, 85–87, 90, 93
speculative fiction, xix, 131–148
 See also feminist pedagogical praxis; relationality, tools for
spirit-based work, 2, 5–6, 12, 145
Spivak, Gayatri Chakravorty, 70
St-Amand, Isabelle, 117–118
Standing Rock, 15, 241
Stanley, Eric, 156
Starblanket, Gina, xii–xiii
Stauffer, Jill, 83
staying with trouble, x, xvii, 47–60
Stein, Gertrude, 163, 174
Stohlmann-Rainey, Jess, 66–67
The Stone Collection, 21
storytelling as witnessing, xix, 115–117, 125–126
stuplimity, 50–51
Sturluson, Snorre, 228
Styres, Sandra, 19–20, 23, 171
Suhm, Peter Fredrik, 235
suicidality as a traditional site of intervention, 69–71

Index   267

suicide-affirmative approach as anti-oppressive methodology, xviii, 63–78
suicide-prevention as harmful, 64–69
Sy, Christine, 24

Talaga, Tanya, 24
Tallbear, Kim, 19, 241
teaching critical literacy, 18–20
Tekakwitha, Kateri, Saint, 114, 121–124
"Tell All the Truth but Tell It Slant," 35
13 Reasons Why, 64, 67
Thom, Kai Cheng, 69, 75–77, 162
Thor, 222, 228–229
"Threshold," 106, 109
The Thunderbird Poems, 180–181, 185, 186
Titchenell, Elsa-Brita, 228
Tobimatsu, Kimiko, xix, 96–97, 101–108
Trans Care, x, xiv, 153, 156, 158
transformative justice in suicide care, 74–78
transgenerational feminism
    See feminism
trans-inclusive feminism
    See feminism
Tremblay, Jean-Thomas, 202
Tronto, Joan, xiv, 68, 74
Trouillot, Michel-Rolph, 215
Trudeau, Pierre, 143
Tuck, Eve, 20
Tuin, Iris van der, 98
Two-Eyed Seeing methodology, 172

"Ugly Duckling Syndrome," 107
Undoing Suicidism, 65
University of Guelph, 1, 6, 8
unlearning, xx, 25, 103, 157, 186
    See also feminist pedagogical praxis
Utopia, 146

Vautier, Marie, 115
Verchère, Madeleine de, 122
violence against women, xviii, 85–87, 90–91, 182–183
    See also Missing and Murdered Indigenous Women and Girls (MMIWG); ongoing legacy of settler colonialist violence
Vizenor, Gerald, 177
Vowel, Chelsea, 26

Wah, Fred, 132, 144, 146
wake work, 37–42
    See also Sharpe, Christina
Ware, Syrus Marcus
    Abolition is Love, 158
    Activist Love Letters, 154, 158–164
    Activist Portrait Series, 154, 158–164, *159*, *161*
    Activist Wallpaper Series, 161–162
    Baby, Don't Worry, You Know That We've Got You, 159
    Every.Now.Then, 159
    I Promise (Illustrator), 158
    Irresistible Revolutions, 161, 162
    Portrait of Queen Tite Opaleke, 161
    Touch Change, 160
Watson, Julia, 116

Webb-Campbell, Shannon, 183, 185–186
Wedlake, Grace, 73
Wehkamp, Cara, 12
West, Lindy, 240
Westen, Thomas von, 220, 222
White, Jennifer, 77–78
Whitehead, Joshua, 26
Wilderson, Frank B. III, 33
Wilson, Nina, 241
Wilson, Robert A., 95
Wilson, Sean, 242
witnessing
    poetry as, 55–58
    queer, 156
    storytelling as witnessing, xix, 115–117, 125–126
    See also Black deaths; Couture-Grondin, Élise; Désil, Junie; ethics; listening; Soros, Erin
Wittgenstein, Ludwig, 167, 185
"Women, Epic, Live Wires," 52, 54, 57–59
Wong, Rita
    "Dada-Thay," 206
    Downstream, 131–132
    "Epilogue," 210
    forage, 196
    "Fresh Ancient Ground," 204–205
    "Holders," 209
    "Lupus, a Doubled Being," 203–204
    "A Magical Dictionary from Bitumen to Sunlight," 205–206
    "Night Gift," 209, 210
    "Remembering the Future," 203
    "Suncorpse," 209
    undercurrent, 193–194, 196–197, 199, 204, 206, 211
Woodward, Kathleen, 99–100
Words for Water, 15
Between the World and Me, 33
Wright, Cortez, 69, 78
writing as heteronormative and patriarchal, 124
Writing Menopause, xviii–xix, 96–97, 101–104, 106–109
Wunker, Erin
    acedia as feminist praxis, 48–50
    investigative lyric as feminist praxis, 51–55
    learning with stuplimity, 50–51
    living with bad feelings, xvii, 47–48
    Notes from a Feminist Killjoy, 162
    poethics as praxis for relationality, xviii, 55–58
    response-ability of witnessing, 59–60

Yang, Wayne, 20
Yee, Paul
    body of work, xix
    Ghost Train, 132, 137–142, 147
    "Justice Aesthetics," 139
    A Superior Man, 132, 137–142, 147

Zimmerman, Stan, 64
Zombie Theory, xv, xvii, 31–34, 35–37, 38

www.ingramcontent.com/pod-product-compliance
Ingram Content Group UK Ltd.
Pitfield, Milton Keynes, MK11 3LW, UK
UKHW050241110725
460656UK00005B/36